Scripted for Change

Joseph V. Hughes Jr. and Holly O. Hughes
Series on the Presidency and Leadership

James P. Pfiffner, General Editor

Scripted for Change

The Institutionalization of the American Presidency

VICTORIA A. FARRAR-MYERS

Texas A&M University Press   *College Station*

Library of Congress Cataloging-in-Publication Data

Farrar-Myers, Victoria A.
  Scripted for change : the institutionalization of the American
presidency / Victoria A. Farrar-Myers. — 1st ed.
    p. cm.
  Includes bibliographical references and index.
  ISBN–13: 978–1–58544–585–1 (cloth : alk. paper)
  ISBN–10: 1–58544–585–1 (cloth : alk. paper)
    1. Presidents—United States.   2. Executive power—United States.
    3. United States—Politics and government.   I. Title.
  JK516.F37   2007
  352.23'50973–dc22   2006029790

To my loving husband,

Jason Myers,

who has given me

the gift of his love,

understanding,

& patience

Contents

Acknowledgments

A person's life is defined by those people and events that one encounters and leave one forever changed in ways that often go unnoticed until one is able to reflect on their consequence. It not surprising then that this book has also been shaped in part by the imprint those same individuals and experiences have left on my life.

While the ideas herein have been germinating for some time, one of the earliest attempts to articulate these theories occurred during my dissertation process. I will never forget my first meeting with my dissertation chair, Bruce Miroff, where I tried pictorially to explain why understanding the "microprocesses of change" in the presidency was a valid place to start. It was the first of many conversations in which he encouraged me to dive below the surface of the premodern/modern divide I began with as a foil and to find my own voice in describing the interplay among institutions. Bruce, your words served me well in taking that rudimentary text with the kernels of ideas to the book you see today.

It was also thanks to Bruce that I met and had the privilege of working with Stephen Skowronek. I will never forget an engaging conversation we had in a sandwich shop in New Haven about the relevance of recapturing the historical moorings of the presidency and our lively debate about the significance of Cleveland's tariff address as an example of laying the groundwork for a new understanding of the role of government. I have not had a richer conversation, and I can only hope that I have done justice to the aspirations we addressed that day. Stephen, thank you for taking on an "unknown" entity and guiding me all these years. Your shepherding has truly been a guiding light in my intellectual development.

While the manuscript is presidency in focus, Michael Malbin never let me forget the importance of Congress in the coordinated scripting of institutional development. Michael, you have been a mentor, friend, champion, and cheerleader. I will be forever grateful for the trust you showed in me by allowing me to serve as your graduate research assistant on the Congressional Historical Database Project. It was in the many hours of reading presidential biographies and texts and coding presidential requests and congressional responses that I truly developed an appreciation for the role that institutional interactions play in the unfolding of our political narrative fundamental to policy and institution creation.

Years before I even understood what a dissertation meant, Mrs. Anne Fobian, my high school social studies teacher, nurtured my love of presidential history. My first "presidency" paper on Theodore Roosevelt was some thirty pages long and won the paper award that year. I will never forget Mrs. Fobian telling me in response to the length that one day I could write a book on the presidency. Well, Mrs. Fobian, I have. As an undergraduate I did an independent study with Stan Lugar on the presidency. We read the classics—Corwin, Cronin, Neustadt, and Rossiter. It was the most challenging course I took as an undergraduate, and I will never forget his quipping at the end of the semester that he had prepared me well for graduate school. Well, Stan, you were right, and little did you know this course planted the seeds that would germinate into this text.

My first true mentor, Sybillyn Jennings, is the reason I became an academic. She nurtured my love of research and encouraged a shy teen to believe she could make a difference in the classroom. Syb, I will never forget what you said when I asked how I could thank you for your mentoring, friendship, and unyielding belief in me. You said the only thanks you would need would be my happiness and the promise that I would do for others what you did for me. Syb, you are the reason I count myself privileged every day to work with the many students I have the honor of teaching. You showed me the power I have to influence their lives, and I strive each and every day to show my appreciation by passing on the mentorship and passion to my own students. I can only hope my impact on them will be as great as yours has been on me.

I owe an intellectual debt to many people who have provided insights or reacted to various versions and iterations of what eventually became the contents of this book. They include David Adler, Peri Arnold, Deborah Avant, Scott Barclay, Meena Bose, Jeff Cohen, George Edwards, Lou Fisher, Ben Fordam, Michael Genovese, Diane Heith, Anne Hildreth, Karen Hult, Scott James, Martha Kumar, John Kushma, Terry Moe, Karen Orren, Mark Peterson, Dan Ponder, Russ Renka, Steven Shull, and Robert Spitzer.

As they say, you never fully understand anything without teaching it, and so I must thank the students in my graduate and undergraduate Separation of Powers, U.S. Presidency, and Presidency and Foreign Policy classes for their penetrating questions and eager responses. Never will they fully appreciate how my thinking has been refined by these interactions, nor will they ever understand that they gave me the "aha" moments along the way. I must also thank the anonymous reviewers for Texas A&M Press, who provided such rich comments. One reviewer in particular challenged me to move beyond just minor changes and strive to achieve a "great" book. I can only hope I have followed the outline provided in doing so. Any shortcomings in this effort are mine alone, but I am grateful for the encouragement to strive for more. Each of these individuals is owed thanks for the cascade of thinking they each set into motion with their alternative perspectives, challenges, and insightful questions. You will never know how much our exchanges have aided me in the production of this work.

There are many others who have also provided support or an ear to bend and have just listened and reflected with me when I have spoken about "the book." They include Molly Alfers, Ira Carmen, Jill Clark, Lori Cox-Han, Michael Gizzi, Nancy Kassop, Bob McMahon, Leah Murray, Troy Smith, and Dale Story, with a very special thanks to Anne Tego. I am also grateful for the UT Arlington faculty development leave that allowed me the time and concentration to finally make this book a reality.

I want to especially thank several people without whose belief in me this book might never have seen the light of day. They include Mary Lenn Dixon, who saw something in that first awkward conversation that made her believe this book was worth pursuing. Through the years of its creation she has been more than an editor; she has become a true colleague and friend. I wish to also thank James Pfiffner, who believed enough in this work to stick with me and find a home for it in his series.

My parents, Sally and John Farrar, taught me to appreciate the value of education and the responsibility that comes with seeking to make the world a better place. They taught me not only to set high goals and strive to achieve them but also to appreciate the effort just as much as the result. They never failed in their resolve, even when faced with a child who never quite grew out of the urge to ask "why" and the curiosity to seek answers. Mom and Dad, your unfailing belief in me and the sacrifices you have made to aid me in my quest mean more than words can convey.

And last but not least, to my husband, Jason Myers, who lived, breathed, suffered through, and edited much of the work that lies between these covers, you are my friend, my counselor, my critic, and my sounding board. You never lost faith in my ability to produce this book or enthusiasm for its content even when I doubted whether it was worth finishing. You truly complete me, and, without you, neither this project nor my life would ever be the same. I love you, admire you, and am honored to call myself your wife.

Preface

The first inklings of this book began with my frustration with the fact that the presidency that most people agreed was worth studying extended from FDR forward. I could not come to terms with the fact that all that came before FDR could be so easily dismissed as mere history. I was bothered by the explanations posited that changes in the presidency occurred because of the president, the times, or the actions of other people and institutions. It struck me that neat explanations from singular vantage points that do not wrestle with the full range of entanglements posed by the organic nature of politics and life would fall short in crafting a dynamic-process understanding of how change occurs.

Like life, institutional actors, it struck me, would seek the easiest means to resolve a situation but in doing so would not realize that they might have set in motion changes whose true consequences would be revealed only in hindsight. It also struck me that new behaviors, while resisted at first, sometimes become so quickly ingrained that many people might articulate, when challenged, that "that is just how we do it." I wanted to understand how a new behavior goes from being resisted to being accepted as "what we do." More importantly, I wanted to understand what consequences these changes have for institutions and actors within them. It is this multifaceted puzzle that drives the present inquiry.

Unlike other works that seek to understand institutional change, this book takes full advantage of its understanding of institutionalization, as changes in expectations and norms, to build a notion of this process conceptualized through the realities of secular events. Through the coordinated scripting that develops between the presidency and Congress during the resolution of a policy issue, a shared understanding of authority (defined as the ability to affect change and the perceived right to do so) emerges. The reaffirmation of the use of this authority over time lies at the heart of explaining the mechanisms that drive the institutionalization process.

This book weaves a dialogue that provides a theoretical bridge between what, to some, appear to be competing "schools of thought" within the study of the presidency and of institutional and political development more broadly. The book provides a theory that demonstrates how the following suppositions are not actually competing but complementary in what they add to our understanding of institutionalization.

- Institutionalization is really a function of the rich layering of new understandings built upon the original framework provided by the Constitution. Understanding it as such explains why various institutions begin and remain at different levels of authority (even across a variety of issue areas), as well as why, due to the separation of powers system, such institutionalization does not take place in isolation but rather through the complex interactions among institutions. Further, although we seem to notice only punctuated changes, development is really an ongoing process occurring within the dynamics of everyday politics and the pursuit of governmental ends. Uncovering the processes that drive these constant changes not only incorporates these instances of punctuated change but also more richly explains their occurrence.
- Using key contexts within history can more readily lay bare the dynamics that underlie the notion of institutional change. The mode of inquiry in this book demonstrates that change is not deterministic toward some prescribed equilibrium (such as the "modern presidency") but contingent on context, policy, individuals, and short-term political imperatives. Ferreting out particular key contexts that call into question original shared understandings provides the best opportunity to isolate the mechanisms that drive institutional change. By considering change in this manner, the artificial boundaries of periodization—that is, the idea that a certain period of time is distinct from all others—fall away and allow for a much richer appreciation of the contributions of actors and institutional relations throughout time.
- Although power and authority, as previously employed in political science literature, seem like competing conceptions, they are really two sides of a coin in a theoretical sense. Reconceptualizing authority in a new way that takes into account (a) the ability to affect change that power (both formal and informal) provides and (b) the perceived right to do so that authority (as previously used) offers results in more theoretically rich understandings of

authority. Such a reinterpretation explains why some actions are acceptable, whereas others are not, regardless of the allocation of powers enumerated in the original constitutional design. Through this reconceptualization of authority one can also see more constitutionally grounded presidency literature begin to speak to scholarship that is more politically and situationally grounded.

- Individuals are important in any given context because their skills, choices, and actions help guide the direction of change. Much of our literature, however, places an overemphasis on "great individuals." Individual action is necessary but alone is not a sufficient explanatory factor for understanding the dynamics of change. Further, political actors are not deterministic creatures; rather, they are motivated by short-term goals that often belie or undermine their long-term institutional interests. These short-term motivations, if left uncovered, make explanation of institutionalization and change seem ad hoc, irrational, and marked by fits and starts. By placing these individual motivations within a historical, institutional context and looking at short-term decision making, one can uncover the understandings that develop between actors within institutions and the expectations that go along with them. These shared understandings and expectations become the "residue" that remains associated with an institution and serve as cues for behavior in subsequent decision making. After a period of time, this "residue" becomes layered upon and inextricable from the original institutional design. Therefore, revealing the underlying dynamic that emerges from everyday interactions—most starkly evident during key contexts when new issues emerge, requiring new understandings—allows the overall dynamism of institutionalization and change to be revealed.

- Our conception of leadership is often equated with being transformational or transactional, as well as individually centered. These notions on their own miss the idea that leadership is inherently a cooperative exercise embedded within institutional structures and is often exhibited through the efforts of a multitude of people within various institutional and political contexts. This work conceives leadership as predicated upon the shared understandings that are reached between institutional actors seeking short-term decisions and the acceptance of such understandings over time.

Further, it unpacks the notion of leadership by conceiving it in two complementary ways. When initiating the creation of new shared understandings, leadership is both proactive and individual. When acting because of the expectations built up through the institution-alization of authority, leadership is reflexive and institutional and is housed within the understandings that develop around institu-tions. Regardless of which aspect of leadership is utilized, each is predicated upon the assent of others in the separated system.

Scripted for Change

CHAPTER I

Institutional Change in the Presidency

> *But I know also, that laws and institutions must go hand in hand with the progress of the human mind. As that becomes more developed, more enlightened, as new discoveries are made, new truths disclosed, and manners and opinions change with the change of circumstances, institutions must advance also, and keep pace with the times. We might as well require a man to wear still the coat which fitted him when a boy, as civilized society to remain ever under the regimen of their barbarous ancestors.*
>
> —*Thomas Jefferson*

Everything changes, and nothing stays the same; it is a matter-of-fact statement but one that tells us little about how change happens in American politics and what these changes mean for the institutions and individuals affected by them.[1] The framework of the Constitution, predicated on the concepts of separation of powers and majoritarian rule, set in motion a complicated choreography of coordinated scripting between the presidency and Congress.[2] This choreography has translated into shared understandings between institutions, the presidency, and Congress, which in turn have led to change in the American political context. Gaining insight into how these shared understandings develop and are transmitted is the key to solving the riddle of how the institution of the presidency has come to look very different from the design provided by the Constitution.

One cannot overlook the fact that the founding dialogue did not merely create an invitation to struggle among institutions,[3] but also produced a framework that fosters a complex dialogue between the presidency and Congress over policy creation. The Constitution brings these two institutions together, for the functioning of government depends on the interaction of the two branches to develop, approve, implement, and evaluate public policy. This dialogue leads to the creation of coordinated scripts that help explain what factors lead to change and innovation in the presidency and more broadly in the U.S. political system. But what are these coordinated scripts? A coordinated script is the majority-based justification provided for the resolution of an issue. One must, however, move beyond the particular policy decision reached to the underlying reasoning and logic for the conclusion. Within the reasoning and logic are the shared understandings that provide the decision cues prescribing behavior in future political interactions.[4]

Furthermore, within coordinated scripting (i.e., the process leading to the creation of these scripts), one can gain a vantage point that reveals how such shared understandings of expected behavior housed within these scripts are created. We also gain insights into how the give-and-take during individual policy interactions can lead to an ebb and flow of authority between institutions. Taking into account both the underlying logic of the coordinated script produced and the process leading to its creation allows us to understand their respective contribution to institutionalization—that is, the process by which these shared understandings develop, become layered upon, and then ingrained into the political institutions.

To begin to unpack the processes that lead to changes in the institution of the presidency, however, poses some issues for presidential scholars. It requires recapturing a historical understanding of not only the institution but also its occupants and its partner in policy making, Congress, at key moments. It requires moving beyond discussions of formal and informal power and to a new understanding of authority that combines power with the right to use such. It requires looking at the coordinated scripts that develop as a part of the institutional interactions and what they mean for how institutions gain authority to act within the political system.[5] It requires examining how attaining this authority guides behavior and, in turn, lends insight into how institutions change and why our institutions today, on one hand, look similar to those crafted on that piece of parchment more than two hundred years ago but, on the other hand, perform so differently in reality.[6]

UNDERSTANDING INSTITUTIONAL CHANGE IN THE PRESIDENCY

The crafting of the Constitution was itself the first experience of coordinated scripting in the U.S. context. The Founders worked together to construct a shared understanding of how the U.S. government should be designed and what parameters would need to be created to ensure its continued functioning. The shared understandings that emerged were formalized into the text of the Constitution, setting into motion a complex, interwoven structure that was to take advantage of self-interested action and rely on institutional interactions to achieve governmental ends.

Within the Constitutional convention various pathways to accomplishing these two goals were explored. The governmental ends of producing policy were key to the necessity of government; therefore, the legislative branch would be the first among institutions, and its formalized power enumerated in the Constitution required discriminate detail. Despite this belief, the Founders worried that the legislative branch had the potential of being a "vortex" to which all government action would be drawn.[7] To avoid such a fate, the Founders needed to craft a counterweight, an institution that would share in some of the legislative power and check the actions of the legislative branch. This counterweight, the executive branch, would be a new conception—one that would have to draw a delicate balance between being powerful enough to play these dual roles, yet not so powerful as to appear like a king that the nation had just rebuffed.

These competing goals proved a bit daunting. At first blush, the understandings about the executive branch that emerged seem quite grand in their simplicity. The Founders created an institution that was indeed a counterweight necessary for good government.[8] Madison believed the enumerated structure of the executive branch provided the appropriate balance to Congress, yet was sufficiently limited through the enumerations in Article II that it would not pose a danger.[9] Hamilton's writings in the *Federalist Papers* (no. 70 in particular) seem to echo this understanding.

Hamilton, however, also lay bare in these papers an alternative pathway not chosen. Discussion of this alternative was necessitated by the need to justify this new institution, the need for which lay in the necessity of a source of energy within the political system.[10] This explanation, in conjunction with the enacting clause of Article II, which states, "The executive Power shall be vested in a President of the United States of America," allowed for a potential alternative notion of the role of the presidency.[11] Within these pathways of understanding, the seeds of change of further institutionalization lay dormant, discarded, and not fully developed. In raising such alternative pathways, the Founders left open a broader notion of the presidency, one that had the potential to emerge at some later time when circumstances would call into question these initial codified structural understandings. Demands for this alternative understanding of the presidency to address the imperatives of the day may result in an institution with more authority and ability to go beyond the limited role prescribed by the Constitution.

Many have argued that the individual president explains the change in the presidency that has taken place since the founding.[12] This may be natural given the enacting clause that vested the executive power in a single president. This inference begs the question, however, of why certain expectations regarding the behavior of the occupant of the office remain long after an administration has ended. In fact, much of this individual-centered perspective dismisses the possibility of institutional memory altogether since each administration is seen as coming into the office with a clean slate. While parsimonious in its assumption, this view of the institution leaves unexplored other potential explanations of both continuity and change in the presidency.

As noted earlier, unpacking the process of institutional change requires examining the presidency in a historical context. A historical understanding of political phenomena allows researchers to transcend a myopic view of a particular event and begin to build comprehensive, dynamic insights into the key factors that offer explanation of long-term interactions. As Theodore Lowi has noted, "political history only insists that the time frame be extended, not only to do justice to the dependent variables but also to pick up the, let us say, intervening variables, such as institutions, policies, and social structures that could never be gotten directly from cross-sectional data themselves."[13] A historical view enables one to develop an appreciation for such intervening variables and other more subtle indicators of change that become evident only when viewed in their context over time. As a result, it allows us to understand not only the factors leading to and the implications of political change but also the processes that drive that change.[14]

Understanding the presidency through a historical lens, in addition to taking advantage of what history has to offer generally, allows for a comprehensive vision of the institution's progress. Many researchers of the presidency choose to break their analysis down into temporal portals of premodern, modern, and postmodern. Although such periodization can be a useful methodological approach and such categories are convenient markers for analysis,[15] this particular technique misses the patterns of behavior and developmental connections that guide the institution to any given point in time and leads some to dismiss what came before the period being studied as mere prologue.[16] Furthermore, this approach glosses over the question of how change occurs. This perspective so defined sees change as full of punctuated events that serve as guideposts that describe the state of the institution at any given time. This viewpoint also means that certain events, presidents, and timing matter. However, it does not allow one to trace trends or patterns over long periods of time, nor does it allow one to trace the microprocesses that lead to these noticeable, punctuated changes, which may otherwise appear to rise unexpectedly and quickly when cut loose and considered in isolation from their historical moorings.

As a simple example of the importance of examining the developmental connections that arise before a noticeable, punctuated change, consider the presidents who have taken office following a realigning election—Andrew Jackson, Abraham Lincoln, William McKinley, Franklin Roosevelt, and possibly Ronald Reagan. Each of these presidents, with the possible exception of McKinley, pushed the nation in a new direction and, in doing so, helped redefine the nature of the presidency as a political institution. Certainly, their tenures in office represent important guideposts in the development of the presidency. Much of the warrant for their actions, however, stemmed from the failure of their immediate predecessors to address the political issues of the day facing the nation.[17] The ability of Jackson, Lincoln, and others to bring about change in the nation and the institution of the presidency was tied to the political events of the day, as well as to events that occurred previously.

Time itself needs to be understood not just as a date marker, for looking at time this way would force one to look at *all* of history to make a full and complete argument. Since this is not very useful in allowing for close dissection of the subtle interactions that rich history allows for, we must regard time as a key context in which the conditions are ripe for the emergence of shared understandings (not just during the presidencies of Jackson, Lincoln, and others but also during not-so-dramatic times). For we need to understand that neither temporal issues nor individuals provide the sole explanation. It is the complex interaction of each along with what was set in motion by the Constitution and the coordinated scripting that developed in the interactions up to that point that provide the fullest picture of institutionalization of the presidency and change in the U.S. political system. The perspective set forth herein, combined with an understanding of key contexts in history, allows for the tracing of the rich institutional layering that develops with each interaction between the presidency and Congress, each policy decision, and each new set of individuals; it is the harmony, or disharmony, evident in the particular action that lends insight into how pathways are opened, closed, and revisited throughout time.

With these principles in mind, this work posits that institutional interactions over public policy between the presidency and Congress produce not only policy but also coordinated scripts. The dynamics associated with the creation of these coordinated scripts lend insight into why particular pathways are chosen at any given time and how those explored but not chosen remain potentially viable for future action. The reasoning and logic underlying these coordinated scripts is made up of the shared understandings of expected behavior, otherwise known as norms, which serve as guides for future behavior. With each subsequent policy interaction where these norms are employed, they, in turn, become interwoven into the fabric of the original institutional framework as authority for the institution to exercise. This authority is the basis of informal institutions that provide acceptable pathways for guiding behavior—pathways, however, that are not fixed in stone. They are tenuous at first, and actors within an institution may be cautious in basing their actions upon them. The key, then, turns on how ingrained these new layers become and how accepted they are as a basis for action. By peeling back the rich layering that develops from the creation of these informal institutions of authority, we achieve an understanding of how institutionalization occurs.

These informal institutions layered upon the original design are subsequently carried forward administration to administration, forming the institutional memory so often not associated with the presidency. Actors in the system must appreciate the full scope of the institution inherited to operate effectively within their given context. Institutional change is not explained by a series of punctuations guided by outstanding individuals, but as an ongoing process in which understandings are constantly developed, modified, discarded, and rediscovered through the complicated interactions of individuals and institutions. This rich layering can best be appreciated within a given key context in which old understandings are strained and may not provide an appropriate guide for action in the current policy dialogue. These policy dialogues are not necessarily over extraordinary issues but rather over ordinary (although often important) policy matters of the time. Change in the political system therefore arises from the coordinated scripting that occurs in policy development between institutions with different levels of authority.

The concept of authority first needs to be clearly distinguished from that of power. There has been much debate over the notion of power, particularly in the context of presidential studies.[18] The formal sense of power, wherein a president can draw upon what is written in the Constitution or in statutes, is juxtaposed against an informal notion of power, which is derived from the interpretation of what is written in the Constitution, left unsaid, or derived from the office or other political and personal sources. Formal power is seen as a source that allows presidents to command action, while informal powers, much like what Neustadt described, are perceived as powers to persuade action.[19]

What these conceptions miss is that the debate should not be solely about formal versus informal powers, for both are potential sources of strength upon which the president can draw.[20] They are not in conflict but complementary as presidents pursue their goals. This debate masks a much richer understanding that can be derived, first, from breaking free of a discussion of formal power since everyone would agree there has been very little change in Article II of the Constitution since the founding, and, second, from unpacking this notion of informal powers since they often become the catchall or residual reservoir that becomes convenient in explaining presidential action.

In addition, past conceptions of authority also need to be refined. Prior views of authority followed two approaches: The first takes a formal, constitutional slant;[21] the second views authority solely in terms of informal expectations and perceptions.[22] Such conceptions are limited, though, much in the same way that the dichotomy between formal and informal power is. Presidents may draw upon both their power and authority (as previously conceptualized) as viable explanations for action.

Neither a power perspective nor an authority (as has been previously conceptualized) alone fully captures what is at the heart of the institutionalization process. Therefore, a reconceptualized notion of authority that takes into account power, both formal and informal, and shared understandings of expected behavior (i.e., norms) is necessary to comprehend the institutionalization process. The term "authority," defined herein as the ability to affect change and the perceived right to do so, encompasses all of these concepts. The first part of the definition incorporates the notion of power, both formal and informal. The second part of the definition refers to the shared understandings (i.e., norms) that are created through institutional interactions.

To appreciate what this reconceptualization of authority offers, consider the following example. In a matter of first impression, in which a president is trying to get Congress to act in a new way or to address an issue for the first time, the president must rely on both the formal powers of the presidency and any informal powers as well, such as a personal ability to persuade. The president needs to push Congress to accept his understanding of the presidency's role in the issue of public policy at hand so as to make the coordinated script that emerges beneficial to the institution, a shared understanding that will facilitate future presidential action. As future interactions employ that understanding, what was personal now becomes institutional, thus allowing us to perceive continuity in presidential action across administrations. The informal institutions of authority that are created, like the one in the example here, are layered on top of the original Constitutional design. As a result of this layering or institutionalization, future presidents are able to justify their actions as being not merely personal but rather as falling within the institution of the presidency. Furthermore, this institutionalization, predicated originally on the coordinated scripting, makes the presidency a more potent actor for facilitating leadership in the political system.[23]

Chapter 2 offers a prime illustration of how the preceding example can play out in real world politics. Theodore Roosevelt's response to the financial crisis in the Dominican Republic constituted the first time that the president sought to apply his Roosevelt Corollary to the Monroe Doctrine. The policy itself and, more importantly, the way in which Roosevelt sought to implement it represented what was seen at the time as an aggressive extension of presidential authority. Ten years later, though, Wilson's actions with respect to Haiti—which were expressly based on and mirrored Roosevelt's actions in the Dominican Republic—went unchallenged. The new understanding that Roosevelt sought to create had been sufficiently established so as to justify Wilson's actions.

This reconceptualization of authority herein further allows us to consider a different notion of leadership that incorporates and then goes beyond the traditional notions of leadership by command or leadership by influence.[24] Such notions on their own miss the idea that leadership is inherently a cooperative exercise embedded within institutional structures and is often quietly exhibited through the efforts of a multitude of individuals within differing institutional and political contexts. This work conceives leadership, therefore, as predicated upon the shared understandings that are reached between institutional actors seeking short-term decisions and the acceptance of such understandings over time.

The notion of leadership herein is both initiating and reflexive, both individual and institutional. These two components, much like power and authority (as previously defined), are not inherently at odds but necessary components to appreciate what is meant by leadership. When seeking to develop new shared understandings, leadership is both initiating and individual. Leadership, however, can also be housed within the understandings that are layered upon the institution. As a result, when acting because of the expectations built up through the institutionalization of authority, leadership is both reflexive and institutional.

From these notions of leadership, we can begin to untangle the confusion that sometimes develops between what is institutionally derived and what is individually contrived. For regardless of which aspect of leadership is utilized, each is predicated upon the assent of others in the separated system. Consider, for example, the differing reactions that Grover Cleveland and William McKinley received with respect to their views on the role of the chief executive in establishing tariff policy (discussed in more detail in Chapter 4). Cleveland made the tariff issue the primary focus of the last year of his first term in office; McKinley, although not quite to the extent that Cleveland promoted, also saw a fundamental role for the presidency in establishing tariff policy. For various reasons, though, Cleveland was unable to persuade others in the political system to share in his view regarding tariff policy and thus was unable to exert effective leadership on this issue. McKinley, on the other hand, had support for his views and effectively exerted presidential leadership. One of the conclusions that this instance shows is that even highly skilled individuals are unable to lead successfully or achieve desired changes devoid of shared understandings. Appreciating the dynamic interaction of the institutionalized structures and the cooperative functioning of individuals within these structures can provide keen insights not only into presidential action but also into the very dynamics that drive change in the U.S. political system.

To comprehend the importance of authority in setting parameters of behavior and driving change in the political system, consider the following example. Imagine a scenario in which the president, in a discrete policy development, asserts that he has the authority to dictate how the policy should be crafted. Suppose this occurs during a time of crisis in which the president calls for a major security overall and provides draft legislation that the president insists Congress must pass right away due to national security concerns. Because of the charged political context and a desire to rally around the president, Congress concedes and passes the policy as dictated by the president. Although Congress may believe it is just making policy in *this instance,* in actuality it has created a coordinated script that provides the basis for precedent for future interactions under similar circumstances. When another comparable national security crisis emerges, the then-sitting president feels justified in leading Congress, Congress may follow suit because it did so in the previous interaction, and the public begins to hold Congress and the president to these behaviors. As a result, a norm develops, and the authority of the presidency is bolstered. The underlying explanation of this change in authority under these circumstances is revealed through the coordinated scripting that emerged from the ongoing interactions between the institutions. Therefore, understanding the changes in authority—that is, the ability to affect change and the perceived right to do so—allows us to uncover the residue left from these everyday interactions between the institutions and layered upon the original institutional structure.

Authority also helps us to understand why the presidency's institutional development differs from that of Congress. The differing levels of specificity regarding the legislative and executive functions in the original Constitution created an asymmetry between the two institutions.[25] Article I of the Constitution provides Congress with formalized power well beyond what is enumerated for the presidency within Article II. Even within the context of Article II, certain of the presidency's powers are better defined than others. One result of this asymmetry is that Congress's role in the U.S. political system was clear from the outset, whereas the presidency's position lacked defined parameters.[26]

Presidents, therefore, have an incentive to seek greater definition and clarity of the institution's role in the U.S. political system. Given the initial asymmetry in the Constitution, however, such clarification cannot be based on power, which has already been allocated in favor of the legislature. Instead, a more defined role for the presidency must be based on some other means. In particular, the second component of authority—the perceived right to affect change—allows the institution to overcome the original asymmetry favoring Congress. As a result, the presidency has a vested interest in building its authority because doing so places the institution in a more meaningful position of influence within the system.

The presidency's position, however, is in some ways more tenuous than that of Congress since the former's additionally acquired authority is not layered upon a well-defined formalized structure. The authority for the presidency's claim to leadership has its roots in these informal institutions of authority crafted through coordinated scripting. Thus, although the presidency has developed to where it appears to be able to exert more leadership vis-à-vis Congress, in actuality it draws its strength from and relies upon these informal institutions.

Further, the presidency's development is contingent on the pathways opened up by the sequencing of policy and context.[27] The complex intersection of policy, context, and the original authority (as defined here, i.e., including both the formal and informal powers and the original shared understandings that emanated from the Constitution) leads to coordinated scripting that develops identifiable patterns of behavior. The range of acceptable behavior at any given time, however, is subject to the sequencing of events and institutional development that has come before—what issues have arisen, what coordinated scripts were employed in addressing those issues, what shared understandings have already been developed. As a result, institutional development in this context is not linear or evolving into any particular end state (such as the "modern presidency");[28] instead, it is an ad hoc, path-dependent process that varies across and even within policy areas.

Within this developmental process, opportunity structures for institutional development may arise as a regular part of the policy-making process. Such opportunity structures may include, for example, the federal government addressing new issues, individual presidents seeking to expand the presidency's role, or members of Congress seeking assistance with respect to a policy matter. Within certain key contexts, opportunity structures will be more exaggerated, providing more and better opportunities to develop new shared understandings regarding the presidency playing broader roles in the system and providing an easier time for these understandings to develop into informal institutions of authority.[29] Thus, for example, one can see that, given that the initial scope of the national government was fairly narrow in focus and much of what needed to be done was clearly enumerated to Congress, opportunity structures for the buildup of any significant authority for the presidency were limited. As greater demands were placed upon the national government, the need to develop new understandings that would affect both the presidency and Congress increased. This, in turn, increased the opportunity structures for the presidency.[30]

We have already seen the incentive for presidents to build the presidency's authority. But what motivates other individual actors within the political institutions, particularly members of Congress, to either grasp more authority or, more importantly, surrender authority? The explanation is more simplistic than it might initially appear. The normal politics of policy making occurs because it is the role of government to produce these ends (i.e., the laws and policies of the nation). The short-term imperatives of electoral concerns of politicians; public outcry for action; and partisan, economic, and/or social contexts that are ripe for change all motivate individual actors to pursue short-term, incremental changes that are the most optimal outcome at that time.[31] The precedents set— that is, the coordinated scripts that are created—are the residual of these everyday interactions. This residual, however, becomes more important over time as patterns of interaction lead to perceptions that certain institutions have abilities to affect change more than the original framework of the Constitutional prescribes.

When this occurs, actors may not even notice the changes or, if they do, they may subordinate concerns related to the surrender of authority to other, more imminent priorities. This occurs because the coordinated script so employed provides the path of least resistance and, thus, the less costly course of action in achieving short-term ends. As individuals within institutions become more focused on short-terms incentives and less concerned with long-term institutional implications, the pace of changes in authority might appear to quicken. The reality is that the unintended consequences, emerging as a result of actors dismissing or not focusing on such consequences, are the very ingredients for authority development.

The creation of the Interstate Commerce Commission (ICC; discussed in Chapter 3) abounds with examples in which the members of Congress sacrificed their long-term institutional authority for the short-term gain of passing legislation needed to address a major political issue of the day. Not only did it formally delegate authority to the ICC itself, but it also carved out a role for the presidency—through the power to appoint and remove commissioners—in the ICC's exercise of this authority. Congressional members at the time emphasized the importance of their intended consequences and downplayed the threat posed by (and raised by some members of) the unintended consequences. Such unintended consequences, however, would later help broaden the authority of the presidency in the area of creating administrative agencies.

To see how the development of authority ties into the institutionalization process, one must begin by unpacking the various key steps that this process entails. As Figure 1.1 shows, the process begins with the current political context at any given time, which includes the formal powers prescribed by the Constitution for the institution, the informal institutions of authority built to date, and the current political pressures and incentives for action. Understanding this temporal context and the state of the existing institution is vital to beginning to trace change. Also, the particular policy over which the president and Congress are interacting needs to be identified. Whether foreign or domestic, broad or narrow, ongoing or new, the type of policy is an important aspect for understanding the coordinated scripting that might take place between the presidency and Congress. Further, this information allows for comprehension of what short-term ends the policy-making branches wish to achieve and what motivations might be impacting their respective behaviors. Although the policy is of importance, our focus here is not on the ends produced but on the process used to achieve those ends. The coordinated scripting employed to achieve the policy formation is most important to comprehending how shared understandings of expected behavior (i.e., norms) are created, which entails the second step of the process as shown in the diagram.[32]

Figure 1.1. The institutionalization process.

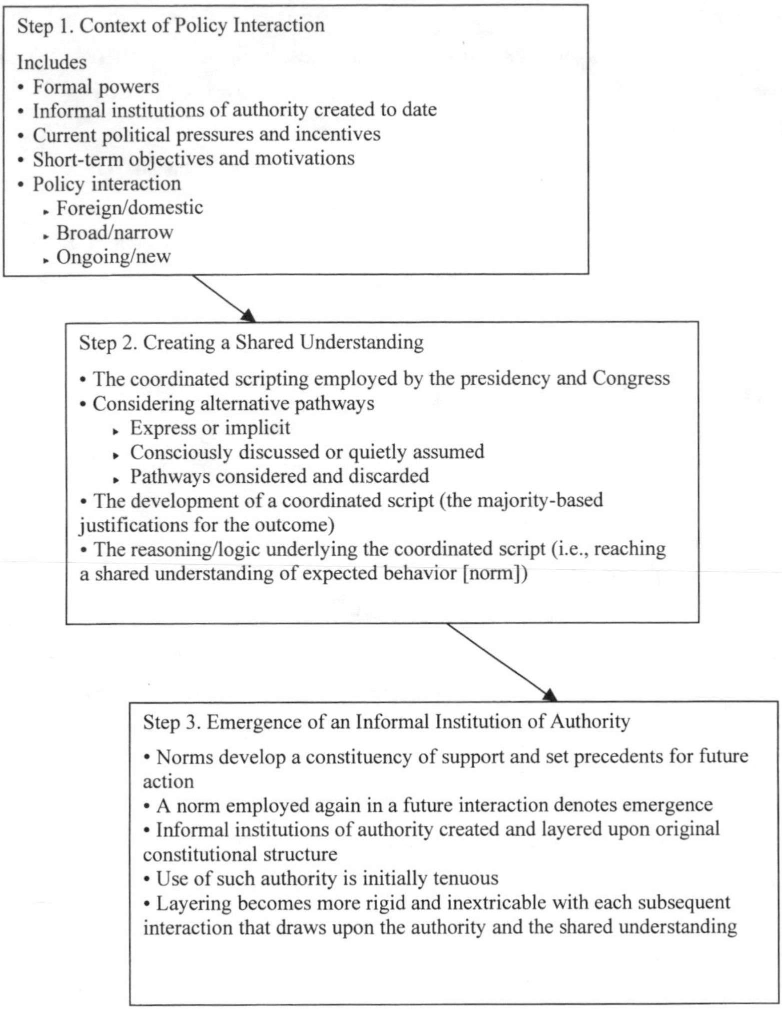

Step 1. Context of Policy Interaction

Includes
• Formal powers
• Informal institutions of authority created to date
• Current political pressures and incentives
• Short-term objectives and motivations
• Policy interaction
  ‣ Foreign/domestic
  ‣ Broad/narrow
  ‣ Ongoing/new

Step 2. Creating a Shared Understanding

• The coordinated scripting employed by the presidency and Congress
• Considering alternative pathways
  ‣ Express or implicit
  ‣ Consciously discussed or quietly assumed
  ‣ Pathways considered and discarded
• The development of a coordinated script (the majority-based justifications for the outcome)
• The reasoning/logic underlying the coordinated script (i.e., reaching a shared understanding of expected behavior [norm])

Step 3. Emergence of an Informal Institution of Authority

• Norms develop a constituency of support and set precedents for future action
• A norm employed again in a future interaction denotes emergence
• Informal institutions of authority created and layered upon original constitutional structure
• Use of such authority is initially tenuous
• Layering becomes more rigid and inextricable with each subsequent interaction that draws upon the authority and the shared understanding

Norms are created out of the interactions between the president and Congress as they, for example, debate principles and agendas, explore potential approaches, trade language, and leverage their support.[33] Within the swirl of all of these dynamics and within the correspondence and dialogue between these players, a coordinated scripting begins—a scripting of how the ends of policy making are achieved. This consideration of alternative pathways for action may be either express or implicit in the actors' behavior, or they may be consciously discussed or quietly assumed. The coordinated script that emerges denotes that the actors involved have chosen an agreed-upon path. This does not mean that once one pathway has been selected, all others are closed forever. The chosen path may be revisited at a later juncture when the costs of employing it become too high and alternatives are sought. The importance, however, of creating such a coordinated script is that the underlying reasoning and logic of this script becomes the shared understanding of expected behavior that is carried forward.

Tracing these scripts is vital to seeing how these norms develop not just within one policy interaction but also among several interactions in the same policy area (the third step in the process).[34] As a norm develops a constituency of support among political actors, it sets precedents that guide future action.[35] A norm that is employed again in a future interaction, as evidenced by the continued use of the previous script, denotes the emergence of an informal institution of authority. This authority structure is layered upon the original framework set out by the Constitution for that institution. At first, these new informal institutions are tenuous, but with each new interaction that draws upon this authority and the shared understandings that underpin them, they become more rigid and inextricable from the original constitutional structure. Further, future actors in similar policy interactions begin not to question why a particular pathway is employed, and the status-quo inertia seems to dictate that that pathway be employed again. What then emerges out of the buildup of informal authority structures is institutional change.

To summarize this process, I focus on the interactions between the president and Congress in terms of the impact that the logic underlying the coordinated scripts that emerge from these policy interactions has in forming shared understandings of expected behavior. Furthermore, as these norms are reinforced through continued action and/or acquiescence by the institutions, they become informal institutions of authority. These informal institutions, created by the buildup (or even the loss) of authority, then set the expectations of acceptable behavior of political actors at any given time, as well as provide the continuing justification for future actions. They are layered upon the original design and become the building blocks of further institutionalization.

Examining institutionalization in this way shows that the process is not deterministic toward some desired ends but rather is ongoing and subject to adaptation and reinterpretation.[36] Institutional change is contingent on the continued viability of the original scripted understandings; if a previous pathway is later discarded, then the viability of all other pathways that subsequently built upon it may also come into question. The full breadth of the change is also contingent upon several factors, such as the extent to which informal authority structures can be attached to the original framework set out in the Constitution and the extent to which they may have already been built up from past interactions.

Further, just as authority can be gained, it can also be lost. Even though a chosen pathway may be continually reinforced through future interactions, other pathways that were dismissed through the original scripting still remain potentially viable options. The cost of returning to previously discarded pathways often is higher.[37] However, as shared understandings become more engrained into the institution, the rigidity that develops may eventually increase the costs of interaction. Thus, the discarded pathways (or perhaps some newly considered ones) may come to provide less costly alternatives than the path that has developed, although the context must be ripe for such a call for innovation and change. This is the natural progression in the dynamic pathway of institutionalization.

Certainly, innovation and change in the presidency can come from individual presidential action. Presidents act within the boundaries outlined in the constitutional framework but may seek to carve out a position when the framework is vague or silent. Further, individual presidents may pursue a leadership role by pushing the boundaries of what they can do, as well as try to seize the advantage or establish a precedent when Congress is acquiescent.[38] Theodore Roosevelt, as Chapters 2 and 3 explain, clearly sought to push institutional boundaries. However, these dynamics from a presidential perspective predicated upon individual action take us only so far in understanding institutional change. Theories of individual action tell us very little about how the actions of one president are connected to those of others or how Congress can bolster the authority of the presidency even when a president may not be seeking it. Furthermore, an individual perspective tends to aggrandize "great men" and downplay the potentially more powerful explanations embedded within the interactions of institutions, contexts, short-term incentives, and policy arenas. The institutionalization process as outlined here, that is, one based upon coordinated scripting between individuals and institutions, allows for greater insights not only into how shared understandings are developed but also how institutions become repositories for authority that guides future interactions.

UNCOVERING INSTITUTIONAL CHANGE IN THE PRESIDENCY

How, then, can one begin to probe the utility of such a notion of institutionalization? Although the process delineated can be predictive, its utility must first be established by determining whether these patterns of coordinated scripting actually occur. While key contexts must be sought, we need to be ever mindful to choose a time period that will allow for several interactions within the same policy area in order to show the development and adoption of coordinated scripts within each policy area. Further, choosing just any time period is not advisable; one that is too early may not uncover sufficient coordinated scripts for analysis, but in a later period the coordinated scripts may be so well established that they also do not fully reflect the institutionalization process. Therefore, a time period that is a key context poses opportunities for calling into question the established practices and the need for innovation to meet the changing demands of the political context. Such a key context is needed to best explore the institutionalization process generally and as it relates to the presidency specifically. The period from 1881 to 1920, from post-Reconstruction through the progressive era, seems to fit these criteria nicely.[39]

At first, this may seem counterintuitive to what we already know about this era, which is generally seen as a time of congressional dominance in the political process[40] and the institutionalization of the House of Representatives.[41] It is sometimes referred to as the modernization period of Congress, so it might appear to be a period of limited usefulness for studying the presidency. However, it provides a key context that is useful for analysis because of a conglomeration of events that would generally make evidence of institutional change more apparent and specifically provide a basis by which informal institutions of authority for the president might develop.

First, within the U.S. political system, there was an increased nationalization of the political discourse. During this period, we see that policy issues and calls for action became nationalized. As a result, we also see the beginnings of an expanded scope for the national government. The growth of the national government's purview also led to the need to create a new administrative apparatus to handle the growing agenda of the national government.[42] Second, we see greater pressure for the United States to look outside itself, an increased awareness of the international realm, and the importance of international interaction. These factors are reflected in the rise of imperialism within the United States. All of these characteristics were important driving forces behind the institutional development of both Congress and the presidency during this time. With these changes at the national and international levels, a greater number of societal needs developed within the nation and were made imperatives for national action. As a result, there were more opportunities for the political institutions either to fill a need in society or to have society expect them to do so.

Further, in the domestic realm, we see additional changes in the political context, such as the breakdown of the party system in the electorate.[43] Further, factors within government, particularly within the interactions between Congress and the president, include the predominance of the House speakership and the subsequent rise of committees following the revolt against Cannon in 1910, the high partisanship exhibited in congressional voting, the use of the tools of the presidency, such as the veto and removal power, and the use of rhetoric by the president to set the public discourse and influence public opinion. As a result of the changes in the political context that were occurring in the government, domestic political system, and international political system, the presidency was poised to break from the nineteenth-century conception of the institution that tended to defer to the legislative branch to start to fill more and broader roles within the U.S. political system, all the while opening the way for a more expansive realm for presidential authority.[44]

The conglomeration of these forces created contextual opportunities in which the Constitution became less useful as a guide in addressing the new issues that were arising. Moreover, the old shared understandings and coordinated scripts no longer effectively met the governing context, which demanded energy, thus rendering the political environment ripe for presidential action, as Hamilton would have predicted.[45] This key context provided a transitional phase for not only the national government but also the national institutions. Therefore, investigating sustained coordinated scripting in various policy area interactions between the presidency and Congress during this period should reveal how the institutions changed and emerged from this governing context.

Investigating different policy areas will uncover important nuances in comprehending the institutionalization process. Since this process is based upon shared understandings that are developed through the coordinated scripting between the institutions over policy making, one should not expect that the coordinated scripts would be the same for every policy. Recall the initial institutional asymmetry set out in the Constitution, in which the legislative branch's powers are highly enumerated and those of the executive branch are less formalized. Furthermore, even within a policy area there may be various levels of coordinated scripting based upon both the differing levels of authority that could be derived directly from the Constitution and whether or not a shared understanding has already begun to prescribe certain behavioral outcomes.

To fully explore these potential coordinated scripting opportunities, we need to select policy areas that provide differing levels of previous institutionalization. Within the policy realms of foreign affairs, domestic issues, and questions regarding control of government operations, for example, one can begin to draw presumptions about authority by examining the initial framework and roles prescribed within the Constitution. For example, based upon the powers granted to the presidency, one can say that the president is expected to be the commander in chief, chief diplomat, and the nation's representative to foreign governments. As a result, given these prescribed roles, we should expect the president to have greater presumed authority in foreign affairs. Congress, on the other hand, is granted the power to form legislation and is expected to serve as the representatives of the people and their particularized interests. Therefore, we would expect Congress, given its prescribed roles, to have greater presumed authority on those issues that most closely affect the people of the nation, namely domestic issues. The presumed authority of each institution in the control of government operations is not as clear as in the other two areas since both institutions are granted powers and prescribed roles within this area. Based upon the powers associated with the chief executive role, the president is expected to serve as the head of government. Congress, with its powers to draft legislation and authorize appropriations, can be expected to oversee how its legislation is executed. Therefore, the presumed authority in this area is mixed and requires continual definition.[46]

Looking at a policy area where (at least initially) more authority appears to be granted to the presidency, one where Congress appears to have more authority, and then an area where neither seems to have an authority advantage allows for a nice test of the full range and potential for the development of different kinds of coordinated scripting. The coordinated scripts that emerge from such analysis will allow us to say something about institutionalization in general and more specifically about how the presidency is institutionalized and what that means for our understanding of institutional relations going forward from this key context.

Within the foreign, domestic, and control of government operations policy realms, interactions related to the commitment of troops abroad, the tariff, and the creation of administrative agencies, respectively, are examined. Within the foreign realm during the era under study, U.S. policy was dominated by the rise of imperialism.[47] Thus, the use of troops overseas was a component of the United States' more expansive international role. In the domestic realm, the United States experienced a growth of industrialization and the nationalization of the economy.[48] Economic issues dominated much of the domestic political discourse with the tariff, as one of the ongoing, important, and divisive issues of this time. Finally, in the government operations realm, the growth of the federal government, both in size and functions, reflected the nationalization of the U.S. political system.[49] As a result, institutional interactions concerning the establishment of administrative agencies are examined. See Table 1.1 for a summary of this discussion.

As an initial step in analyzing the coordinated scripting in these policy areas and the development of presidential authority, we need to develop an appreciation of the political and institutional context of the era between 1881 and 1920. Doing so will provide us with a picture of the political universe of the time related to the policy issue, as well as an understanding of the types of issues and interactions that occurred between the president and Congress in these policy areas. To this end, I have developed a database of all of the potential institutional interactions within each policy area (see "Procedure for Collecting Data and Creating a Database" in the Appendix). Potential institutional interactions refer to those instances in which at least one institution, either the presidency or Congress, addressed one of the policy areas discussed here—actions such as executive requests that go unanswered or die in committee; executive initiatives without congressional response; con-

TABLE 1.1.
POLICY REALMS AND ISSUE AREAS

Policy Realm	Foreign	Domestic	Control of government operations
Issue Areas	Commitment of troops	Economic	Operation of executive branch
Area of Interactions	Committing troops abroad	Tariff	Creation of apparatus
Presumed Authority	Tends toward the presidency	Tends toward Congress	Mixed (both have claims)

gressional initiatives that do not succeed; and interactions that produce resolutions, concurrent resolutions, bills, statutes, confirmations, and ratified treaties.[50] With the total universe of potential and actual institutional interactions that took place during this time period so identified, specific case studies were culled.

To examine the institutionalization process, a set of indicators of institutional change needed to be developed. The first is a set of indicators for determining whether a coordinated script has developed into a shared understanding of expected behavior, or a norm. Norms are recognized by their breadth rather than their frequency (i.e., the number of times a behavior occurs). In other words, behavior can be considered a norm because an array of actors (e.g., the president, congressional leaders, other members of Congress, members of the president's administration) all express a shared understanding of how to behave or what role they play in any given interaction. The wider the array of actors that share this understanding, the more evidence that a norm exists.

The delivery of the State of the Union address serves as an example of a presidential norm that has changed throughout history, with an important change occurring before 1921 that persists today. Starting with Thomas Jefferson, the established norm was that presidents would deliver their annual messages to Congress in written form. However,

Woodrow Wilson started the current practice of delivering the message directly to Congress (actually restarting a practice that had been followed by Washington and Adams). As the presidency had greater behavioral expectations being placed upon it, presenting the State of the Union message in a more visible forum was a way in which to fulfill the expectations of the office. Furthermore, a coordinated script developed between the presidency and Congress whereby the State of the Union address became an important vehicle by which the president would try to set the legislative agenda. As time progressed, the practice of the president appearing before Congress to deliver the speech became institutionalized, and doing so thus became another expectation of and source of authority for the presidency.[51]

Given this conception of norms, we would expect to find indications of these shared understandings in the communications of the president and members of Congress and within the larger political system as well. Since we are interested in the coordinated scripting taking place between the presidency and Congress during their interactions, it is important to look at sources that will lay bare these communications. Evidence for the case studies used here was collected from primary sources such as public and private presidential papers; private papers of congressional members, particularly leaders; the *Congressional Record;* party platforms; and other relevant sources regarding the policy issues at hand. We can examine the rhetoric of the president and members of Congress in the course of their interactions during specific policy events to determine, for example, their understanding of the institution of the presidency at that time and whether it differs from prior and later shared understandings. Behaviorally, we can view the role the president plays as tending toward either proactive (which would indicate that the president either views the institution's role as having the authority to lead or wants the presidency to have such authority) or reactive (which would indicate that the president views the presidency as not having a great deal of authority to lead). To the extent that Congress supports or combats the president's actions is an indication of the shared expectations of the role of the presidency. We will examine these sources for evidence of common dialogues, shared justifications, and references to precedent to determine the existence of a shared understanding and its level of acceptance, thereby allowing us to determine the level of institutionalization within each policy arena.

We also need to develop a set of indicators utilizing the substance and process of the institutional interactions, such as the way the outcomes were affected by the process, the way in which the interaction itself developed, who initiated the interaction, the way each institution responded, and how these interactions differed from or remained the same within or among policy issues. For example, specific indicators could include whether the president starts addressing issues that had previously been within Congress's domain; whether the president addresses and places new issues on the national agenda; whether Congress accepts presidential initiatives without debate over the president's right to propose them; whether Congress, through its actions, places responsibility for addressing an issue on the president; or whether Congress in any way formally codifies the shared understandings regarding the role of the presidency.[52]

Since this study examines the dynamics and processes through which coordinated scripting becomes institutionalized, several data points are needed. Thus, multiple cases are examined within each policy area to determine whether particular shared understandings regarding the role of the presidency exist and become institutionalized.[53] Specifically, since we are interested in seeing how coordinated scripts are transferred from one policy interaction to the next (i.e., whether they become informal institutions of authority), we will need to isolate three cases in each policy area—one at the beginning of the key context, one at the middle, and one at the end. For the purpose of the study, the 40-year period from 1881 to 1920 was divided into three periods of approximately the same length: 1881–1893 (13 years); 1894–1907 (14 years); 1908–1920 (13 years). One case was selected from each segment.

As stated earlier, norms are recognized by their breadth, that is, patterned behavior exhibited by a wide array of actors. Such evidence can be found in any one interaction. By having three data points, the dynamics of coordinated scripting can be addressed: whether the scripting remains the same; whether it changes; how the shared understandings derived from the scripting (once established) affect future behavior; and how these shared understandings may turn into informal institutions of authority. In other words, using multiple cases allows us to track coordinated scripts in order to investigate both the development of shared understandings and the process of how such understandings become informal institutions of authority.[54]

Given the extensive time period under study, we will not be able to control for a number of random variables that will be different for each case (e.g., different members of Congress, different presidents, other intervening variables). One important factor, however, can be held constant: the specific policy reason for the interactions. Given the importance of holding policy goals constant among the cases in each policy area, the logic for selecting the specific cases needs to be developed. Three criteria guided this process. First, all of the cases in each policy realm had to be comparable in scope and magnitude.[55] This criterion will therefore exclude interactions that might be considered outliers and will focus on interactions closer to a median position. Second, the cases should concern issues that are ongoing in nature because this will better allow for the inclusion of three or more observable interactions. Finally, the interactions should be identified as significant issues in the time period within each policy area. This criterion thus permits the inclusion of cases in which actors may be more willing to question existing shared understandings, given the importance of the issues involved.

The process of selecting cases was geared to maximize these three criteria for all of the cases.[56] Certainly, the individual cases selected for each policy area are not the only ones that could be examined. In other words, one could argue, for example, that another interaction over the tariff may be better than one selected. However, since the goal is to maximize the criteria, the selection process is designed to establish *a set of cases* that are just as good as (if not superior to) *any other set of cases.*[57]

Based on the universe of institutional interactions in this area and the case selection process just discussed, the following were selected for further study:

COMMITMENT OF TROOPS

Year	President	Event
1888	Cleveland	Samoa
1905	Roosevelt	Dominican Republic
1915	Wilson	Haiti

Year	President	Event
1887	Cleveland	Interstate Commerce Commission
1903	Roosevelt	Department of Commerce and Labor
1914	Wilson	Federal Trade Commission

TARIFF

Year	President	Event
1890	Harrison	McKinley Tariff
1897	McKinley	Dingley Tariff
1913	Wilson	Underwood Tariff

Within the three issue areas under examination, we would not expect the informal institutions of authority to develop uniformly. Given prior understandings developed from previous institutional actions and judicial decisions regarding the commitment of troops,[58] one would expect that, with the increased importance of international affairs coupled with the rise of imperialism, the nation might look to the president to exercise more authority within the foreign policy arena. Thus, one might expect the president, for example, (1) to become more proactive in committing troops during this period; (2) to assert more authority and be willing to undertake more significant uses of the military with the understanding that it is within the president's authority to do so; and (3) to find an increased understanding of the president as the nation's leader in international affairs. On the other hand, Congress, while it may initially assert its authority as a decision maker in international affairs, might be expected to be more acquiescent of presidential initiatives or encourage the development of understandings along these lines.

Presidential and congressional activity in creating administrative agencies should reflect the fact that both institutions can be said to have presumed authority in this area. Thus, we should expect both institutions to be involved with the creation of agencies throughout the entire period. Given their respective sources of initial authority, we might expect each one to be involved in the creation of agencies at different levels. For example, the president's involvement as chief executive might be related to determining the need for or general purpose of a new agency, whereas

Congress may be more involved with determining its exact responsibilities, powers, and structure. We should generally expect, however, that the president's role in the creation of administrative agencies should increase throughout the era under study, with Congress possibly becoming more responsive to presidential initiatives while maintaining a significant role for itself.

In terms of the tariff, we should expect that any expansion in the presidency's role in this area would be the most difficult to achieve and the most limited in scope given Congress's constitutional power of the purse. Overall, we should expect to see a general trend moving from congressional dominance in this area toward a more coequal governance between Congress and the president. More specifically, while Congress should be expected to maintain a high level of its presumed authority, we also should expect to see increased signs of the president's role as chief legislator, such as increased proactive behavior by the president and greater congressional acquiescence and support of presidential initiatives.

PLAN OF THE BOOK

This chapter lays out a theory and the necessary building blocks for understanding institutional change in the presidency. Armed with the concepts of coordinated scripts and coordinated scripting, as well as the recast notions of authority, norms, and informal institutions, we are set to examine the driving mechanisms behind the institutionalization of the presidency. We are also then in a position to explain the underlying mechanisms of change in the U.S. political system. Further, the methods that are used in the subsequent chapters to empirically examine the theory set forth have been delineated, allowing us now to turn toward examining the development of the presidency between 1881 and 1920.

Chapters 2, 3, and 4 explore the coordinated scripting between the presidency and Congress during this period in the areas of foreign affairs, government operations, and domestic affairs, focusing specifically on policy interactions over the commitment of troops abroad, the creation of administrative apparatus, and the tariff, respectively. Each chapter begins with an overview of the key economic, partisan, regional, philosophical, and institutional contexts and events of this period with respect to the applicable policy area. Doing so not only helps explicate the universe of interactions from which the specific cases for analysis were drawn but also offers an appreciation of the short-term forces that may have been affecting each institutional interaction between Congress and the presidency. From there, each chapter delves into the cases described earlier to explore the coordinated scripting employed in each interaction and the shared understandings that emerge from it. Each chapter concludes by analyzing the coordinated scripting across the case studies and its implications for the creation of informal institutions of authority for the presidency within the specific policy area.

Chapter 5 assesses the implications that the findings have for the presidency during the key context of 1881 to 1920. Further, it explores what the cases collectively tell us about the institutionalization process of the presidency. More importantly, however, the process of institutionalization identified through this analysis lends insight into what the findings mean for the current state of the presidency and interinstitutional relations within the system of separation of powers and checks and balances.

CHAPTER 2

Commitment of Troops

The period from 1881 to 1920 was defined by the struggle between America's traditional noninvolvement in European wars and its avoidance of entangling alliances on the one hand and the country's growing role as an international leader on the other, and the tension between whether to temper the expansion of U.S. interests and limit it to North America or instead to expand more aggressively on a level and sometimes in competition with European powers.[1] The period was characterized by the desire of some to spread the U.S. political system widely abroad and greatly expand U.S. economic interests, while others were reluctant to pursue such a role. Although certain events throughout the era reflected the less active role for the United States abroad—from Grover Cleveland's call for "peace, commerce, and honest friendship with all nations; entangling alliances with none" in his first inaugural address to the rejection of the League of Nations by the Senate after World War I—the primary trend in U.S. foreign policy was toward a more involved, more assertive, and broader role in international affairs, especially in the Western Hemisphere.[2]

THE CONTEXT: THE DEBATE OVER EXPANSION ABROAD

The expansionist objective behind the shift toward increased international activity stemmed from three sources. The first was a revival of the concept of manifest destiny and the philosophical belief in the superiority of the U.S. political system. Under this view, the United States had the responsibility as a great nation to act as a "civilizing agent of the world."[3] Religious leaders sought to expand the political, commercial, and cultural influence of the United States abroad to benefit foreign countries. In doing so, they provided a "moral justification to the new Manifest Destiny."[4]

The desire to increase the nation's stature in the world provided a second source for the expansionist thrust. To compete and negotiate with the European powers, proponents argued that the nation needed the prestige associated with having colonies. As Sen. Henry Cabot Lodge (R-MA) stated, for example, "The possession of the Philippines made us an Eastern power, with the right and, what was equally important, the force behind the right to speak. Mr. Hay, as Secretary of State, has obtained from all the great powers of Europe their assent to our demand for the guaranty of all our treaty rights in China and for the maintenance of the policy of the open door. I do not belittle one of the most important and most brilliant diplomatic achievements in our hundred years of national existence when I say that the assent of these other powers to the propositions of the United States was given to the master of Manila. They might have turned us aside three years ago with a shrug and a smile, but to the power which held Manila Bay, and whose fleet floated upon its waters, they were obliged to give a gracious answer."[5]

Related to the need to compete with European powers was the need to limit the influence of European powers within the Western Hemisphere. This position had been a long-standing fundamental tenet of U.S. foreign policy in the guise of the Monroe Doctrine. Theodore Roosevelt, however, extended the Monroe Doctrine through the Roosevelt Corollary (discussed in more detail in the Dominican Republic case study). The corollary further heightened the tensions between the broader and tempered views of America's international role; it emphasized the difference between the expansionist view that called for increased U.S. presence throughout the world and the anti-imperialist view that considered it an extreme form of jingoism. The effect of the Roosevelt Corollary, however, was that it provided a policy basis that justified greater U.S. involvement in the affairs of countries in the Western Hemisphere.

The third reason behind the nation's expansionist drive related to the need for economic expansion and the industrialization of the nation's economy.[6] An economic crisis that occurred in the early 1890s was blamed, in part, on the lack of sufficient markets for U.S. products. As a result, many manufacturers and bankers pressed for an aggressively expansionist U.S. foreign policy to open export markets. On a more intellectual level, the need for economic expansion abroad was seen as the logical extension of the continental expansion upon which U.S. democracy and economic prosperity thrived for the first century of the nation's history. As William Appleman Williams concluded, "In response to the Crisis of the 1890's, therefore, Americans developed a broad consensus in favor of an expansionist foreign policy as a solution to their existing troubles and as a way to prevent future difficulties."[7]

Williams's term "broad consensus" is important to note because the expansionist belief was widely held, even among the nation's political leaders. Although some of the most prominent imperialists, such as Theodore Roosevelt and Henry Cabot Lodge, were Republicans and the leading critic of imperialism—William Jennings Bryan—was a three-time Democratic candidate for president, the issue was not a strictly partisan one. Both Democrats and Republicans favored increased expansion and the greater international role associated with it.

Although this consensus was broad, it was not universal. Critics of U.S. imperialism formed the American Anti-Imperialist League. Created largely in response to the United States' acquisition of the Philippines after the Spanish-American War, this league consisted of "farmers . . . labor leaders . . . politicians seeking partisan advantage, and liberals who felt that a colonial policy would threaten American democratic traditions."[8] Midwestern farmers and labor leaders in the East had economic concerns about U.S. internationalism (namely, competing with colonial agriculture and the immigration of cheaper labor, respectively). The liberals who opposed U.S. expansion saw the exporting of the nation's political system as contrary to their belief in the country's tradition of self-determination. Despite this economic and philosophical opposition to expansion, the United States expanded its political and economic interests abroad.[9] By the end of the period under study, the tension between the two views of America's international role, while not fully resolved, clearly favored greater expansionism tied to economic interests.[10] As a result, U.S. foreign policy tended toward a more involved, more assertive, and broader role in international affairs.[11]

Although the president and Congress often agreed on internationalist policies throughout the era of 1881–1920, one area of institutional interactions repeatedly resulted in conflict. The Senate guarded the role it perceived for itself in setting foreign policy through its constitutional power to advise and consent to treaties. The Senate specifically voted down six treaties during this period and caused others to not be perfected.[12] This conflict was steeped in arguments of constitutionality and separation of powers. The result, however, was that it at times impeded U.S. involvement and entanglements with foreign nations.

Despite these institutional conflicts over treaties, there were numerous efforts to formalize U.S. interests abroad through the use of treaties and executive agreements. These efforts reflect the nation's growing interests overseas and range over a wide area. Some of the efforts were issue and country specific, such as the Frelinghuysen-Zalava Treaty (1884) regarding a canal through Nicaragua. Others were broader in scope, such as arbitration treaties negotiated under Theodore Roosevelt and Taft[13] and the "cooling off" treaties negotiated under Wilson,[14] all of which were sets of bilateral agreements designed to resolve disputes without using the military. Finally, some were international collaborative efforts, such as the Pan American Trade Conference[15] and the Hague conferences.[16]

One way in which the growth of the nation's international interests can be measured is through the increase in the number of treaties and executive agreements concluded during this era (see Table A.1 in the Appendix). In the final thirteen-year period of the era under study (1908–1920), an average total of 15.85 treaties and executive agreements were concluded per year. This total compares with an annual average of 13.79 treaties and executive agreements from 1894 to 1907 and 7.31 treaties and executive agreements from 1881 to 1893.[17] Clearly, the growth of U.S. interests abroad required presidents to enter into international agreements, which to some spelled "entangling alliances."

During this period, U.S. foreign policy can best be described as a movement from a general policy of expansion to one of annexation and finally to a protectorate policy. These broader trends can be seen by examining the manner in which the nation committed the military as part of its foreign policy. The deployment of troops was consistently used as a tool to achieve the nation's goals internationally. During the 1881–1920 period, two wars were formally declared (the Spanish-American War and World War I), and sixty-seven other incidents occurred in which U.S. troops were committed abroad (see Table A.2 in the Appendix for a more detailed reporting of these events).[18] Largely dominated by its concern with the Western Hemisphere, the United States became involved in a total of forty events (sixty percent) in Latin American or Caribbean countries, with another four events occurring in Pacific Island nations.

The Spanish-American War has been called a turning point for the nation, an important marker in the transition from an isolationist nation to an active participant in world affairs. It too was a reflection of the imperialist forces that were driving the nation to pursue its manifest destiny. Anti-imperialist critics considered the new U.S. foreign policy as jingoism and opposed the extension of the nation's involvement to other parts of the world. Debate notwithstanding, the consequences of the war for U.S. involvement internationally were twofold. First, it provided a basis for an increased role in the Western Hemisphere, through both its formal acquisition of interests throughout Latin America and the Caribbean (most notably Cuba,[19] Puerto Rico, and Guam[20]) and its increased role as the sole world power in the hemisphere. Second, it expanded the nation's influence and interests into the Far East through the acquisition of the Philippines.[21]

As for World War I, although a detailed description of the events relating to the World War is beyond the scope of our discussion, several important facets of the United States' role in the war are worth noting. First, the country tried to remain neutral at the outset of the war. Despite the growth of America's international role, the nation still did not want to be involved in European affairs. This may be one of the last remnants of the traditional policy of nonentanglement. Only when Germany increased its use of submarines, which the United States viewed as threatening its interests and violating its rights of neutrality, did the nation become directly involved in the war. Second, even with the restraint placed upon U.S. involvement by its official neutrality in the first part of the war, Wilson still tried to play a role in the conflict and settle the war diplomatically. In other words, although the nation was not fighting, Wilson still saw a role for the United States within the international crisis.

The third point relates to the League of Nations. Despite the fact that the United States came out of the war as a world power, the League of Nations suffered a backlash from those who opposed increased involvement with European countries. For example, leading critics of the League of Nations in Congress formed the League for the Preservation of American Independence and campaigned against Wilson and the League of Nations.[22] One should consider, however, that the League of Nations was not defeated solely because of this opposition. Its opponents (or at least nonsupporters) included people who were disillusioned with the peace process, particularly with hostilities occurring in Russia and Cen-

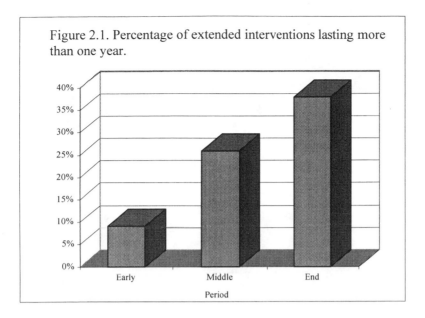

Figure 2.1. Percentage of extended interventions lasting more than one year.

tral Europe right after the war; people who favored an international role for the United States but did not agree with its collective security provisions; people who resented Wilson's efforts promoting it when there were domestic issues such as inflation, strikes, and race riots that required attention; and Republicans who opposed the League of Nations simply because it was Democratic President Wilson's vision for the world.[23] In other words, much of the opposition was along simple policy lines rather than a philosophical difference regarding the role of the United States.

In examining the commitments during the period 1881–1920 overall (other than the two declared wars), troops were generally deployed for what could be termed defensive reasons.[24] In seventy-five percent of the cases, the troops were utilized to protect U.S. lives and/or interests abroad, often during times of political or civil unrest in the other country. As the era progressed, however, the military was also used for other reasons, such as suppressing rebellions, establishing some form of control or protectorate, and serving as a neutral international third party in an area of potential conflict.

The commitment of troops during the period was generally for brief, isolated events. In a majority of cases for which information was available, fewer than one thousand troops were deployed. Furthermore, most

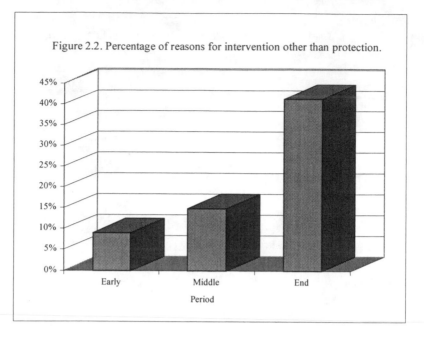

Figure 2.2. Percentage of reasons for intervention other than protection.

(fifty-seven percent) of the events lasted less than two months. In addition, as these events were not declared acts of war, they did not necessarily require congressional authorization. As a result, in only twenty-two cases (thirty-three percent) can we say that Congress had authorized the usage of the military. Most of these, however, were done pursuant to the terms of a treaty or an existing law. In only one case does it appear that Congress had explicitly authorized the specific commitment of troops absent a prior treaty or law.[25]

Breaking down the entire period from 1881 to 1920 into smaller eras, however, starts to unmask several trends evidencing greater international activity by the United States with a greater diversity of purpose throughout the period (see Table A.3 in the Appendix). From 1881 to 1893, troops were utilized abroad in eleven instances.[26] This number increases to 27 and 29 for the periods 1894–1907 and 1908–1920, respectively (exclusive of declared wars). Furthermore, not only were there more commitments in the latter years, but the interventions were more likely to last longer (Figure 2.1). During the first period, only one commitment lasted more than a year; on the other hand, seven ended in less than two months. During the middle period, although a majority (sixty-three percent) of the interventions lasted less than two months, seven interventions (twenty-six percent) lasted for more than a year. Finally, the number of interventions between 1908 and 1920 that lasted more than one year was eleven, which represents thirty-eight percent of the total during that period.

Another important trend is the increasing percentage of interventions that were carried out for reasons other than the protection of U.S. lives and/or interests (Figure 2.2). Whereas in the earliest subperiod the interventions were related to protecting U.S. lives and/or interests,[27] by the middle period (1894–1907), other reasons associated with the usage of the military were employed; some of these, such as suppressing a rebellion or establishing some form of control or a protectorate, are more offensive, rather than defensive, in nature. During the end period, military interventions were carried out to establish some form of control or protectorate, suppress a rebellion, serve as a neutral international third party, and pursue Mexican bandits.[28] Although the protection of lives and interests was the reason in a majority of the interventions, twelve (forty-one percent) were carried out for other reasons.

We can conclude from this review that the United States accelerated its foreign involvement during the era of 1881–1920. Although the nation's interests were starting to spread beyond its borders and needed protection by the U.S. military even during the earliest part of this period, the government was still trying to limit its involvement abroad in scope, magnitude, and purpose. As the United States, however, started moving away from these initial tendencies, the use of the military as a tool to move toward the increased expansion of U.S. interests was still tempered by anti-imperialist sentiments. Nevertheless, there is a subtle, but clear, change in how the military was used during the middle period. This change reflected the growing power and influence of the increased international role in U.S. foreign policy. Such a change continued into the end period, where we see a continued movement toward a more involved, more assertive, and broader role for the United States in international affairs.

The nation's movement toward an expansionist and more active role in foreign affairs also created an environment in which opportunity structures for increased presidential authority could arise. In this policy area where the presidency has the strongest Constitutional claim for authority, both the increased amount of U.S. activity abroad, as well as the nature of that activity, played into the president's roles as chief diplomat and commander in chief. Further, with many international commitments lasting less than two months, the need for quick and timely decisions, particularly when Congress would not be in session, allowed the presidents during this period ample ability to exercise the authority of the institution and build upon it.

CASE STUDIES

Turning now to the specific cases selected (Samoa in 1888, Dominican Republic in 1905, and Haiti in 1915),[29] we see that the period under study began with a president who had a conception of a limited presidency. Cleveland's rhetoric and behavior both reflected an understanding that the presidency and Congress were coparticipants in developing long-term policy. He was willing to share all of the information his administrators collected about the situation in Samoa and even stated that he could go no further in establishing long-term policy without congressional input. He took firm action, however, in the original commitment of troops to Samoa, which went unchallenged by Congress, both in rhetoric and behavior. Therefore, not only are there indications of a shared understanding regarding the president's ability to commit troops but there also appear to be indications that coparticipation is the understanding regarding long-term policy development.

The middle of this period saw the most contentious interaction over authority in this area, as President Roosevelt sought to rewrite the existing coordinated script by pushing the boundaries of the understandings regarding proper presidential behavior. Once again, the issue of contention was not the commitment of troops per se. In this case the issue in dispute was the president's ability to implement an international agreement without the "advice" of the Senate. After much contention by Democratic opponents in Congress, the treaty was finally renegotiated (so that the Senate could have its "input") and ratified. By 1915, the commitment of troops and the handling of the Dominican Republic by Roosevelt was considered a success. Despite the wrangling that went on and the disagreement of some Democratic congressmen, the shared understanding that emerged from this interaction was that proactive movements like Roosevelt's in committing troops and activating the treaty, thereby setting some long-term policy on his own, will eventually be rewarded with congressional approval. Despite the two years of wrangling, the presidency emerged victorious, thus leaving future presidents with precedent to follow.

The final period saw President Wilson acting proactively in committing troops and in negotiating and attaining unanimous consent by the Senate to the ratification of a treaty establishing longer-term policy in Haiti. Congress, on the other hand, was silent. Unlike some members of Congress in the Dominican case, who after reconvening took it upon themselves to challenge Roosevelt's actions, this Congress did not debate the subject at all upon reconvening. In fact, its preoccupation with other affairs, such as the impending European conflict and the trouble with Mexico, made the silence over the Haiti case appear not out of the ordinary. In light of the many comparisons made between this Haiti intervention and the Dominican one a decade earlier, however, the silence takes on new meaning—the coordinated script had already been written and provided a cost-effective way of addressing the issue at hand.

Samoa: History

The Samoan Islands were viewed as being of "considerable commercial and strategic importance to the United States."[30] U.S. commerce with Samoa itself was seen as small but valuable, particularly to Pacific coast trading interests. Samoa's significance also lay in the fact that it was situated on a route between the United States and Southern Pacific trading partners such as Australia. The nation itself is composed of nine islands, with Savaii, Upolu, and Tutuila considered the most important. Savaii is the largest, while Upolu was the richest in terms of population and natural resources. Apia, on Upolu, was a prominent harbor, the seat of government, and the residence of most foreigners. The United States had treaty rights to the Tutuilan harbor of Pago Pago. These interests stemmed from a treaty with Samoa in 1878, while Germany and England signed similar treaties in 1879.

The string of events that led to the U.S. commitment of troops to Samoa in 1888 started in the summer of 1887, when Germany was able to get Tamasese, the Samoan vice king, "elected" king and recognized him as the proper ruler of Samoa. The United States and Great Britain, however, did not recognize the installed Tamasese government. After the former king, Malietoa Laupepa, surrendered to Tamasese,[31] his supporters, led by a new chief, Malietoa Mataafa, engaged in war with Tamasese's forces. In the words of Sen. Joseph Dolph (R-OR), a member of the Foreign Relations Committee, in this conflict, "the lives of [U.S.] citizens have been endangered, their property destroyed; they have been subjected to personal indignities by the German authorities at Apia."[32] The tensions in Samoa increased in September 1888, such that on September 4, 1888, U.S. Vice Consul Blacklock sent a telegram to Secretary of State Bayard that read: "Samoans at war. General revolt against Tamasese. Affairs more serious than ever."[33] On September 15, 1888, Bayard sent a letter to Secretary of the Navy W. C. Whitney, stating, "In view of the possible need of protection to the American interests in that region, I would suggest that, if possible, a discreet officer in command of a Government vessel should visit Samoa at the earliest possible day and report fully upon the condition of affairs."[34]

The USS *Adams,* under Commander Leary, was sent to Apia. On October 9, 1888, Leary transmitted a report to Secretary Whitney in which he concluded, "The present condition of affairs at this place, with a general uprising of the natives against a so-called government, and the utter disregard of foreigners and their property by the Tamasese forces, renders the situation a most critical one for American residents."[35] In subsequent correspondence from Commander Leary to Secretary Whitney, the commander advised the secretary that "The presence of a war vessel here during the existing difficulties is of the utmost importance, if our flag is to be respected or our countrymen's lives protected."[36]

On November 7, 1888, the USS *Nipsic* arrived in Samoa, while the *Adams* returned to San Francisco in early December. During this period in late 1888, Germany bolstered its military forces in Samoa by increasing the number of its vessels from one to three.[37] In addition, German forces continually engaged in skirmishes with the Samoans who opposed Tamasese. The most significant event was reported by Commander Mullan of the *Nipsic* to Secretary Whitney via a telegram: "Three German war ships at Apia threaten to disarm Mataafa; landed at Lalengo to prevent Mataafa's retreat. Engagement followed. Germans lost 20 killed 30 wounded. Germans swear vengeance; shelling and burning native villages. Neutral property not respected. Protests disregarded. American property in danger. Consul reports American in boat flying American flag seized in Apia harbor by armed German boat, but released after (?)investigation.

German captain says no flag was shown. State affairs so serious request additional force."[38]

On January 10, 1889, President Cleveland sent a cablegram to Rear Adm. Lewis A. Kimberly responding to the request for additional force: "Proceed at once to Samoa and extend full protection and defence to

American citizens and their property. . . . Protest against the subjugation of the country and the displacement of native government by German rule enforced by German arms and coercion, as in violation of the positive agreement and understanding between foreign powers interested, but inform the representatives of the German and English Governments of your readiness to co-operate in causing all treaty rights to be respected and in restoring peace and order on the basis of a recognition of Samoan rights to independence."[39]

As a result, the warships USS *Trenton* and USS *Vandalia* were sent to Samoa. Although tensions continued to rise between German and U.S. forces in Apia harbor throughout the first part of 1889, the foreign powers prepared to meet in Berlin to try to reach a diplomatic solution. Before the conference, a major hurricane struck Samoa in March, destroying or badly damaging the German and U.S. ships and killing approximately one hundred men. The destruction caused by the hurricane facilitated a nonviolent resolution to the entanglement by establishing a tripartite protectorate over the Samoan Islands.

Shortly after Cleveland committed the naval vessels to Samoan waters, he sent a message to Congress, consistent with his personal view of the presidency, stating that he thought that he had reached the limit of his presidential authority and that Congress should provide him with legislative guidance. In other words, although Cleveland believed he had the authority to utilize the military in the way he did, Congress needed to make any long-term policy decisions. Congress took up the challenge Cleveland presented to it and appropriated $500,000 for the protection of U.S. interests in Samoa and $100,000 for the construction of wharves and buildings in the harbor of Pago Pago. Quite importantly, however, Congress left the actual expenditures to be made to the president's discretion. Other than these appropriations, Congress explicitly chose to give the president no other instructions or guidance than for Cleveland (and then President Harrison, after he assumed office) to do what he thought best. Regardless of Cleveland's lame-duck status, Congress decided to grant the presidency this authority.

Samoa: Analysis

In terms of the decision to commit military forces to Samoa, Cleveland clearly behaved proactively, as if he had no question about his authority as president to commit military forces in this manner. Acting out the role of commander in chief, he personally issued the order to his military commander in the region to proceed to Samoa and gave him explicit mission objectives once the forces arrived there. Although he continually updated Congress throughout 1888 and provided members with background information about the events as they unfolded in the island nation, Cleveland did not provide Congress an opportunity to participate in the military decision to commit troops. Furthermore, Congress, as an institution, did not seek such an opportunity, as evidenced by its silence on the matter.

Cleveland's understanding of presidential authority limited such unilateral actions to the initial commitment of troops; in other words, his authority to behave proactively ceased at the point of troop commitment. Beyond that, Cleveland believed he required legislative involvement and determination. Cleveland's January 15, 1889, message to Congress provides the key rhetoric for understanding his conception of presidential authority:

> The information thus laid before the Congress is of much importance, since it has relation to the preservation of American interests and the protection of American citizens and their property in a distant locality and under an unstable and unsatisfactory government.
>
> In the midst of the disturbances which have arisen at Samoa such powers have been exercised as seemed to be within Executive control under our Constitution and laws, and which appear to accord with our national policy and traditions, to restore tranquility and secure the safety of our citizens. . . .
>
> Acting within the restraints which our Constitution and laws have placed upon Executive power, I have insisted that the autonomy and independence of Samoa should be scrupulously preserved according to the treaties made with Samoa by the powers named and their agreements and understanding with each other. I have protested against every act apparently tending in an opposite direction, and during the existence of internal disturbance one or more vessels of war have been kept in Samoan waters to protect American citizens and property.
>
> These things will abundantly appear from the correspondence and papers which have been submitted to Congress.

A recent collision between the forces from a German man-of-war stationed in Samoan waters and a body of natives rendered the situation so delicate and critical that the war ship *Trenton,* under the immediate command of Admiral Kimberly, was ordered to join the *Nipsic,* already at Samoa, for the better protection of the persons and property of our citizens and in furtherance of efforts to restore order and safety.

The attention of the Congress is especially called to the instructions given to Admiral Kimberly dated on the 11th instant and the letter of the Secretary of State to the German minister dated the 12th instant, which will be found among the papers herewith submitted.

. . . [This information regarding] Samoa is laid before the Congress, and such Executive action as has been taken is fully exhibited.

The views of the Executive in respect of the just policy to be pursued with regard to this group of islands, which lie in the direct highway of a growing and important commerce between Australia and the United States, have found expression in the correspondence and documents which have thus been fully communicated to the Congress, and the subject in its present stage is submitted to the wider discretion conferred by the Constitution upon the legislative branch of the Government.[40]

A number of key statements emphasize Cleveland's understanding of his institutional role vis-à-vis Congress. His statements that his orders to commit naval vessels to Samoa fell within executive power under the Constitution and laws reflect an understanding that he had the authority as president to do so. In other words, the military commitment reflected an application of the authority granted to the institution of the presidency as codified by the Constitution and subsequent laws. Cleveland understood, however, that this authority has limits and restraints. Most importantly, his concluding statement, that the intervention required legislative involvement for any further action, demonstrates a conception that the presidency shares authority with Congress in setting policy—in other words, a norm of coparticipation. Cleveland's statement seems to indicate that, while the president may have the authority to initiate a military intervention abroad in response to changing international events, the president is expected to seek legislative guidance with respect to any long-term policy making subsequent to the military intervention.

Congress's involvement in the institutional interaction over the commitment of troops to Samoa can be termed "active-reactive." Congress, particularly the Senate, took an active position regarding U.S. policy in Samoa throughout 1888 and 1889. During 1888, prior to the increased hostilities that led to Cleveland's January 10, 1889, order to Admiral Kimberly, the Senate Foreign Relations Committee continually received President Cleveland's reports and, given the level of detailed information the committee members included in their debate on the floor of Congress, reviewed the material. Moreover, after President Cleveland placed the issue in the institution's purview, Congress provided the authorization Cleveland sought through the passage of the two appropriations related to Samoa. Despite this activity, however, Congress as an institution was responding to the signals that Cleveland provided. In addition, the signal Congress sent Cleveland in return was that he was expected to pursue the policy he considered the most appropriate. Most importantly, and easily overlooked, Congress did not question Cleveland's decision to instruct Admiral Kimberly to proceed to Samoa, either from a foreign policy standpoint or as an issue of institutional authority. Cleveland's authority to commit troops was understood and respected by Congress, whose members generally seem to have shared Cleveland's understanding that he was expected to respond to foreign events but participate in the long-term policy-making process with Congress.

An examination of the debates among the members of Congress demonstrates their understanding of the institutional roles of Congress and the presidency. Overall, most of the congressional debate occurred in the Senate and occupied approximately thirty pages in the *Congressional Record*. Although the Senate addressed the Samoan intervention in one way or another throughout the events just described, much of the discussion was concentrated in the period January 29–31, 1889. The primary spokesmen in favor of Samoan intervention included Senators John Sherman (R-OH), Joseph Dolph (R-OR), and Eugene Hale (R-ME); leaders against the proposal included Senators John Reagan (D-TX) and John Morgan (D-AL).[41] All told, twenty-one senators participated in the debate on the floor of the Senate, some of whom were Senate Foreign Committee members.[42] Deliberation in the House regarding the affairs in Samoa occurred in February 1889 (after the Senate had passed a version of the appropriation bills) and was limited to approximately five pages in the *Congressional Record*. The substance of the debate primarily involved settling differences with the Senate's version of the bill or occurred within the context of debate on other issues.

Although some members of Congress had a conception of the institutional roles that differed from Cleveland's (i.e., that Congress had a significantly greater authority in establishing policy than the presidency), most of the members viewed the level of shared authority between the two institutions as more balanced. For example, as early as December 10, 1888, during a debate of a resolution that the Committee on Foreign Relations be instructed to inquire into the situation in the Samoan Islands, Sen. George Gray (D-DE) stated:

> Whether the Government of the U.S. under this impulse of jingoism (which I use for want of a better word to characterize the feeling which seems to be rampant now in regard to our foreign affairs) should interfere in the matter that concerns the islands of the Pacific Ocean and should embroil itself with the powers of Europe, governments where foreign affairs are controlled by the executive entirely, without the intervention of the legislative branch of the government, is a question to be determined by the people of the United States through the Senate and House of Representatives in Congress assembled.
>
> . . . [B]ut there is certainly no power lodged with the Executive or in any of the Executive Departments to commit the Government of the United States to a policy that involves the assertion of physical force in interference in matters of that kind without the consent of Congress and without legislation by the Senate and the House of Representatives.[43]

Although Senator Gray's position was embraced by neither his colleagues in the Senate during the debate nor President Cleveland in the context of the Samoan intervention, similar sentiments were enunciated by other senators regarding the appropriation of funds related to Samoa. More specifically, some senators utilized President Cleveland's words in his January 10 message to argue that Congress had the responsibility to set the specific policy direction for the nation in its affairs in Samoa. For example, Sen. John Reagan (D-TX) argued, "I would give the President power to insist on our rights under the treaty stipulations and correspondence between these governments, and the power to assert our rights in such a way that there could be no mistake about what his meaning and his powers are.

. . . If we do not put some such declaration in the [appropriations] bill, we leave the President when we have passed the act exactly where he is now, in which position he regards himself as powerless to vindicate the rights of American citizens or to discharge the duties of the American Government to the people and Government of Samoa."[44]

Furthermore, Reagan stated, "It seems to me that while this money is given to the President, who has stated to us in substance that he has exhausted his constitutional authority and asks Congress for further direction in the matter, we are either shirking responsibility ourselves or intending to place the President in a false position by appropriating money for him to do something with and refusing to tell him what to do with it. This proposed action does not enlarge the President's power. It does not indicate the policy of Congress on this subject. It simply leaves the whole question open and throws the President upon his own discretion, which he says he has already exhausted. What is he or his successor to do with this money without Congressional direction?"[45]

Despite Senator Reagan's arguments that the president needed explicit congressional direction, the majority of senators disagreed. They viewed the course of action that Congress had proposed—to authorize $500,000 to be immediately available and expended at the president's direction for the protection of U.S. treaty interests in Samoa—as providing the president with the proper authority to proceed in Samoa and as being the appropriate action for Congress to take in its institutional policy-making role. Although Senator Reagan offered an amendment that he felt would have provided the president with additional guidance, it was defeated.[46]

The leading advocate for the majority position was Sen. John Sherman (R-OH). As one of the most prominent members in the Senate generally and as chair of the Senate Foreign Relations Committee, which had legislative jurisdiction over the appropriations bills under consideration and the situation in Samoa, specifically, Sherman was in a position to influence and lead the Senate in determining U.S. policy in Samoa. In the context of the Samoan appropriations bills, Sherman stated:

Now, sir, I say therefore, first, we want to assert our rights and maintain and uphold them, and nobody will call them in question. Next, we want to do what we ought to do to these poor people there who first treated with us, who have leaned upon us, and who have reminded us over and over again that we promised them our good offices, and they understand by that something more than a diplomatic note. This we can accomplish. Therefore, Mr. President, I am willing to vote any sum of money to enable the President either to conduct negotiations, to make surveys of the harbors, or to get better information in regard to the country there. I am willing to vote the sum named here and place it at the discretion of Mr. Cleveland or of General Harrison, and I have no doubt with the powers thus given to them to send agents there or to send ships there they will bring about a prompt solution of this small controversy.[47]

A member of the Senate Foreign Relations Committee, Sen. Joseph Dolph (R-OR) added that "the questions which have arisen between the U.S. and Germany are questions which should be settled diplomatically. If Congress were to interfere and to give direction in the matter, something very different from these proposed [appropriations] amendments would be required."[48] Finally, Sen. Eugene Hale (R-ME), a member of the Appropriations and Naval Affairs Committees, added, "[A]nd I expect that when the executive power of this Government, which is to deal with this important subject by negotiation, is confronted with the issue it will find itself confronted with the German authority and the policy of the German Empire. Out of that I hope a wise course will be pursued, and that we shall not be unnecessarily involved in important steps that will lead to grave and it may be deplorable results unless it is clear that the rights of American citizens have been interfered with and that everything is necessary to protect those rights."[49]

When the debate in Congress concluded, the final wording of the appropriations amendments as they were passed by Congress and signed by President Cleveland left the $500,000 and $100,000 expenditures to the discretion of the president. This simple fact alone reflects the belief held by a majority of those in Congress that such wording was the appropriate response by Congress, as an institution, after President Cleveland placed the Samoan affair before it.

This response and the rhetoric its supporters provided also reflect on the broader issue of the expectations and views of institutional authority held by members of Congress. First, after Cleveland instructed Admiral Kimberly to send additional forces to Samoa, no member of Congress questioned Cleveland's use of these forces. Given this, Cleveland's actions can be seen as not violating any expectations or extending beyond his institutional authority; in other words, Congress shared Cleveland's understanding of his authority.

Second, Congress's decision to address the Samoan situation by appropriating funds to be used at the president's discretion reflects a certain understanding of its own institutional authority vis-à-vis the presidency. Congress clearly understood that its role required it to work with the president to set policy with regard to Samoa and Germany. In the determination of a majority of its members, however, the resolution to the affair should lie in the diplomatic realm, where the president is presumed to have greater authority. Each of the three speakers quoted earlier who reflected this view (Sherman, Dolph, and Hale) exhibited a belief that the presidency should be the political institution that resolved the issue and Congress should not be. They indicated that they expected the president to behave in a specific manner and, through the passage of the appropriations, provided a sufficient signal that he had the authority necessary to proceed.

Samoa: Conclusion

The institutional interaction that occurred over the commitment of U.S. military forces in Samoa in 1889 can be seen as driven by the shared understandings held by President Cleveland and a majority of members of Congress generally and several key members in particular. At the heart of the interaction was a widely held expectation that permitted the president to commit troops abroad into a known and potentially dangerous engagement when U.S. interests were imminently threatened by the intervention of a European power. Cleveland acted as if he had no uncertainty about whether he had the authority to commit troops; he merely ordered their commitment. The members of Congress could have easily expressed opposition to Cleveland over this commitment or questioned his right to do so but chose not to. From this interaction and the indicators uncovered, we can conclude that a widely held shared understanding existed—that when in the course of international events

U.S. interests and property are threatened abroad, the president can be expected to commit troops to protect them.

Another shared understanding helped drive the interaction as well—namely, that the president should interact with Congress to establish long-term policy. Cleveland not only recognized the limits of his authority but also initiated the institutional interaction by placing his limited authority before Congress. Cleveland realized that the presidency shares the policy-making process with Congress. As a result, he placed the process squarely in Congress's collective lap. Although Congress shared the expectation that it would be included in the decision making, it decided that the presidency was best suited to resolve the issue. Congress's view of its proper role in the process was to step back and let the executive branch negotiate a settlement.

These shared understandings and the way in which they played out in the Samoan affair reflect what appears to have been an established pathway that the two institutions followed to address the issues at hand. This pathway points toward a solid basis of authority for the presidency to commit military forces to nations in which U.S. interests are threatened by a European intervention. Essentially, the presidency is expected to interact with foreign governments to protect U.S. interests abroad; inform and engage Congress when long-term policy decisions need to be made; and, after receiving some indication of congressional support, resolve issues related to U.S. interests. Connected to these expectations, the presidency possesses the necessary authority to fulfill them. Through this case, we see that Congress expects to play a part in crafting policy but is willing to delegate many of the specifics of doing so to the presidency. However, even though the presidency may have greater authority to commit military forces abroad, the president must recognize that the authority of the institution to decide long-term policy is shared with the legislative branch of the government.

Dominican Republic: History

The U.S. intervention in the Dominican Republic (sometimes referred to at the time only by the name of its capital, Santo Domingo) stemmed from the financial troubles and debt that the island nation had developed over a period of thirty-five years. Jacob H. Hollander, a special commissioner sent to investigate the Dominican financial condition, calculated Santo Domingo's total indebtedness as of June 1, 1905, including interest in arrears, to be $40,269,404.83.[50] Although a portion of this debt was owed to the United States and U.S. citizens, most of the outstanding debt was owed to European investors. As a result, European powers, including Germany and Italy, threatened to intervene in Dominican affairs to protect their interests and those of their citizens.

The U.S. intervention in 1905 represented the first application of the Roosevelt Corollary to the Monroe Doctrine. This doctrine, which guided the nation's foreign policy in the Western Hemisphere, sought to keep European powers from exerting influence in this part of the world. Roosevelt enunciated his corollary to the Monroe Doctrine in his 1904 annual message in December, shortly before the U.S. intervention in Santo Domingo. Roosevelt stated that "chronic wrongdoing, or an impotence which results in a general loosening of the ties of civilized society" required intervention from a more "civilized" power.[51] Furthermore, when such wrongdoing occurred in Latin America or the Caribbean, the Monroe Doctrine essentially required the United States to exercise an international police power, however reluctantly it did so.[52]

Under this worldview, Roosevelt considered the financial rehabilitation of Santo Domingo to be the United States' responsibility. Roosevelt contended that "[t]he justification for the United States taking this burden and incurring this responsibility is to be found in the fact that it is incompatible with international equity for the United States to refuse to allow other powers to take the only means at their disposal of satisfying the claims of their creditors and yet to refuse, itself, to take any such steps."[53]

Roosevelt entered first into an agreement with the Dominican Republic and then a more formal "Protocol of an Agreement between the United States and the Dominican Republic, Providing for the Collection and Disbursement by the United States of the Customs Revenues of the Dominican Republic, Signed on February 4, 1905." The protocol, which expressly recognized the Dominican Republic's inability to pay even the interest on its debt and the desire of the United States to keep that nation free from European control, called for the United States to attempt to adjust the obligations of the Dominican Republic and allocate revenues according to a formula defined in the protocol; to take charge of the existing custom houses; and, at the request of the Dominican government, to provide whatever assistance it deemed proper to preserve the order and advance the material progress and welfare of the Dominican Republic.[54]

News of the protocol appeared in U.S. newspapers in late January, at which time Roosevelt had not informed Congress of this foreign policy initiative. Many members of Congress, particularly Democrats, were opposed to the policy, both for its content and the process of its development. Both before and after Roosevelt submitted the protocol as a treaty to the Senate in February 1905, the Senate engaged in sometimes acrimonious debate over it, often for partisan reasons. When Congress adjourned from its regular session on March 4, the Senate had not taken action on the treaty, which was still lacking the two-thirds majority necessary for ratification.

Roosevelt called the Senate back for a special session that lasted from March 4 to March 18, 1905. The Committee on Foreign Relations reported the treaty, laden with Democratic amendments, to the floor of the Senate. When the amended treaty still appeared to be lacking the necessary votes for passage, Roosevelt let the Senate adjourn without taking action rather than let the measure be defeated outright. Roosevelt, however, considered himself "left to shoulder the responsibility for [the Senate's] failure" to ratify the protocol.[55]

The threat of European intervention became more real when, on March 14, an Italian naval vessel arrived at Santo Domingo to obtain payment on the debt. To stave off foreign creditors, the Dominican government requested a modus vivendi: The United States would temporarily implement the terms of the protocol until the Senate could vote on the treaty. Roosevelt, after conferring with Senate Republican leaders, proceeded with this course of action. In late March, Roosevelt sent Jacob Hollander to Santo Domingo to examine the government's debt situation. Furthermore, intent on preserving order in the Dominican Republic, Roosevelt committed military forces to the island nation and instructed the secretary of the navy to "tell Admiral Bradford [the naval commander in the area] to stop any revolution. I intend to keep the island *in statu quo* until the Senate has had time to act on the treaty, and I shall treat any revolutionary movement as an effort to upset the *modus vivendi*. That this is ethically right I am dead sure, even though there may be some technical or red tape difficulty."[56] The use of the U.S. military to preserve the status quo in the Dominican Republic lasted for the entire two-year period in which the modus vivendi was in effect.

When Congress returned to session in December, the Senate still opposed the ratification of the treaty and made the competition over institutional authority explicit. Although Senate Democrats argued against the treaty in early 1906, they eventually lost some of their intensity. As a result, the treaty was not brought to a floor vote, and the modus vivendi continued in place throughout 1906. Secretary of State Elihu Root was able to renegotiate a new treaty with the Dominican Republic that addressed the concerns of those in the Senate. The revised treaty was concluded in early February 1907 and ratified by the Senate shortly thereafter.

Dominican Republic: Analysis

The institutional interaction over U.S. involvement in the Dominican Republic was particularly acrimonious. The differences between the president and members of Congress sometimes stemmed from partisan allegiances, and the animosity that was displayed often turned personal. At the base of this conflict, however, was the belief of some members in each institution that the other body was either shirking its institutional responsibility or violating the roles it was expected to play. Through the process of this interaction and the behavior and rhetoric of these actors, we can see that the Dominican case started as an implicit competition over authority and transformed into an explicit one in 1906. Existing pathways were being challenged, as Roosevelt sought to establish a new script when the old one did not work to his satisfaction.

The process of the institutional interaction in the Dominican case shares significant similarities with the Samoan affair. Most specifically, U.S. interests were at risk in a nation in which at least one European power was threatening to intervene in that nation's affairs. Unlike Samoa, where President Cleveland responded to international events by committing military forces first and then placing the long-term policy decision before Congress, in the Dominican case, the U.S. interests potentially at risk were not seen as facing an immediate threat. Thus, President Roosevelt needed to address the long-term policy question prior to the commitment of troops.

The understanding that many members of Congress held at this time was that if policy decisions needed to be made, then Congress would participate. When the members of Congress learned that Roosevelt started protocol/treaty negotiations with Dominican leaders via an article that appeared in the January 22, 1905, edition of the *Washington Post* rather than directly from Roosevelt or an executive branch official, many believed that Roosevelt's behavior violated their understanding of what was expected of the president in such a situation.[57] Other members, however, did not adhere to this view and generally supported both the policy of President Roosevelt and his right to initiate it.

Although the Senate adjourned from both its regular session and a special session without voting on the treaty, a change in international events provided Roosevelt with the opportunity to achieve his policy goals, which included the use of U.S. troops to help preserve order and protect U.S. interests in the Dominican Republic.[58] Even though the Senate returned to session in December, 1905, a renegotiated treaty that addressed many of the Democratic concerns was not ratified until February 1907. All the while, the "temporary" arrangement in the Dominican Republic continued. During this period, the long-term policy questions remained the focus of the institutional differences. Roosevelt's commitment of the military and implementation of the terms of the treaty until a final decision could be reached, however, was not questioned. Roosevelt's supporters in the Senate, in fact, claimed that the modus vivendi was an extension of executive prerogative.[59]

The substance of this interaction came down to one set of key questions: Does the president have the authority to direct a long-term foreign policy initiative without congressional input and consent prior to finalizing the terms of the deal? In other words, are the members of Congress expected simply to accept and approve treaties and other foreign policy initiatives the president places before them, or are they supposed to be active participants in crafting such policies? Thus, Roosevelt (with his supporters in the Senate) and those members of Congress who favored a more active role for that institution can be seen to have been engaged in an implicit competition over authority—the authority to establish long-term policy relating to Western Hemisphere countries threatened with intervention by European powers.

Roosevelt's behavior indicates that he assumed he had the institutional authority necessary to behave as he did. First, he had negotiated with Dominican officials to create a formal role for the United States in managing Santo Domingo's collections and debt problem without formally notifying Congress (or even those committee members that would have jurisdiction over such a treaty). Second, he proceeded with the implementation of the terms of the treaty via the modus vivendi, even knowing the concerns that some members of Congress had raised.

Roosevelt's behavior was proactive; he initiated the policy and pushed the policy-making process, thereby demonstrating an expansive understanding of the presidency's institutional authority.

Roosevelt's understanding, which is supported by the eventual outcome of the institutional interaction, held wide support in Congress but still had detractors. In 1905, however, congressional opponents, largely Democrats, did not focus directly on the competition for authority between the institutions but instead chose to address this issue in other ways, such as focusing on the narrower issues of learning of the treaty through the press and possible procedural violations of the treaty-making process. By 1906, however, the competition over institutional authority developed to the point that it was an explicit topic of debate in the Senate.

This institutional competition was played out on the floors of Congress and in the rhetoric of Theodore Roosevelt. Roosevelt's rhetoric reflected a strong belief that he as president had the authority to undertake, initiate, and implement the policy he crafted. Furthermore, in his belief, Congress should be expected to follow the president's foreign policy initiatives.

In a message to Congress, Roosevelt described the intervention into Dominican affairs as "a practical test of the efficiency of the United States Government in maintaining the Monroe Doctrine."[60] In doing so, Roosevelt considered the U.S. intervention to be the nation's responsibility, which consequently meant that Congress's obligation was to pass the treaty necessary to implement this policy clearly based on the Monroe Doctrine. In Roosevelt's view, "Every man who votes against this treaty by his vote invites foreign nations to violate the Monroe Doctrine, and refuses relief and protection to a struggling American republic which has appealed to us for aid."[61]

Roosevelt tried several ways to persuade the Senate to ratify the treaty. At the start of the special session, he sent a message to "state to the Senate that the condition of affairs in Santo Domingo is such that it is very much for the interest of that Republic that action on the treaty should be had at as early a moment as the Senate, after giving the matter full consideration, may find practicable."[62] In this message, Roosevelt outlined the benefits that the treaty would afford to the Dominican Republic, which included relief and assistance and "the method most like to secure peace and to prevent war on the island."[63] Roosevelt also individually addressed specific key senators who were blocking the ratification of the treaty. For example, Roosevelt wrote to Sen. John C. Spooner (R-WI), a member of the Senate Foreign Relations Committee, "You can have no idea of the way in which we are hampered by any such amendment as this in trying to carry out any kind of decent and effective foreign policy. Personally, I of course feel very strongly that there was no need of amending the Santo Dominican treaty."[64]

Roosevelt vented his frustration stemming from the Senate's not ratifying the treaty at both the individual and the institutional levels. For example, he referred to Senate Democrats and "men like Spooner" as "prize idiots," while saying that "the necessity for a two-thirds vote in the Senate and the power to amend treaties by the Senate together with the Senate's limitless capacity for delay combine to render it a very poor body to compose part of the treaty-making power."[65] Furthermore, he warned against "the wrong that will be done the United States Government to defeat the Santo Domingo treaty on partisan grounds."[66] From this rhetoric we can infer that Roosevelt expected the Senate to follow his lead in establishing a policy that he saw as entirely consistent with the Monroe Doctrine. When the Senate failed to ratify the treaty, he saw the body as in some way shirking its responsibility to pass laws to protect and benefit U.S. interests.

Roosevelt's rhetoric also demonstrates that he understood his own institutional authority to be sufficient to implement the modus vivendi. He recognized, however, that some in the Senate might not share this understanding with him (although he clearly did not agree with them). Roosevelt described the process by which he decided to pursue the implementation of the modus vivendi as "There has been rather a comic development in the Santo Domingo case. Morales asked us to take over the custom houses pending action by the Senate. I decided to do so, but first of all consulted Spooner, Foraker, Lodge and Knox. All heartily agreed that it was necessary for me to take this action."[67]

Furthermore, in an April 2, 1905, letter to Secretary of State Hay, Roosevelt stated matter-of-factly, "In Santo Domingo, we have taken the necessary step," but concluded, "I do not think that Santo Domingo itself will give us much trouble; but the fool vote and the timid vote will both be greatly alarmed at home."[68] Roosevelt's labels of the "fool vote" and the "timid vote" reflect that he knew that some members of

Congress would oppose his actions, as well as his personal perception of those opponents.

Perhaps the key word in both of the preceding quotations from Roosevelt is "necessary," which added a component of immediacy that may have been lacking previously; as such, it required the president to respond to the situation and commit resources as he thought best. In other words, the president can be expected to respond as he deems necessary when U.S. interests in a Western Hemisphere nation are under threat of imminent European intervention.

The Senate's initial debate of issues related to the Dominican intervention and treaty, including the fact that the senators learned of the protocol through the press, took place in large part among members of the Senate Foreign Relations Committee, including Chairman Shelby Cullom (R-IL), Henry Cabot Lodge (R-MA), Joseph B. Foraker (R-OH), John C. Spooner (R-WI), John T. Morgan (D-AL), Augustus O. Bacon (D-GA), and Hernando D. Money (D-MS). Other prominent participants in the debate included Henry D. Teller (D-CO), a member of the Appropriations, Finance, and Rules Committees, and Edward W. Carmack (D-TN).[69]

In addressing Roosevelt's policy initiative and behavior, the Senate did not initially concern itself with many of the issues that Roosevelt had broached. Most senators did not question either his policy or even his authority to craft it. The primary issue to which some Senators took exception was the fact that Roosevelt engaged in treaty negotiations without conferring with the Senate. As Sen. Henry M. Teller, the most outspoken critic of Roosevelt's tactics in the course of this interaction, said, "[U]nder the Constitution of the United States the President of the United States can not make a treaty; he can not make a protocol; he can not make an agreement that amounts to a treaty without the approval of this body, and it is not possible for the President of the United States to change the character of a document by calling it a protocol or calling it an agreement if it is a treaty."[70]

A few senators made isolated remarks about the appropriateness of Roosevelt's proposed policy. For example, Senator Teller said, "I shall defer . . . until some favorable opportunity, when I shall endeavor to show that the suggestion made in the President's message that the Monroe doctrine requires certain conduct on our part, is sustained neither by precedent nor by the principle of the Monroe doctrine."[71] In addition,

Sen. Hernando Money (D-MS) argued that "I take it this is one of the cases where the President must act by and with the advice and consent of the Senate. It is a very important matter to undertake the suzerainty of a republic, for it means nothing else, on account of its debts. We are under no obligation to run the fiscal affairs of anybody but ourselves."[72]

Despite these concerns, the primary focus of debate in the Senate in both the regular and the special sessions was what information regarding the treaties the president could and should give to Congress. Much of the initial discussion on this question stemmed from a January 24, 1905, resolution offered by Senator Teller that required the president to inform the Senate whether any agreement with Santo Domingo had been reached and, if so, to disclose the nature of the accord. Roosevelt's supporters were able to see that "the resolution . . . [took] its proper course . . . referred to the committee and reported back in a proper form, and then sent to the President for his answer."[73]

The debate regarding what information the president should submit to the Senate continued and intensified in the extra session. It was primarily carried on by Senator Teller and Senator Lodge. The most specific enunciations from these senators of their respective positions are as follows:

Senator Teller:
Mr. President, in my judgment when the Senate comes to consider a treaty the Senate is entitled to everything that has taken place prior to the sending of the treaty to the Senate. I do not think the President of the United States can, under those circumstances, refrain from sending the correspondence and all the details, because we are as much a part of the treaty-making power as is the Executive. We have the final veto on whatever he may do; we have the power to amend, to change or to reject as we see fit.

It is an absurdity, Mr. President, to say that the President can have in his possession facts and information which were necessary for him to negotiate the treaty that we can not have before the Senate when we come to consider this question. We do not consider the form of the treaty alone. We consider the propriety of the proposed treaty. We consider whether the American interests will be promoted by it—not only the form, but all the surroundings and its effects are a matter of consideration for the Senate.[74]

Senator Lodge: "The Constitution intrusts to the President the sole power of negotiating treaties. In the course of negotiation many notes are interchanged, many interviews are held of which brief reports are made to the Government, and much is done in an informal and unofficial way in order to bring the treaty to pass. In that process of negotiation we are not concerned. We begin to act only when the treaty is sent to us for approval or disapproval."[75]

Senators Lodge and Teller even appealed to historical precedent and previous pathways of understanding in outlining what was expected of the president in relation to Congress's need for information about the treaty. In the course of debate, Lodge stated, "I have never known a case where the correspondence or the reports of interviews, the process of negotiation by which the treaty was brought into being, had been requested from the President."[76] Teller responded shortly thereafter, "Why . . . old George Washington, without any precedent before him, was brave enough, when he thought a paper should not go to Congress, to say so; and I think practically that every President since has been able to say that."[77]

When Congress returned for the first session of the 59th Congress, the Senate debated, on and off, issues relating to the Dominican affair for a month. From January 8, 1906, through February 7, 1906, the debate comprised 105 pages of the *Congressional Record* and saw fourteen senators participate at one point or another. While many of the leaders (e.g., Senators Lodge, Cullom, Spooner, Teller, and Money) in this debate continued in that role from the previous session, a few became embroiled in the issue, whereas they had not done so previously. The most active was Sen. Benjamin R. Tillman (D-SC), a member of the Naval Affairs, Appropriations, and Interstate Commerce Committees, while others included Francis Newlands (D-NV), Jacob H. Gallinger (R-NH), Isidor Rayner (D-MD), and Thomas M. Patterson (D-CO).

The debate that occurred during the early part of 1906 turned the implicit competition for authority into an explicit one. For example, Senator Spooner argued that the Senate should consider treaties only via a vote of the body and not a "public discussion of current foreign relations, including treaties," which Spooner saw as "not a healthy precedent to establish."[78] Senator Newlands immediately responded, casting the policy issue as one between the institutions of the presidency and the

Senate: "May I ask the Senator a question? . . . It is whether he does not think it advisable to open the discussion of this question in the Senate? Does he not think it involves something beyond mere treaty relations with the Government of Santo Domingo; that it involves the possible consideration of a new policy on the part of the United States, affecting our relations not only with Santo Domingo, but with all the Caribbean States, Central American and South American Republics? And inasmuch as that departure is threatened, would it not be wise for us to take the entire country into our confidence and discuss it with the aid of a discussion upon the outside by newspapers and periodicals?"[79]

Newlands placed on the table the concerns of a number of members of Congress that, if Congress allowed Roosevelt to continue the modus vivendi, then Roosevelt would be able to pursue similar policy goals in other Western Hemisphere nations under the guise of the Monroe Doctrine. In other words, Newlands feared the establishment of a norm that would enhance presidential authority at the expense of the Senate.

Sen. Hernando Money most explicitly considered the Dominican case from the perspective of presidential authority. Near the start of a lengthy speech on Santo Domingo, he framed the question as one of the "authority . . . of the President to carry into operation a treaty negotiated but failing of ratification."[80] Money further argued, "I say the President of the United States is really carrying out the treaty which this Senate has failed—I used the mildest word possible—to ratify, and that he has no such authority whatever to do it, and nobody, I will venture to say, can successfully contend that he has. It is not a question of whether it is desirable that this thing shall be done. It is totally dissociated from that question, absolutely differentiated. . . .

But the point I am coming to now is that we are in this condition, that the President of the United States is carrying out a treaty which has never been ratified. If he can do that in one instance, he can do it in another; if he can do it in another one, he can do it in five hundred, and the effect will be that he need not pay any attention whatever to the Senate in the matter of treaties."[81]

Money concluded, "in my opinion, the Senate has lost very directly and substantively a part of its authority when it permits—I will use that word—without a protest the President to carry into effect a treaty which never has been here ratified, and no euphemism in the English language can conceal the fact that that is being done."[82]

The remainder of the debate over the Dominican Republic focused on specific components of the treaty and the issues that surrounded it: Roosevelt's application of the Monroe Doctrine, the issue as a partisan one, presidential prerogative, the necessity to prevent foreign intervention in the Dominican Republic, and so on. However, other than a brief procedural reference to the treaty in April, the matter was not discussed after February 1906. In the meantime, Secretary of State Root renegotiated the agreement, taking into account some the concerns raised in the Senate. Most significantly, Root and Roosevelt provided an opportunity for the Senate to "advise" as well as "consent." With the primary institutional concern—namely that the Senate was kept out of the original process—eliminated, the Senate ratified the treaty in 1907 without debate.

Roosevelt can be seen as trying to expand the presidency's authority so that the president can set policy in relation to countries in the Western Hemisphere that are being threatened with European intervention. His approach is a forward-looking, proactive one. Those senators, however, who opposed or questioned Roosevelt's approach reacted solely to his behavior. Although Roosevelt's opponents were able to block ratification of the treaty for nearly two years and then forced it to be renegotiated prior to passage, the United States continued to control Dominican customs and manage Santo Domingo's debt in the interim. While Roosevelt strove to expand the presidency's authority, his opponents protested loudly. At the conclusion of the interaction, however, it was Congress who had allowed the presidency this authority by acquiescing in Roosevelt's general position through the ratification process.

Dominican Republic: Conclusion

From a policy standpoint, Roosevelt has been said to have won a limited victory for his efforts in the Dominican Republic.[83] The incident, however, can also be seen as a significant victory for the institution of the presidency. At the start of the interaction, President Roosevelt had a particular understanding of presidential authority as it related to the application of the Monroe Doctrine. In his view, the president could establish the nation's policies in situations in which, under the guise of the Monroe Doctrine, U.S. intervention into a nation's affairs was considered necessary to stave off European intervention, as evidenced by his behavior in this case.

Roosevelt recognized that this particular understanding was not shared by all members of Congress, for, in part, it did shift some of Congress's institutional authority to the presidency. Whereas the president was previously expected to engage Congress in a more balanced policy-making process, Roosevelt sought to be able to set policy in situations such as the Dominican Republic more freely. Despite finally acknowledging the institutional issues involved, Congress allowed the modus vivendi to be implemented for two years without ratifying the treaty and, in the end, supported Roosevelt's policy. The outcome of this competition for institutional authority served only to strengthen presidential authority in this area. Senator Money was correct: The Senate lost very directly and substantively a part of its authority.

The presidency maintained its authority to commit military forces to protect U.S. interests in such nations. More importantly, Roosevelt was able to push the boundaries such that the president was expected to play a greater role in determining and implementing long-range policy decisions in such nations. On the other hand, by letting Roosevelt guide the process, Congress essentially established a precedent for future presidential action of a similar nature.

The Dominican Republic case study represents a tangible and dramatic example of the coordinated scripting process. Roosevelt and the members of Congress openly debated alternative pathways for action and the reasoning for such. The participants understood that the resolution of this matter would directly affect the authority of both the Congress and the presidency. From this interaction, a new coordinated script emerged, and a new understanding of expected behaviors started to develop. As a result, a new layer of informal authority was placed on the institution of the presidency.

Haiti: History

As Secretary of State William Jennings Bryan concluded in a letter to President Woodrow Wilson dated January 7, 1915, "the financial affairs of the country [Haiti] are in bad shape."[84] Of specific concern to Secretary Bryan was the National Bank of Haiti, a French institution largely owned by U.S. investors.[85] For example, the Haitian government attempted to obtain the money remaining in the bank after its officers had removed $500,000 in gold and sent it to New York aboard a U.S. government ship. In addition, the government issued money, which was contrary to the contract it had with the bank, and threatened to undertake other activities that would have violated the terms of the contract. Worried about the financial and political instability in Haiti, Bryan recommended that "the success of this Government's efforts in Santo Domingo would, it seems to me, suggest the application of the same methods to Hayti whenever the time is ripe."[86] Wilson, in his response to Bryan, concurred with the recommendation, stating that "it is our duty to take immediate action there . . . [as] the United States cannot consent to stand by and permit revolutionary conditions constantly to exist there."[87]

In addition to the political unrest in Haiti, Wilson and Bryan were concerned about the prospect of European influence in Haitian affairs generally and European control of the harbor Mole Saint Nicholas specifically. Germany had used the harbor as a supply base; both France and Germany indicated that they wanted to share the control of Haitian customs, similar to the U.S. arrangement in the Dominican Republic. Wilson and Bryan were determined that Mole Saint Nicholas "should not be permitted to pass into the hands of other foreign governments, or foreign capitalists. . . . As long as the Government is under French or German influence American interests are going to be discriminated against there as they are discriminated against now."[88] In a letter to Bryan two days later, Wilson made his position regarding Haiti even clearer:

First. The time to act is now.

Second. We must make certain demands and make them as conditions of recognition, backed by the intimation that we will not take No for answer:

1) The use and control of Mole Saint Nicholas, or, at the least, the exclusion there of foreign control;

2) An advisor . . . to speak the conditions upon which this Government will support the government of Haiti, our object being, not merely to safeguard foreign interests on the island with entire impartiality, but also to prevent the constant recurrence of revolution there and the assistance then of revolution in San Domingo. Our support and countenance to be depended on so long as the government there honestly sought to represent and serve the Republic.

In this connection we ought to let them know that the management of the customs was the point of danger which we would watch, and through our Advisor control, with the greatest vigilance.[89]

In May 1915 Paul Fuller Jr. was sent to Haiti as the president's special representative and was, among other responsibilities, to inform the Haitian president that Haiti was protected from European intervention under the Monroe Doctrine. As part of Wilson's policy in Haiti, the USS *Connecticut* was sent to Port-au-Prince, Haiti, in late July 1915 and arrived there as the political instability was increasing. President Vilbrun Guillaume Sam was murdered and mutilated by a frenzied mob out of retribution for his role in the slayings of prisoners who were political opponents of Sam's government. This left all of Haiti in complete turmoil as warring factions could no longer be held in check. Further, the lives and property of Americans and other foreigners in the island country were increasingly in jeopardy.

Another threat to the Haitian government's stability was the possibility of the default on foreign debt owed to European creditors. These were loans held by German, French, and English creditors that, if defaulted upon, would provide inroads these powers would need to interfere with Haiti. In particular, these loans were secured by the customs revenues; therefore, default by the Haitian government would give the European powers the necessary avenue to seize control of the Haitian custom houses.

As Robert Lansing, who became secretary of state following Bryan's resignation in June 1915, would later recall,[90] "The restoration of order and government in Haiti was as clearly the duty of the Government of the United States as was the landing of the marines. If the United States had not assumed the responsibility, some other power would. To permit such action by a European power would have been to abandon the principles of the Monroe doctrine. The United States had no alternative but to act, and to act with vigor."[91]

Despite some concerns shared by Wilson and Lansing that the president might not have the legal authority to do what he thought was necessary, Wilson instructed Lansing to send enough military forces to occupy Port-au-Prince and the surrounding areas. Rear Adm. William Banks Caperton commanded the landing of four hundred marines and sailors in Port-au-Prince; on August 11, 1915, he notified Wilson that the landing forces had assumed control and been reinforced.[92] By September, a puppet government had been established under a treaty between Haiti and the United States. After Congress returned to session, the Senate unanimously ratified this treaty on February 23, 1916.

Haiti: Analysis

The U.S. intervention into Haiti in 1915 was strictly a presidency-driven process. President Wilson and his advisors structured and implemented the control of Haiti's finances to protect U.S. interests in the island nation and to stave off any possible European intervention. Although Wilson expressed concern about proceeding with such a plan, he recognized the need to take immediate action in Haiti. As a result, Wilson and his advisors set forth on a course similar to the one President Roosevelt had pursued in 1905 with the Dominican Republic. Although Congress was not in session during the period in which much of the international events and associated decision making occurred, it had the opportunity to debate or oppose Wilson's actions but did not do so.

Haiti's situation in 1915 was quite similar to the Dominican financial and political troubles in 1905. This similarity was not lost on either Wilson or his original secretary of state, William Jennings Bryan. As early as January 7, 1915, Bryan suggested to Wilson that he believed "that there will be no peace and progress in Hayti until we have some such arrangement as we have in Santo Domingo."[93] By the end of March, Wilson recognized the need "to take a very decided stand with the government of Haiti."[94]

Wilson was prepared to take a very proactive stance with regard to Haiti. He and his second secretary of state, Robert Lansing, however, were having difficulty doing so. On August 3, 1915, for example, Lansing wrote Wilson that "The situation in Haiti is distressing and very perplexing. I am not sure at all what we ought to do or what we can legally do. . . . I do not think we can let the present condition continue too long. . . . I hope that you can give me some suggestion as to what course we should pursue."[95]

Wilson's response to Lansing the next day, which provided the secretary of state the guidance he sought, also reflects the crux of the institutional dilemma that the president believed he faced:

> I fear we have not the legal authority to do what we apparently ought to do; and that if we did do what is necessary it would constitute a case very like that of Mr. Roosevelt's action in Santo Domingo, and have very much the same issue.
>
> I suppose there is nothing for it but to take the bull by the horns and restore order. A long programme such as the enclosed

letter suggests involves legislation and the cooperation of the Senate in treaty-making, and must therefore await the session of our Congress.

In the meantime this is plain to me:

1. We must send to Port au Prince a force sufficient to absolutely control the city not only but also the country immediately about it from which it draws its food. I would be obliged if you would ascertain from the Secretary of the Navy whether he has such a force available that can reach there soon.

2. We must let the present [Haitian] Congress know that we will protect it but that we will not recognize any action on its part which does not put men in charge of affairs whom we can trust to handle and put an end to revolution.

3. . . . . [W]e consider it our duty to insist on constitutional government there and will, if necessary (that is, if they force us to it as the only way) take charge of elections and see that a real government is erected which we can support. I would greatly value your advice as to the way in which all this can be done.

Number One can be done at once."[96]

From this quotation, we can see that Wilson wanted and felt he had to implement a policy similar to the one Roosevelt had crafted for the Dominican Republic but worried that he might encounter challenges to his authority similar to those Roosevelt experienced. Wilson's "taking the bull by the horns" comment, however, demonstrates that he recognized that immediate action was *necessary* to rectify the situation.[97] Furthermore, both his comments and those of Lansing demonstrate that the precedent Roosevelt set with the Dominican case was still untested. Although Wilson kept the possibility of congressional resistance in mind, he proceeded with the knowledge that both the perception of the successful Dominican case and the odds against resistance to his exercise of authority were in his favor.

Even after the U.S. forces had the situation in Haiti under control, Secretary of State Lansing continued to express concern about the president's authority to take the action he did: "I have not been unmindful of the possible criticism which may be aroused in the Senate in case this treaty should be signed and submitted to them for action. As I said, it seems a high handed procedure, but I do not see how else we can obtain the desirable end of establishing a stable government in Haiti and maintaining domestic peace there."[98]

Wilson's and Lansing's concern about the presidency's authority and interaction with Congress was apparently all for naught. After Congress returned in December 1915, the treaty "negotiated" with the Haitian officials was submitted to the Senate for consideration. Unlike Roosevelt's two-year effort to get his treaty with the Dominican Republic passed, Wilson's agreement with Haiti passed the Senate *unanimously and with no debate* slightly more than a month after it was introduced.[99]

Perhaps the lack of opposition to Wilson's application of the policy used in the Dominican Republic to the situation in Haiti lay in the general perception that it was a worthwhile course of action. As Rep. John J. Rogers (R-MA) stated in regard to the Dominican treaty in 1905, "after two years' operation the success of [the] Roosevelt-Morales interim agreement became so clear that the Senate consented to ratify" the treaty.[100] Regardless of the reason for the senatorial silence on the Haitian treaty, however, Wilson did not experience the challenges to his authority that Roosevelt did. The Senate did not debate the treaty, its terms, Wilson's policy, or his authority to act as he did. The members of the Senate could easily have protested Wilson's action or contested the treaty if they thought the president had exceeded his authority, as some senators did in the Dominican case a decade earlier. Instead, the senators chose to remain silent and wholeheartedly accept the policy Wilson laid before them.[101] The only debate in Congress related in any way to the Haitian intervention consisted of six pages in the *Congressional Record* of May 4, 1916, when the House considered a bill designed to implement the terms of the ratified treaty.[102]

The chairman of the House Military Affairs Committee, James Hay (D-VA), wrote generally (although not specifically in the context of Haiti) that "military command vested in the Executive is limited by, and must be executed in accordance with, such rules as may be prescribed by Congress in the exercise of the power vested in it by the Constitution."[103] In relation to Haiti, Congress in its silence did not prescribe any rules or otherwise limit either the executive's military command or Wilson's ability to set a long-term policy regarding Haiti. Whereas in the case of Samoa, Congress was characterized as "active-reactive," in regard to Haiti, Congress's collective action can be considered "passive-reactive." Whereas the norm regarding the setting of a long-range policy in Samoa was one of coparticipation, the norm here was one of presidential control. Perhaps the fact that other international events occurring at approximately the same time as those in Haiti garnered more attention lessened any opposition that Wilson might have incurred otherwise.[104] The bottom line, however, is that Wilson committed the military and established a long-term policy in relation to Haiti, and all that Congress chose to do, without question or opposition, was to give its formal legislative approval for those portions of the policy that required it. In other words, Wilson acted within the scope of the presidency's now expanded authority in relation to the situation in Haiti.

Haiti: Conclusion

In and of itself, the institutional interaction concerning Haiti is straightforward. Wilson identified a problem and knew of a way to resolve it. Although he was concerned about his level of authority, he ultimately did not need to be. By so unquestioningly approving the treaty with Haiti and having no debate on the U.S. intervention there, the Senate can be seen as agreeing to Wilson's assertion and application of presidential authority.

The Haitian intervention, however, taken in the context of the Dominican Republic a decade earlier, reflects the further development of the shared understanding of the expected behavior in relation to this policy decision. Although Roosevelt's use of the military to preserve order in Santo Domingo was accepted without question, his attempt to set policy in regard to the Dominican debt met with resistance and challenges. He was trying to broaden the realm of presidential authority in order to drive the development of this type of policy more freely; as a result, the congressional role in the decision-making process would be limited to simply approving an already-crafted policy. Roosevelt can be seen as trying to modify the shared understanding of setting policy in this area. Although a number of vocal senators did not adhere to this new understanding, in part for partisan reasons only, Roosevelt ultimately won. Wilson, in almost an identical position ten years later, followed the same pathway but did not meet with the resistance or challenges his predecessor did. Although Wilson may have benefited by Congress's not being in session at the time of the intervention, Congress clearly did not express any dismay or concern about the presidential actions upon its return to session—Congress chose not to challenge the script employed.

In the new understanding that was apparently widely held, not only is the president unquestionably able to commit troops but he is also able to proactively pursue long-term policy initiatives, with Congress quietly endorsing the initiative.

COMMITMENT OF TROOPS: CASE STUDIES CONCLUSION

Utilizing the cases of Samoa in 1888 and 1889, the Dominican Republic in 1905, and Haiti in 1915, we see that the presidency already had a sufficiently high level of institutional authority to commit troops.[105] In the Samoan affair, President Cleveland and the members of Congress shared an understanding that the president had the authority to commit troops without question. Such an understanding was reflected and supported in the Dominican Republic and Haiti case studies as well. Despite the varying contexts in which each event took place, each president (Cleveland, Roosevelt, and Wilson) acted similarly in terms of the actual commitment of troops, thus reflecting the presidency's high level of institutional authority in this specific area. Further, Congress's silence on this issue in each case provides additional evidence of this shared understanding.

These cases do not demonstrate the expansion of the presidency's role in this area; however, they do reflect the existence of a norm regarding the commitment of troops in specific situations. To draw this out further, the presidency's role did not need to expand, nor did it have room to, since the presidency's level of authority allowed the president to commit troops in such situations without much, if any, opposition in Congress.

The cases also allow us to draw some tentative conclusions about the shared understandings of the Washington community regarding the president's authority to engage the military in more significant uses. In each of the cases, military forces were used to protect U.S. interests in a nation threatened by the intervention of a European government. With Samoa, protection was an end in itself—it was part of the mission's objectives. In the latter cases, however, the commitment of troops and the protection of interests were part of a larger policy aim—protection was a means to help achieve a broader policy goal. Thus, the cases provide sufficient preliminary evidence that the president was able to assert more authority and was willing to undertake more significant uses of the military with the understanding that it was within his authority to do so.

The cases provide initial evidence that the understanding of the president as the nation's leader in international affairs expanded during this era specifically with respect to interactions involving the commitment of troops to a nation where U.S. interests are threatened by a European intervention. We see through the cases studied that an understanding that placed expanded international affairs leadership expectations on the presidency developed throughout this era, specifically in the context of setting policy direction toward the specific nations. With Samoa, President Cleveland and the members of Congress shared an understanding that the president led jointly with Congress in the creation of long-term policy interests. While Cleveland was ultimately granted the discretion to resolve the issue, his authority to lead was curtailed by the fact that Congress needed, in effect, to authorize through legislation continued U.S. involvement beyond the initial troop commitment.

With the Dominican Republic, the institutional competition that occurred was, in part, about the president's ability to lead in setting policy, more specifically through treaties devoid of congressional involvement. The ultimate outcome of this interaction was the development of a more expansive understanding of the president's ability to direct the nation's foreign affairs more freely. Finally, with Haiti, the president's ability to serve as the nation's leader in international affairs appeared unquestioned and expected, as demonstrated by the unanimous ratification and lack of congressional debate on the treaty Wilson placed before the Senate. Thus, in these cases, we see a definite expansion of the president's role—as the Washington community understood it—as the nation's leader in protecting U.S. interests and in setting national policy in regard to nations facing a threat of European intervention.

Finally, the cases also seem to provide evidence that, although Congress initially asserted its authority as a decision maker in international affairs, its members became more acquiescent of presidential initiatives as short-term imperatives fostering expedient decisions overrode other institutional concerns. We find evidence that members of Congress moved away from the institution's joint status in the decision-making process (in the Samoan case) to a position in which they did virtually nothing except merely ratify the treaty that Wilson presented (in the Haitian case).

In other words, as the norm regarding the presidency shifted toward active-proactive behavior, the norm for congressional behavior shifted from coparticipation to being passive-reactive. This shift was not an easy one, as demonstrated in the contest over authority between Roosevelt and some Democratic members of the Senate in the Dominican Republic case. The evidence from all three cases taken as a whole, however, reflects that the members of Congress came to accept a more limited role in the decision-making process, as it relates to long-term policy issues associated with the commitment of military forces to nations in which U.S. interests are threatened by European intervention.

From the cases presented here, we can begin to draw two basic conclusions about the presidency's authority in this area. First, the Washington community understood the presidency to have great authority to commit military forces unilaterally to areas in which U.S. interests were imminently threatened by European powers. Such an understanding was consistently demonstrated throughout these cases by presidents and members of Congress alike. Second, the understanding of the president's role to set long-term policy related to the commitment of military forces expanded throughout the era.

The cases also demonstrate the coordinated scripting process in action. Established pathways provide a low-cost mechanism for addressing a political issue and will generally be followed, as was the case with Samoa. Because those existing pathways, however, did not satisfy Theodore Roosevelt's desire for timely support for his policy in the Dominican Republic, he challenged them. The members of Congress debated alternative pathways, but those promoted by Roosevelt ultimately won out, and a new coordinated script emerged. That script remained tenuous at first until tested by Wilson in Haiti. Wilson and Lansing seemed more concerned about whether the president had the authority to replicate Roosevelt's actions than Congress did. In the end, the interaction, or rather the lack of interaction, between Wilson and Congress reinforced the presidential authority developed during the Dominican Republic episode.

CHAPTER 3

Creation of Administrative Apparatus

The nationalization of U.S. politics between 1881 and 1920 provided a rich context for the creation and enhancement of the federal government's administrative apparatus. During this time, the U.S. political system shifted from one that was local in nature to one in which the issues, debates, and decision-making processes were national in focus. Correspondingly, the national government broadened the scope of its areas of governance. It expanded its powers to address new national issues that arose[1] and assumed power in areas that had traditionally been left to the states as these areas, too, took on added national importance.[2] As a result, the federal government required a greater administrative apparatus in order to function within the context of its newly expanded scope.[3] Various administrative departments, bureaus, commissions, and so on were created to address the issues that arose during the era.[4]

THE CONTEXT: THE NATIONALIZATION OF ADMINISTRATION

Between 1881 and 1893, thirteen agencies were created, and four were elevated to a higher position through the passage of a statute. This period includes two of the most important acts in the nation's history creating an administrative agency: the Pendleton Act, which created the Civil Service Commission in 1883, and the Interstate Commerce Act (ICA), which created the Interstate Commerce Commission (ICC) in 1887.[5] This period also saw the creation of subdepartmental agencies that dealt with issues of health, safety, and education—areas traditionally considered state governmental functions. Although the number of agencies created was rather limited, they nonetheless represented and signified the increased scope of federal government activity.[6]

In the middle period of 1894–1907, nine agencies were created, and twelve were elevated by law. At a closer glance, however, only two new agencies were created between 1894 and 1900, under Cleveland and McKinley, while the remaining seven were established during the three-year period from 1901 to 1903. Of the new agencies, the most important clearly was the Department of Commerce and Labor (and the Bureau of Corporations within it), a Cabinet-level agency reflecting the importance of a nationalized economy. In addition to this, the other agencies created indicate a growing diversity in the scope of areas within the federal government's jurisdiction. Furthermore, several existing agencies were given new or modified responsibilities.

The period of 1908–1920 is most notable for the growth of independent regulatory commissions, such as the Federal Reserve Board, the Federal Trade Commission (FTC), and the Federal Power Commission.[7] In addition, several agencies were created in response to the outbreak of World War I.[8] Further, the scope of federal government activity, as reflected in its administrative agencies, continued to expand. All in all, forty-two agencies were created, and three were elevated by law.

The various administrative agencies created between 1881 and 1920 (see Table A.4 in the Appendix for a complete list) were not established according to a grand scheme or philosophical conception of how the government should be structured. Instead, these agencies were generally created in reaction to specific events, circumstances, or needs.[9] For example, the Bureau of Animal Industry was created in 1884 to address the problem of "dangerous communicable diseases in livestock, particularly in connection with foreign trade," only after rumors of such diseases provided European nations the rationale to limit or ban the importation of U.S. livestock, particularly pork.[10]

Furthermore, the formation of specific administrative agencies during this time was largely a particularistic issue in the sense that many of them were created in response to the needs of specific groups.[11] In the preceding example of the Bureau of Animal Industry, the U.S. meat and pork industry supported efforts by the federal government to eliminate livestock diseases and to open European markets. The elevation of the Department of Agriculture to Cabinet-level status, seen by some members of Congress as "class legislation" and an inappropriate topic for the national government,[12] reflected the national power that organizations such as the National Grange and the Farmers' Congress started to wield and the pressure they exerted on the federal government for a Cabinet-level official to represent their interests. Bureaus such as the Children's Bureau and the Women's Bureau were set up to address issues related to the labor of those specific groups. Even the creation of regulatory agencies, those administrative organizations that are designed to limit unfavorable business practices, if opposed were generally done so only by those businesses that were being regulated.[13]

As the preceding examples illustrate, though, the creation of administrative agencies mirrored the increased scope of the national government during this period in the area of economic regulation. Closely related to the nationalization of U.S. politics were the growth and industrialization of the U.S. economy. This era saw the "most rapid expansion of capital and industry over any long period of U.S. history, reaching a peak in the decades of the 1880s and 1890s, and leveling off during the first decade of the century."[14] This era, particularly between 1890 and 1916, has been defined as the one in which "corporate capitalism" emerged and in which capitalism passed from "its propriety-competitive stage to its corporate-administered stage."[15]

This period, also known as the Progressive and/or Reform Era, witnessed the emergence of groups that sought to address the ills that the nation was experiencing. Along with the benefits provided by the expansion of the economy came economic uncertainty and inequality, unfair business practices, and unsafe working conditions. These negative consequences not only fostered divisions within the nation but also provided both an opportunity and a need for government regulation at the national level. For example, Theodore Roosevelt noted that, taken together, the Hepburn Act[16] strengthening the powers of the Interstate Commerce Commission, the Meat Inspection Act, and the Pure Food and Drug Act[17] marked "a noteworthy advancement in the policy of securing Federal supervision and control over corporations."[18]

At first blush, these two concepts—corporate capitalism and reform efforts—may seem contradictory; the reformers of this era sought to regulate the economy and the business practices of the emerging corporate structures.[19] Certainly, the business leaders of the day did not favor all regulation. Some regulation went beyond what the corporate leaders, such as Morgan and Rockefeller, may have wanted; as such, they adjusted to the regulatory environment as best they could.[20] Not all business interests, however, opposed these reform efforts. Instead, they saw some national government regulation of the economy as a means to provide stability to their prices and markets.[21] The Federal Reserve Act, for example, represents an instance in which, with President Woodrow Wilson balancing "the interests of corporate capitalism and the need of ordinary Americans to have their opportunities protected," Congress passed a "surprisingly balanced compromise measure."[22]

The business community, however, was not a unified entity during this era. Business interests were divided by many differences, including those between urban centers and small towns, regions, the size of business enterprises, and the competing functions that businesses performed in the economy.[23] In each of these divisions, Eastern financial interests, trusts and monopolies, and the largest capitalists provided foils for which many groups would define themselves in opposition. In addition to these divisions within the nation's business interests, corporate capitalists faced fierce opposition from an increasingly organized and vocal labor movement.[24]

The Progressive movement emphasized the need to reform the ills brought about by these economic conditions and interests. The desire to regulate the economy "to distribute more widely its benefits" served as the Progressives' most important concern.[25] Further, this broad movement consisted of a diverse group who, in addition to economic regulation, focused on government representational reforms and humanitarian assistance for the nation's poor and disadvantaged.

The Progressive movement stretched across party lines, with its leaders including Republicans Theodore Roosevelt and Robert La Follette and Democrat Woodrow Wilson. As a bipartisan movement, the Progressives did not change the landscape of partisan politics.[26] They did, however, lead to some internal divisions within the Republican Party that resulted in Theodore Roosevelt running as a Progressive Party (Bull Moose) presidential candidate in 1912. The split within the Republican Party aided Wilson's election to the presidency. Once in office, however, Wilson extended the Progressives' desire to regulate the economy and address the other problems facing the nation.

Before examining specific interactions that led to the creation of various administrative agencies within the executive branch, we must address the issue of civil service reform. Although not directly linked to the general creation of administrative agencies, this issue reflects a movement away from a bureaucratic system based on patronage and the spoils system toward a depoliticized one in which government employees were selected on the basis of their merit. The goal of this movement was to develop a more competent, efficient, professional bureaucracy. Thus, the establishment of new executive agencies had to take place within this environment.

Although the movement for a less partisan civil service system was under way, the assassination of President James Garfield in 1881 by a person who was not given a patronage job served as a catalyst for reforming the system. Garfield's successor, Chester A. Arthur, supported civil service reform, which is somewhat ironic in that he had long benefited from patronage jobs. In the Senate, the Pendleton Act, originally introduced by Sen. George Pendleton (D-OH) in December 1880, eventually worked its way through Congress after gaining support from Republicans for political reasons and was signed into law in January 1883.[27]

The Pendleton Act limited the exposure of government employees to political strong-arm tactics by forbidding compulsory contributions or performance of services by employees on behalf of political parties or elected officials, as well as solicitation by government officers on government property. In addition, the act established the Civil Service Commission, a three-person panel whose members were appointed by the president and confirmed by the Senate but whom the president could remove. The commission was vested with the power to make rules, subject to presidential approval, designed to oversee and implement the provisions of the act. In the years that immediately followed the passage of the act, the commission established standards for entrance examinations, promotional examinations, efficiency records, salary classifications, and apportionment.[28]

Although civil service reform started with personnel issues and the Pendleton Act was probably the most significant piece of reform legislation passed, attempts at administrative reform did not rest solely on personnel issues. A number of highly regarded scholars of the day called for efforts to reform the organization and methods of administrative agencies and emphasized the need for scientific management to separate politics and administration.[29] Such calls found their mark in attempts to reorganize the national administrative agencies. These attempts included President Taft's Commission on Economy and Efficiency in 1912, the elevation of the Bureau of Efficiency in 1916, and the establishment of the Joint Committee on Reorganization on December 29, 1920. These attempts, however, were too isolated to produce any reorganization of the bureaucracy within the time frame of this study; however, such a restructuring was accomplished shortly thereafter.[30]

The growth in the activity of the national government and the corresponding growth in its administrative apparatus afforded the presidency opportunity structures to enable the institution's authority to grow. The sheer number of administrative agencies created between 1881 and 1920 meant that the president was in charge of a broader, more active federal bureaucracy. Further, as chief executive, the president could be expected to influence the way in which the executive branch would be organized.

CASE STUDIES

With the U.S. political system undergoing a process of nationalization between 1881 and 1920, Congress and the presidency responded to the new issues and needs that arose by creating administrative agencies to address them. As we will see, the institutional interactions that led to the specific agencies under examination here did not take place in isolation. Instead, they were shaped by political forces—regional, economic, partisan, and ideological—as well as institutional ones. Within the political context and policy debates, however, Congress and the presidency addressed and reshaped (either directly or indirectly, explicitly or implicitly) the authority of both institutions. The creation of the Interstate Commerce Commission, the Department of Commerce and Labor, and the Federal Trade Commission cannot be considered totally separate from the political forces that shaped them. We can focus, however, on the substance and processes of the institutional interactions that led to their creation and examine what the coordinated scripting that took place meant for the shared understandings of expected behavior that developed from these interactions.

Within this specific focus, we will observe a growth of presidential authority in the area of creating administrative agencies. Further, we will also see varying degrees of participation by the presidency and Congress in setting up these agencies, with presidential efforts ranging from minimal involvement to micromanagement. In addition, we will see Congress, although willing to delegate authority to surrogates, expressing reticence about the direct control of their surrogates' operations by "outside interests," including the presidency.

At the beginning of the period under study, the Interstate Commerce Commission was established as a tool to regulate interstate commerce, an issue that involved a congressional power as defined by the Supreme Court. The debates in Congress reflected a regional division, as business interests in the Northeast favored the creation of a commission, while Southern agrarian concerns preferred a legislative approach. In the end, the commission approach won out, and the national government's first independent regulatory agency was created.

President Cleveland seemingly had little to say about this issue and the formation of the Interstate Commerce Commission. Congress, on the other hand, had to consider among many policy-specific questions whether it should be developing policies to regulate the economy broadly and, further, whether it had the authority to create a surrogate related to those policies. In addition, once deciding in the affirmative to both questions (with the assistance of the Supreme Court), Congress became concerned with how the surrogates it created should be used and who should influence their direction. Congress also needed to consider how much "outside influence" could be permitted in the surrogates' subsequent functioning. Despite these concerns, Congress's response to these questions provided pathways, however limited, for future presidential involvement.

During the middle part of this period, the presidency and Congress established the Department of Commerce and Labor, which provided commercial and labor interests with Cabinet-level representation, something for which both sets of interests had longed. The department, particularly the Bureau of Corporations created within it, also provided President Theodore Roosevelt with the executive agency he wanted to be able to fight trusts.

Within the institutional interaction, President Roosevelt was quite active and even escalated the presidency's role by writing the legislative provision establishing the Bureau of Corporations. While Congress voiced some concern over the potential impact this new department might have on issues of presidential authority, it crafted a piece of legislation consistent with the general vision provided by Roosevelt. The larger issues of whether Congress had the authority to create such a surrogate and the necessity for it, as were found in the ICC interaction, generally were not addressed in the creation of the Department of Commerce and Labor. These questions appear to have been resolved during the creation of the ICC.

The growth of presidential influence in the functioning of this surrogate was an underlying concern of some members of Congress throughout the interaction. The creation of the Department of Commerce and Labor demonstrated the understanding that the president should be involved and have input regarding executive agencies. The question remained, however, of how much input the president should be allowed to have and how far this input should go: Should it end at the creation stage, or should it extend to the functioning of the agency? The new department was an executive agency and contained Roosevelt's Bureau of Corporations, thereby affording the presidency, at least for a time, direct control of the agency's functioning.

In the final period, the government's efforts to fight unfair business practices took shape in the form of the Federal Trade Commission. As with the creation of the ICC, Congress eventually faced two bills—one from the House and one from the Senate. The House proposal would have restructured the existing Bureau of Corporations under a new entity, while the Senate called for a stronger, independent commission. To end this impasse, President Woodrow Wilson switched positions— away from the traditional Democratic stance favoring states' rights and a limited national government—and helped close the deal.

Institutionally, President Wilson took what Roosevelt began in the previous case a step farther by not only requesting action for creating the Federal Trade Commission but also actively participating in the writing and editing of the legislation itself. The members of Congress both accepted and actively sought President Wilson's assistance. To the extent that authority questions were specifically discussed, they were considered in the context of the wisdom and ability of Congress to delegate its legislative authority to the new commission. In seeking to establish an independent body that could effectively regulate unfair business practices, Congress readdressed the question of the presidency's direct control over the Bureau of Corporations. Congress eliminated the bureau and transferred its powers to the FTC, thereby depoliticizing and "depresidentializing" the new commission.

Although authority issues were only part of the political and institutional forces that shaped the outcome of the legislation establishing these three entities, these interactions had lasting effects on the authority of the presidency and Congress.[31] Moreover, they not only demonstrate a growing involvement by the presidency in guiding and designing the creation of these surrogates but also indicate Congress's hesitation to relinquish full control of the functioning of these surrogates to the presidency. Since Congress was delegating its own powers and authority to these surrogates, it sought to limit the political influence of "outside forces," including the presidency. Thus, while Congress allowed the presidency to help define the scope of the federal government's sphere of economic regulation, it was not willing to allow the president to have direct control of the sphere itself.

Interstate Commerce Commission: History
One cannot separate the creation of the ICC from the larger effort to regulate interstate commerce. The railroad industry developed during the nineteenth century in large part due to government concessions and assistance. In an effort to develop a national transportation system, the federal government granted 158 million acres of land for the railroads.[32] In addition, local governments, thinking that a railroad through their town would be the key to their economic prosperity, paid great prices to bring in a railroad.[33] As the industry developed, the pricing practices it utilized were seen as arbitrary and unfair. In large cities where competition among railroads and with water transportation was greater (e.g., Chicago, St. Louis), railroad rates were low.[34] In addition, railroad companies would give lower rates to larger businesses or preferred shippers. This practice resulted in higher rates for everybody else—smaller businesses and farmers who could not afford to pay high rates, small towns in the Midwest and West that paid dearly to bring in a railroad, and so on.

The first attempts to regulate the railroad industry were at the state level, most aggressively in states such as Illinois, Iowa, Michigan, Minnesota, Missouri, and Wisconsin.[35] However, state regulation of the railroad industry was soon challenged because of its impact on interstate commerce. In 1886 the Supreme Court struck down such state regulation as an unconstitutional restraint of interstate commerce in *Wabash, St. Louis, and Pacific Railway Company v. Illinois*. As a result, only the federal government—specifically Congress—could regulate the railroads.

Although the Interstate Commerce Act became law on February 4, 1887, Congress had been trying to address the issue of railroad regulation for two decades. In fact, "between 1868 and 1887 over 150 bills were introduced in Congress providing for federal regulation of railroads."[36] However, out of this vast array of legislative attempts, only two pieces of legislation were of any major significance. In the House of Representatives, Rep. John Reagan (D-TX) introduced legislation in 1878, which was passed by the House but did not make it out of committee in the Senate. Afterward, Reagan introduced modified versions of the "Reagan bill," as it was referred to, each year through 1886.[37] Reagan believed that the "aggregations of capital, of power, of influence, and of privilege in the great railway corporations of this country" needed to be "controlled by law."[38] Furthermore, he called the issue of regulation of interstate commerce "the greatest with which the legislators and statesmen of this country have ever had to grapple. I doubt, indeed, if any single question of greater importance ever came before a legislative body."[39]

The other major piece of legislation regarding the regulation of railroads came from the Senate under the leadership of the chairman of the Senate committee with jurisdiction over the bill, Sen. Shelby Cullom (R-IL). The Cullom bill was initially introduced in 1883 and passed by the Senate in 1885. Cullom echoed the importance that Reagan placed on regulating the railroads: "[W]ith this changed condition of affairs in the commercial world [stemming from the development of the railway industry] came new questions of the greatest importance for the consideration of those upon whom devolved the duty of making the nation's laws."[40]

The Reagan and Cullom bills differed in several key ways. In terms of policy issues, the primary areas of differences stemmed from rates for short hauls and long hauls, as well as pooling, or the "agreement between competing railroads to apportion the competitive business."[41] More importantly for consideration here, another key difference between the Reagan and Cullom bills rested in the creation of a regulatory commission. Reagan, representing Southern agrarian views, believed that the judiciary should enforce the regulations set forth in his bill and proclaimed that "the machinery of the courts is already in existence, and will require no additional expense, and is within convenient reach of the people everywhere, and is fully able to adjudicate all cases which may arise under this bill."[42] Cullom's bill, on the other hand, reflected the position of Northeastern urban and industrial interests and structured an interstate commerce commission designed to administer the general provisions set forth in the Interstate Commerce Act.

The Senate once again passed the Cullom bill in 1886. When the bill was referred to the House, the Committee on Interstate and Foreign Commerce, chaired by Representative Reagan, substituted the Reagan bill, which the House approved after a series of legislative and parliamentary maneuvers by both supporters and opponents of the Reagan bill.[43] The two houses first met in conference committee in June 1886.[44] While the two bills were under consideration in the conference committee, the U.S. Supreme Court decided in the Wabash case that, if interstate commerce were to be regulated, only Congress had the authority to do so.[45] This decision only increased the public's desire to have some form of railroad regulation adopted. The members of the conference committee reconciled their differences in December 1886, but with concessions on both sides.[46] The conference report modified the Cullom bill and, as such, created the Interstate Commerce Commission, consisting of five commissioners appointed by the president with the advice and consent of the Senate (Section 11).

In addition, "any Commissioner may be removed by the President for inefficiency, neglect of duty, or malfeasance in office" (Section 11). The act placed several requirements and restrictions on railroad companies, such as prohibiting special rates, rebates, and drawbacks (Section 2) and mandating that common carriers print their rates (Section 6). One of the more hotly debated provisions of the act was Section 4, which stated that "it shall be unlawful for any common carrier . . . to charge or receive any greater compensation in the aggregate . . . for a shorter than for a longer distance over the same line, in the same direction, the shorter being included within the longer distance." Although this language was similar to the original Cullom bill, the conference report also granted the ICC the authority to allow common carriers to charge more for shorter distances and to "prescribe the extent to which such designated common carrier may be relieved from the operation" of those provisions. This language raised the most concern among some members of Congress.

The other highly debated provision of the conference report prohibited pooling among the railway carriers (Section 5). The Reagan bill included such a provision, and Reagan insisted in having it in the final legislation.[47] Although many senators spoke out against the pooling section in the debate on the Senate floor, they ultimately accepted the packaged bill.

The act also defined the authority and powers granted to the ICC, as well as the scope of its jurisdiction, including:

1. investigating the business management of railroad companies, with specific powers to receive the information it requires to do so (Section 12)

2. being required to investigate a common carrier if a person, business, or other entity files a complaint against it and that common carrier fails to satisfy the complaint; investigating any complaint forwarded by a state railroad commission; or instigating an investigation on its own (Section 13)

3. being required to prepare a report of any investigation it undertakes, which would be deemed prima facie evidence in all judicial proceedings (Section 14)

4. issuing notices to railroad companies to cease and desist from any violation of the act within a specified time frame (Section 15); or, in the event that a railroad company violates, refuses, or neglects to obey an order or requirement of the commission, having the ability to petition to the federal judiciary alleging such violation or obedience (Section 16)

Interstate Commerce Commission: Analysis

In terms of the institutional roles played by Congress and the presidency, the creation of the Interstate Commerce Commission was a decidedly one-sided interaction. Other than the constitutionally prescribed act of signing the bill into law, President Cleveland was mostly silent on the issue of railroad regulation generally and the creation of the ICC specifically.[48] The only input that Cleveland had on the subject was in his annual message in December 1886, when he simply stated, "By a recent decision of the Supreme Court of the United States it has been adjudged that the laws of the several States are inoperative to regulate rates of transportation upon railroads if such regulation interferes with the rate of carriage from one State into another. This important field of control and regulation having been thus left entirely unoccupied, the expediency of Federal action upon the subject is worthy of consideration."[49]

Cleveland's silence during the development and crafting of the Interstate Commerce Act and his lukewarm support for the idea of federal action imply an understanding that the authority for addressing this issue rested in Congress and clearly not with the presidency.[50] Although the politics of the Interstate Commerce Act may have been geared toward enhancing Cleveland's electoral chances in the 1888 election,[51] the presidential inactivity in the process surrounding the act speaks to Cleveland's perception of his institutional authority. If Cleveland viewed presidential and congressional authority regarding the creation of this new agency or the regulation of railroads differently, one would expect his behavior to reflect that. For example, if he considered the presidency as having authority on these issues, he would have been more active and would have worked with Congress in shaping the legislation.

The interesting result of the creation of the Interstate Commerce Commission is that, despite Cleveland's lack of involvement, the presidency was granted some degree of authority over interstate commerce—an area where the presidency previously had no authority at all—through the power to appoint and remove commissioners.[52] The commissioners, however, were to serve staggered six-year terms, a structure designed as a check on the influence that any individual president could have on the commission.[53] At the institutional level, however, the members of Congress codified the expectation of presidential leadership with the power of appointment and removal of commissioners. In other words, notwithstanding President Cleveland's personal inactivity, the presidency grew as an institution through the passage of the Interstate Commerce Act. The presidency went from having no authority in the area of regulating interstate commerce to having the codified, albeit limited, authority to influence the government's policy in this area.

Since the institutional authority to address this issue rested with Congress, we should consider how the members of Congress viewed the authority questions involved, particularly as they related to the creation of the Interstate Commerce Committee.[54] In the first session of the 49th Congress, the House took up the issue of railroad regulation on five occasions, covering a total of 35 pages of substantive debate in the *Congressional Record*. In the second session, when the Interstate Commerce Act was passed, the House debated the issue six times, representing 38 pages of debate. Between the two sessions, approximately fifty different members spoke on the matter. The Senate debated the issue more extensively. In the first session, it took up railroad regulation twelve times for 148 pages of debate; in the second session, discussion ensued eight times for 68 pages. Overall, fifty-six senators spoke at one time or another on the issue.

The most vocal opposition to the creation of a commission came from House Democrats, led by Rep. John Reagan. Throughout the course of the debate, these members set forth several, sometimes overlapping, sets of arguments against the creation of the commission. As we will see, the intensity of the opposition to the creation of the ICC was much stronger than the intensity of the support; however, it was concentrated in the minority.

Possibly the most significant concern regarding the establishment of the commission related to the perception that the act bestowed upon the ICC legislative and/or judicial powers. The commission, as it was understood by the majority in Congress who approved its creation, was designed to function as an agency that administered the laws but did not create or adjudicate them. A number of members of Congress, however, expressed concern that the ICC would have a level of codified authority greater than one might expect an executive agency to have.

The most direct attempt to address this issue came on May 12, 1886, the day the Senate passed the Cullom bill. Almost immediately before the final vote on the bill, Sen. John Morgan (D-AL) offered an amendment that would have added a section to the bill that read, "The commissioners appointed under this act shall be considered as being executive officers, and shall not exercise either legislative or judicial powers." Morgan argued: "I think it is our duty to be able to expound what is our view of [the commissioners'] authority that we are conferring in this bill and not leave it as a matter of litigation and dispute to be fought out at the expense of people who go before the commissioners hereafter. It is the first bill I have ever known to be brought into the Senate—and in that respect this bill is unique—where the authors of it were not willing to enter into a definition as to whether the powers they conferred on the bill were conferred upon officers of the executive department, officers of the legislative department, or officers of the judicial department of the United States."[55]

Morgan's arguments met with resistance among his colleagues. Sen. Orville Platt (R-CT) responded that the commissioners "cannot exercise judicial powers because they have no life tenure."[56] Sen. George Edmunds (R-VT) countered that "[the commissioners] ought to exercise exactly the power that the bill confers; that is, an executive, discretionary power."[57] Finally, Sen. Samuel Maxey (D-TX) stated, "I see no necessity whatever for the amendment proposed by the Senator from Alabama."[58]

Despite the fact that the Senate rejected Morgan's amendment on a voice vote, his arguments highlighted a stream of thought that persisted in the floor debates up until the final vote accepting the conference report in January 1887. For example, on January 20, 1887, the day before the House accepted the conference report, Rep. William C. Oates (D-AL), in discussing the discretionary powers the commission would be granted in regard to the short-haul/long-haul provisions in Section 4 of the act, stated that, "In my judgment that provision makes this feature of the bill a great deal worse than if no such proviso were incorporated in it. . . . I believe that it is absolutely unconstitutional and void, because to my mind it is a blending of the legislative, the judicial, and perhaps, the executive powers of the Government in the same law."[59]

Rep. Samuel Dibble (D-SC) added that the "gravest object to the bill" was that it conferred legislative powers on the commission, while "under the Constitution the three departments of the Government are to be kept distinct in their operations in their agencies."[60] Furthermore, Dibble argued that when the act provided that, if the party who brought a case to the ICC lost and could not appeal that decision, it provided the commission with a judicial power in that it would be the final adjudicatory body for that one side (instead of a higher court, including the U.S. Supreme Court).[61]

As this discussion demonstrates, many of the most vocal opponents of the creation of the ICC were Southern Democrats (Reagan, Morgan, etc.). They preferred a legislative approach with the judiciary being the final arbiter of the law rather than an administrative one to regulating interstate commerce. They reflected an ideological position that distrusted the transfer of authority from Congress—from the people's branch—and a concentration of authority in the executive branch.[62] These positions helped shape the political context and the final outcome of the Interstate Commerce Act. For the purposes here, however, in pursuing their political and ideological positions, these Southern Democrats raised an important issue related to presidential and congressional authority.

On one hand, the question of how one views the powers that Congress conferred on the ICC—whether legislative, judicial, executive, or some combination thereof—was at the heart of these particular Southern Democrats' criticisms of the Interstate Commerce Act. On the other hand, theirs was a minority position; the majority of Congress (seventy-one percent of Senators who voted, and eighty-three percent in the House) approved the ICA and thus supported voluntarily granting a portion (however small) of its authority to the commission. Interestingly enough, however, the grant of authority to the commission apparently had little effect on the vote of the conference report. Most of the opposition in both houses came from members from the Northeast, a region where a commission approach was more widely supported but that would suffer economically if the act's long-haul/short-haul provisions were strictly interpreted. By comparison, Southern representatives generally supported the bill (because of these same provisions) despite its creation of the ICC.[63] Although authority issues were subordinated to policy issues in the final votes on the ICA, Congress's grant of authority to the commission set a foundation from which a norm could potentially emerge—specifically, that Congress could delegate some of its own authority to the administrative agencies it creates.

The opponents of the creation of the ICC also questioned Congress's ability to delegate its authority and the wisdom of providing discretionary powers to the commission. As Rep. John Reagan pointed out, "This is an attempt to delegate the authority of Congress to the railroad commission to make law. I do not understand that the power to legislate can be so delegated."[64] Furthermore, Sen. Johnson Camden (D-WV) stated, "In framing a general law for the benefit of the whole people of this country to regulate its vast carrying interests, is it not better to make the rule uniform and of general application, in which the interests of the vast body of the whole people are to be affected, rather than to make exceptions that apply only to isolated cases, and which expectations may affect so materially the purposes of the bill? . . . In order to get at the exceptions it becomes necessary to delegate to the commission appointed under the provisions of the bill a dangerous discretion, which virtually places in their hands the essence of the whole question of discriminations intended to be remedied by the bill."[65]

Moreover, those who opposed creating a commission were concerned about the dual issues of the discretionary powers provided to the commissioners and the possible abuse of those powers. As Rep. John Martin (D-AL) stated, "I am not willing to invest the commission with such extraordinary and dangerous discretionary power. General laws, we know, derive value from their uniform operation, not being the subject of either discretion or caprice. . . . Such a temptation is both terrible and cruel; and we can find no justification, as I can conceive, for creating such a dangerous office."[66]

Providing the ICC with the powers proposed in the Interstate Commerce Act would result in a lack of control by Congress over the commissioners' behavior. These members were expressing concern about the level of independence of the agency the legislative branch was creating. They acknowledged the potential impact this independence might have in terms of both implementing the policy of the act and from an institutional perspective. Even though John Reagan agreed to the conference report in the end, he still made the most succinct statement during the course of the debates opposing the creation of the ICC: "I want no commission. The Congress of the United States is the commission created by the people for the enactment of laws, and the courts of the country the tribunals for their enforcement."[67] In other words, according to this view, the institutions that already existed had sufficient authority to decide and adjudicate the regulation of railroads involved in interstate commerce without creating a new administrative agency.

Given this view, one may ask why Congress would be willing to create an agency and grant this new entity some of its authority. One simple answer is, as already mentioned, that, while this delegation was one concern the members of Congress debated, it was not as important as others. Thus, even though some members of Congress fought to limit the grant of authority to the commission during the legislative process, they did not base their votes at the end of the process on this consideration. Perhaps they recognized that, regardless of the approach they took to regulating interstate commerce (i.e., administrative or legislative), the members of Congress would have to delegate authority to another entity.[68] The fact that the members of Congress based their decisions on other factors does not diminish the importance of Congress's grant of authority when examining the impact of the ICA on the institutional development of the presidency and Congress.

Further, in answering the question above from the perspective of political authority, two other possible answers emerge. First, the Interstate Commerce Act can be seen as broadening congressional authority overall. Many congressmen in the debates surrounding this legislation recognized that Congress was entering a new field.[69] In doing so, Congress exercised the authority that only it had, as indicated by the Supreme Court. The members of Congress recognized that, as a body, however, it did not have the technical and detailed knowledge to assess the reasonableness of rates, adequately investigate possible violations of the act, and employ the other powers eventually granted to the ICC. Arguing that Congress was "limited necessarily in practical knowledge in railway movements," the minority report of the House Committee on Commerce stated that "It is the province of legislators to ascertain by intelligent experience the legislation required, and that experience can best be secured through the proposed commission."[70] Furthermore, for example, Sen. John Ingalls (R-KS) stated, "I think that if we intend to deal with certain evils and propose to place this subject under the control of a commission to deal with them we should not limit or impose restrictions upon their power, but leave it with them to determine in the light of circumstances as they arise. I am entirely willing to say in general terms what shall be the duties of this commission; but the more we deal with the subject mentioned in this fourth section [the long-haul/ short-haul provisions] the more inextricably we are befogged, the more apparent it is that nobody understands or can comprehend the result of the various provisions that have been up to this time introduced in that section."[71]

Therefore, although Congress had the authority to pass the act, its members recognized that they did not have the functional ability to implement it. As a result, they can be seen as making a trade-off. To expand its authority, Congress recognized its institutional limitations and delegated a portion of that authority to the new commission.

The second reason that Congress may have been willing to grant away some of its authority stems from the fact that Congress's authority is grounded in and flows directly from the people via the Constitution. Underlying the grant of authority, Congress is expected to reflect the interests and opinions of the mass public, particularly when they are well defined. One theme that pervaded the floor debate in Congress was the public's demand for congressional action on the issue of railroad regulation. As Sen. Shelby Cullom stated, "there is no subject of a public nature that is before the country about which there is so great unanimity of sentiment as there is upon the proposition the National Government ought in some way to regulate interstate commerce."[72] Many members were responsive to this demand to the point that it was their overriding concern. As Rep. Charles Crisp (D-GA), a member of the conference committee, stated as the House considered the conference report,

"I say with the utmost frankness, that, as an individual, I preferred the bill without the commission, but I say also in the same breath that I am not to be classed with those who will not take anything unless they can get all they want, and that, with all respect I submit, must be the attitude of those gentlemen who oppose this bill because of the commission."[73]

Rep. William Fuller (R-IA) added that "the bill as presented by the conference committee should, in my judgment be amended in several particulars, but rather than have this session close without some legislation on this great question I shall vote for the bill."[74] These statements reflect a sense that the public would hold Congress accountable if it did not pass some form of legislation; creating the ICC was an available means to achieve that end.

Interstate Commerce Commission: Conclusion

The creation of the Interstate Commerce Commission was shaped by a variety of political forces. From an institutional perspective, however, it was strictly an exercise of congressional authority. This is due, in part, to the fact that the formation of the commission was housed in the context of railroad regulation rather than being the focus of the Interstate Commerce Act itself. Although one might expect both the president and Congress to play a role in establishing administrative agencies, the act was geared more toward an issue of domestic politics and thus more toward congressional action; this position was buttressed after the U.S. Supreme Court declared that the matter rested explicitly in the realm of congressional authority.

This understanding of congressional authority was widely shared, both within and outside the Washington community. In the process of creating the ICC and regulating railroads, Congress established a new set of expected behaviors regarding the creation of administrative agencies, some of which were codified into statute. First, as discussed earlier, Congress both expanded and relinquished its authority. It set the foundation that would allow Congress and the national government to expand their powers and influence to respond to the nationalization of the U.S. economy.

In terms of creating administrative agencies, the specific focus here, Congress set the foundation that would provide for the formal delegation of authority to an executive agency. As Congress and the national government expanded into new areas, they created the need to have experts deal with the technical issues associated with implementing the general policy set by Congress. By delegating authority to the ICC, Congress implicitly stated that, although it may have the perceived right to affect change, it did not have the full ability to do so, for as Rep. John Findlay (D-MD) claimed, "there are limitations even upon the omnipotence of an American Congress."[75]

Furthermore, Congress placed the exercise of one form of authority under the president's jurisdiction. Even though the ICC was designed to be more independent than other executive agencies, the president's ability, as set forth in the act, to appoint commissioners and remove them with reason provided the presidency with the opportunity to influence the direction of the commission. Although some members of Congress tried to resist this transfer of authority, most of them shared the understanding that this transference was not of sufficient concern, especially given other issues, and/or that it was an appropriate and necessary action to take regardless of the future ramifications it might hold for presidential authority, which at the time seemed limited, well defined, and checked.

Department of Commerce and Labor: History

The creation of the Department of Commerce and Labor was the culmination of various efforts to create new Cabinet-level agencies to represent those interests. Much like the Interstate Commerce Commission, the idea of creating a Department of Commerce had been bandied about in Congress for two decades prior to actually establishing the agency.[76] As the nation's economy grew and became more national in focus, however, it became more apparent that the federal government should create a formal organization to reflect the growing importance of this area. Similarly, the role of labor interests in U.S. politics continued to grow during the late nineteenth century. The organization of the national government reflected this growing importance as a Bureau of Labor was created in the Department of the Interior in 1884 and a sub-Cabinet-level Department of Labor was created in 1888. Despite these formal structures, labor interests continued to press their need to have a Cabinet-level secretary to represent their concerns.

The effort to create a Department of Commerce received a significant boost when Theodore Roosevelt became president. In both of his annual messages in December 1901 and December 1902, he specifically requested that Congress create such an organization with a Cabinet-level secretary. In 1901 Roosevelt stated, "There should be created a Cabinet officer, to be known as Secretary of Commerce and Industries, as provided in the bill introduced at the last session of Congress. It should be the province to deal with commerce in its broadest sense; including among many other things whatever concerns labor and all matters affecting the great business corporations and our merchant marine."[77] The day after Roosevelt's December 3, 1901, annual message, Sen. Knute Nelson (R-MN) introduced the legislation that eventually became the bill that created the Department of Commerce and Labor more than a year later.[78]

Nelson cited four premises that served as the rationale for a Department of Commerce, in a manner that reflected Roosevelt's statements in his annual message. First, it would provide for the development of a department with jurisdiction over the care, promotion, and development of the nation's "commercial, manufacturing, mining, and other industrial enterprises."[79] Second, it would allow the United States to achieve an equal standing with European nations that had similar entities. Third, it would meet the demands for such a department made by commercial and industrial interests, a position that Nelson explicitly noted the president recognized and supported. Finally, it would improve the efficiency of some government organizations, many of which were "overloaded and overburdened with work and duties foreign to their main and chief purposes and not germane to their principal functions."[80]

The original bill contained a provision that the Department of Labor would be transferred to the new agency but remain subordinate to the secretary of commerce—a situation that received mixed support by labor interests.[81] However, by the time the Senate passed an amended version of the Nelson bill on January 28, 1902, its full title was "A bill to establish the department of commerce and labor." At that point, the legislation was referred to the House and placed with the Committee on Interstate and Foreign Commerce, where it sat until January 1903. When the committee's version was introduced to the House, it differed from the Senate's version in regard to which existing bureaus would be transferred to the new department. After the House passed the bill on January 17, 1903, the measure was sent to the conference committee.

The Senate and House conferees presented a modified version of the original House bill to the two houses.[82] Prior to the final vote in the House, Rep. William Richardson (D-AL), one of the House conferees, dissented from Section 6 of the conference report, which was a substitute amendment for the original Section 6 in the House version. This section, referred to as the "Nelson Amendment" and written by Theodore Roosevelt, created and established the powers of a Bureau of Corporations. Section 6 stated, in part, that the head of the bureau, a commissioner of corporations, "shall have power and authority to make under the direction and control of the secretary of commerce and labor, diligent investigation into the organization, conduct, and management of the business of any corporation, joint-stock company, or corporate combination engaged in commerce among the several States and with foreign nations."[83]

The amendment also provided that the president would decide what information obtained by the bureau would be made public. Although Richardson criticized the amendment's language as being too weak,[84] the House overwhelmingly approved the bill 252 to 10; the Senate followed suit by approving the bill by voice vote.

Aside from the creation of the Cabinet-level department reflecting commercial and labor interests,[85] the most significant provision of the bill was the establishment of the Bureau of Corporations, which served as the "keystone of Roosevelt's strategy" to ensure that "the national government—or at least *his office*—possess[ed] power that matched (and, in a showdown, exceeded) that of the corporate giants."[86] President Roosevelt pushed for the inclusion of this bureau in the newly created department, arguing that "the creation of [the Department of Commerce and Labor] would in itself be an advance toward dealing with and exercising supervision over the whole subject of the great corporations doing an interstate business; and with this end in view, the Congress should endow the department with large powers, which could be increased as experience might show the need."[87] Furthermore, Roosevelt "regard[ed] the Nelson Amendment on account of the supervision and publicity clauses as the most important of all" of his efforts related to trusts.[88]

Department of Commerce and Labor: Analysis
The political context that surrounded the creation of the Department of Commerce and Labor was filled with a variety of regional and partisan differences, although not quite to the same extent as during the creation of the ICC. The interaction between President Roosevelt and the members of Congress, however, also concerned issues related to presidential authority. When examined in this light, the process that led to the forma-

tion of the Department of Commerce and Labor is both similar to and different from the one that brought about the creation of the ICC. The primary purpose of the legislation that created the ICC was to address a problematic segment of the nation's economy (i.e., railroads); the ICC was a tool to achieve that end. With regard to the legislation that created the Department of Commerce and Labor, establishing a new administrative agency was the end itself. One objective of the new department, however, was to address a problematic segment of the nation's economy (i.e., trusts). The potential of using the creation of the ICC as a model was not lost on President Roosevelt, who stated in his December 1901 annual message that "I believe that a law can be framed which will enable the National Government to exercise control . . . profiting by the experience gained through the passage and administration of the Interstate Commerce Act."[89]

On the other hand, the most significant differences in the processes of creating the two agencies lay in the level of presidential involvement. Unlike President Cleveland, who did not participate significantly in the creation of the ICC, President Roosevelt led the efforts to create the Department of Commerce and Labor and, to a greater extent, the Bureau of Corporations within it. Some would say Roosevelt's efforts with regard to the Bureau of Corporations were somewhat dubious. As the House and Senate conferees were revising the legislation, Roosevelt called for Senator Nelson and showed him a substitute amendment he had drafted regarding Section 6 of the bill. After Nelson somewhat reluctantly submitted the amendment to the conferees for their consideration, Roosevelt planted with two White House correspondents a news story that John D. Rockefeller opposed the Nelson Amendment. When the correspondents broke the story based on Roosevelt's word, members of Congress received numerous telegrams from their constituents, which "had their effect" as the Nelson Amendment and the conference report were ultimately accepted.[90]

After the fact, it was revealed that the story Roosevelt had planted was in actuality his own fabrication. Regardless of his tactics, however, Roosevelt's involvement was an important component of the bill's passage and the creation of the Bureau of Corporations. As he wrote a friend in late summer of 1903, "I think it is well to recall that on this labor and capital question the following are the important steps *I have taken:* . . . Securing the enactment of the law in reference to a Bureau of Corporations."[91]

The difference between Cleveland's and Roosevelt's respective behaviors can be attributed in part to their different personal legislative styles and also to the slightly different focuses of the two pieces of legislation. The explicit focus of creating a new agency provided Roosevelt, as chief executive, with an opportunity to mold the executive branch more directly. Roosevelt, however, also utilized and advanced the federal government's authority to address national economic problems—the authority that Congress codified in the Interstate Commerce Act—and sought to extend it to the presidency.[92] Roosevelt can be seen as blending that general authority, his specific authority as chief executive, and his personal style to lead the nation on this issue by directing Congress to take further steps to create the Department of Commerce and Labor. His behavior had the effect of establishing a new pathway by assuming greater authority for the presidency, not just in creating administrative agencies but also in addressing economic issues.[93]

Although Roosevelt may have led on this issue, it was not one of complete presidential dominance. Congress maintained and exercised its own authority in designing the exact structure and jurisdiction of the new department. Between the 57th Congress, first and second sessions, the Senate debated the creation of the new department ten times, covering sixty-four pages of the *Congressional Record* with more than twenty senators speaking. The House took up the issue on four occasions in the second session and had more than forty members speak on it, covering fifty-seven pages of debate. Other than Roosevelt's influence on the Nelson Amendment, Congress primarily decided what bureaus would be transferred under the bill, including the transfer of the existing Department of Labor into the new department. As the members of Congress, particularly in the Senate, debated this measure, however, they examined among other things its implications for presidential and congressional authority.

A number of senators opposed the transfer of the Department of Labor, which had been outside any executive department, to the new department and therefore directly under the presidency's control for two reasons. The first related to the transfer of authority from Congress to the presidency. As Sen. Frank Cockrell (D-MO) asked his colleagues, "Why shift the responsibility for the administration of the Department of Labor from Congress to the head of an executive department?"[94] After some debate on this issue, Sen. Stephen Elkins (R-WV) provided

Cockrell with an answer: "I think Congress has a good deal to do with-out managing executive bureaus."[95] Elkins's statement reflects a view similar to one that Congress had relied upon in the creation of the ICC; in both cases, Congress demonstrated a willingness to formally grant a portion of its authority to an executive agency because of a limitation of institutional resources (in the ICC, it was knowledge of the issue; in this instance, it was time and workload capacity).

The more important concern certain members of the Senate expressed regarding the transfer of the existing Department of Labor into the new department was that it would become the political tool of the presidency instead of being an independent body representing labor interests. If placed in the new department, the labor entity would be under the con-trol of the head of that department and, as such, subject to presiden-tial control as well. As Sen. Hernando Money (D-MS) argued, "Every-body knows that this department chief, the secretary of commerce, like the Secretary of the Treasury and other Secretaries, will be a political appointment. Such officers are the political advisers of the President on all questions of public policy. They are his advisers as to appointments to be made to carry out and execute the laws of Congress. In the Depart-ment of Labor, as it now exists to-day, no sort of political influence is exercised as far as I know."[96]

Money continued:

You can not put a bureau under a political department and make it independent and nonpartisan. . . . [W]e all know and feel that politi-cal influence ramifies every single branch of the service, military and civil. It has shown itself so repeatedly and so persistently that it is impossible for anyone, however, dull, to ignore the fact. . . .

I know that Alexander Hamilton, whose principles are espoused by the other side of the Chamber, said the nearer we could come to the monarchy of Great Britain the better for us; that it was impos-sible for the plain people to govern themselves; that it must be a government of the better class, the "better class" always meaning the people having money. . . . And so to-day it is becoming more and more obvious that the people are not to speak for themselves. We need at least one grand, impartial, nonpartisan bureau or depart-ment that will give the facts in which they are concerned without any coloring or any direction from any political chief whatever.[97]

Money's argument reflects a position held by many Southern Democrats, as discussed earlier in connection with the ICC. Once again we can see a distrust of delegating authority from Congress to the supposedly nonpartisan administrative agency. The essence of Money's argument (which also underlies part of Cockrell's argument) is that, in reorganizing the government's administrative agency relating to labor interests and the collection of labor data in this manner, Congress was providing the president with a political tool.

The understanding shared by a majority of the members of Congress, however, was that the reorganization of the labor interests was an appropriate grant of authority to the presidency—that the government's labor data collection agency should be under the presidency's control. Most members agreed with the statement of Sen. Thomas Martin (D-VA) that, "as a general proposition, for the efficient administration of the business of the Government I believe that every bureau should be classified under some Cabinet officer and should be controlled by a Cabinet officer in direct communication with the President and directly responsible to the President."[98]

Part of the reason that many members of Congress downplayed the threat of presidential use of the data collection function for political reasons was that it was not a likely political reality. Senator Elkins argued that, "In the multifarious duties that rest upon the shoulders of the President he can not give these bureaus any attention whatever, and for this reason we believe that it is better to put them in the hands of a responsible Cabinet officer, notwithstanding the claim of the political complexion that might attach to the administration of the Labor Bureau."[99]

Sen. John C. Spooner (R-WI) added, "[E]very right-thinking citizen of the United States with public duties and fit to hold public office, knows that the statistical information that reveals to the people our growth, the condition, of our industries—general statistical information—must be honest in order to be of any use or value, and I never expect to see a President elected who will put a tool in such a position or who may be expected to be willing to so prostitute his position as to give political coloring to investigations of this sort and to the collection and compilation and report of statistical information."[100]

In other words, the widely shared understanding regarding the Department of Commerce and Labor was that it would not be used for political purposes and that its value as an administrative organization rested in its being a neutral collector and disseminator of information. The president was expected to conform with this understanding because to do otherwise would be an abuse of the authority that the institution was granted.

Although the House did not touch upon this issue to the extent that the Senate did, Rep. Edgar Crumpacker (R-IN) expressed a similar argument concerning the threat of presidential misuse of the institution's authority. Crumpacker drew an analogy between the creation of both the Department of Commerce and Labor and the Department of Agriculture. He stated, "The importance, however, of the agricultural interests became so great . . . [as] to justify Congress in elevating the Bureau of Agriculture to the dignity of a Department and making the head of that Department eligible to admission into the President's council of advisors. But this action of Congress did not and could not change or add to the powers of the Chief Executive."[101] In other words, even though the new department would provide the president with another Cabinet-level advisor, it would not significantly alter the presidency.

The provisions of the Nelson Amendment most directly raised the issue of increased presidential authority. The original House bill provided that the Bureau of Corporations would "gather, compile, publish, and supply useful information concerning such corporations." The Nelson Amendment, on the other hand, charged the bureau with "gather[ing] such information and data as will enable the President of the United States to make recommendations to Congress for legislation for the regulation of such commerce, and to report such data to the President from time to time as he shall require; and the information so obtained, or as much thereof as the President may direct, shall be made public."[102]

In other words, the power of publicity—that is, making the information collected by the bureau public and therefore a tool against improper business practices—shifted under the Nelson Amendment to be entirely within the president's discretion. For this reason, Representative Richardson launched into his verbal assault on the revised Section 6 (as discussed earlier).[103] Representative Mann, another of the conferees, retorted that "the Nelson substitute confers a greater power upon the commissioner of corporations to make investigations of so-called trusts than has been proposed in any other bill or in any other proposition brought before Congress."[104]

Overall, the members of Congress exhibited both reactive and proactive behavior in their efforts to pass the legislation to create the Department of Commerce and Labor; they followed the guidelines that Roosevelt set for creating the department and echoed his sentiments, while at the same time setting forth most of the specific provisions in the legislation. Roosevelt stated that he would like the new department to be "one phase of what should be a comprehensive and far-reaching scheme of constructive statesmanship for the purpose of broadening our markets, securing our business interests on a safe basis, and making firm our new position in the international industrial world; while scrupulously safeguarding the rights of wage-worker and capitalist, of investor and private citizen, so as to secure equity as between man and man in this Republic."[105] Congress responded to the policy direction set forth by Roosevelt and crafted an executive agency that addressed the concerns of "wage-worker and capitalist."

Department of Commerce and Labor: Conclusion

The creation of this new department was an example of cogovernance between the presidency and Congress, although President Roosevelt could certainly be seen as directing key elements of the process. The general behaviors exhibited by Roosevelt and members of Congress were consistent with this supposition. Roosevelt, as chief executive, provided the framework; Congress, with its legislative powers, filled in the details.

The institutional interaction, however, was driven in part by Roosevelt's use of his institutional authority more expansively than one would expect from reading the Constitution. In pushing for the creation of the new department, he did not simply act as the head of the executive branch; he acted as the head of the nation, trying to put forth the first stage of a solution to a broader problem. He did not let Congress merely enact the plan he presented; he used the tools of his office and his personal skills to direct that process to his satisfaction.

The members of Congress responded to Roosevelt and his exercise of the presidency's authority. Not only did they pursue the path Roosevelt laid out for them, but they also did so specifically because of Roosevelt. In describing the purposes of creating the Department of Commerce and Labor, Sen. Knute Nelson stated, "The President of the United States has seen the necessity and demand for such a department, and hence in his last annual message recommended the measure to Congress"—a sentiment expressed by other members as well.[106] Furthermore, the legislation also formally enhanced the presidency by codifying specific grants of authority to it, most significantly through the establishment of the Bureau of Corporations and the presidency's control of its powers of publicity.

Authority can shift from one institution to another to address an existing need in society or be granted to an institution as a new need arises. The authority that the presidency seems to have gained through the institutional interaction over the creation of the new department is tied more to a new societal need that had developed: specifically, controlling the trusts that had emerged due to the expanding U.S. economic system. This new need presented an opportunity structure that Roosevelt took full advantage of in order to foster the writing of a new script. As a result, both the formal and informal grants of authority to the presidency did not come at the direct expense of congressional authority. Instead, the grant of authority reflected the emerging expectation that the presidency would coordinate the government's responses to those needs and the problems caused by a nationalizing economic system.

Federal Trade Commission: History

The growing problems related to business trusts, coupled with the federal government's inability to create a method to address them, provided the foundation that led to the creation of the Federal Trade Commission. Since the Sherman Antitrust Act of 1890 proved to be a failure and the Bureau of Corporations only an investigative body and therefore too weak to prevent business combinations, many in government and the business community started calling for a more powerful government entity to be created.[107] By the 1912 election, both the Progressive and Republican parties included platform planks on this issue. The Republican platform read: "In the enforcement and administration of Federal Laws governing interstate commerce and enterprises impressed with a public use engaged therein, there is much that may be committed to a Federal trade commission, thus placing in the hands of an administrative board many of the functions now necessarily exercised by the courts. This will promote promptness in the administration of the law and avoid delays and technicalities incident to court procedure."[108]

The Progressives, in their platform, "urge[d] the establishment of a strong Federal administrative commission of high standing, which shall maintain permanent active supervision over industrial corporations engaged in inter-State commerce, or such of them as are of public importance, doing for them what the Government now does for the National banks, and what is now done for the railroads by the Inter-State Commerce Commission."[109]

The Democrats did not include a specific provision in their platform. President Wilson, however, took charge of the issue and in a special address to Congress on January 20, 1914, called for the creation of an interstate trade commission—"an administrative commission capable of directing and shaping . . . corrective processes, not only in aid of the courts but also by independent suggestion."[110] Wilson's call was taken up in Congress as both House and Senate committees began drafting legislation.

Despite having what would seem to be strong bipartisan support, with congressional Republicans and Democrats joking on the House floor about the Democrats taking the Republicans' ideas,[111] the members of Congress embarked on a legislative journey that lasted several months before they passed the final version of the Federal Trade Commission bill. The House of Representatives was the first chamber to pass a version of this legislation. This measure, however, provided for a commission with only limited authority to investigate, which was seen by some as doing little more than slightly enhancing the existing Bureau of Corporations and removing it from the direct control of the president.

The Senate took a longer time to debate its version of a trade commission bill but produced one with greater authority and stronger powers. A significant portion of the debate in the Senate regarded what constituted unfair trade practices—the bill's key provision. The differences in the House and Senate versions stemmed in large part from the question of how strong the new commission should be.

President Wilson played a key role in resolving this issue, although in ways that conflicted with the Democratic Party's long-standing preferences for limited government and states' rights and opposition to economic concentration.[112] Wilson originally argued that unfair practices "can be explicitly and item by item forbidden by statute in such terms as will practically eliminate uncertainty."[113] As the Senate stalled over how to handle unfair practices, however, Wilson switched his position and surmised that "such precise definition had proved impractical; and the President, in consultation with Congressional leaders, had concluded that it would be necessary to formulate a broadly worded prohibition against 'unfair competitive trade practice' and to give to the proposed trade commission the quasi-judicial job of applying this prohibition in concrete cases."[114]

The Senate debated other issues, such as whether the legislative branch could provide the new commission with quasi-judicial powers; the relationships between the new commission and the presidency, attorney general, and the ICC; and the potential success of the bill as a piece of antitrust legislation. In addition, a vote on the bill was held so that it could be considered along with two other pieces of legislation, the Clayton Act and the Rayburn Act.[115] After the Senate passed its version of the measure, the issue went to conference committee. The Senate and the House passed the conference report on September 8 and 19, 1914, respectively, and the bill was signed into law on September 26, 1914. The primary provisions of the law included creating the Federal Trade Commission, which would be composed of five commissioners appointed by the president with the advice of the Senate; eliminating the Bureau of Corporations and assuming all its employees and workload into the FTC; and allowing the FTC, after some investigation, to provide cease and desist orders against unfair business practices, along with other data collection and regulatory powers.

Federal Trade Commission: Analysis

The institutional interaction surrounding the creation of the Federal Trade Commission was similar in structure to that of the Department of Commerce and Labor with respect to issues of authority. In both cases, the idea for establishing a new government agency had been floating in the political system for some time without really taking hold. The president's specific call for creating a new agency, however, served as a crystallizing force that helped spur Congress into decisive action. Furthermore, the president worked with congressional leaders, including the sponsor of the Senate's version, to formulate key provisions of the legislation.

The substance of the interaction, as it related to the potential shifting of authority and expectations, was more akin to the interaction that led to establishing the Interstate Commerce Commission. Specifically, as with the ICC, there was some concern about the president's ability to appoint commissioners. Unlike the ICC case, however, Congress explicitly removed potential authority from the presidency by eliminating the Bureau of Corporations and placing its power within an entity perceived as more "independent." In doing so, Congress signaled that, while it might allow for greater presidential involvement in the legislative process creating the new commission, it was unwilling to permit continued direct presidential control of the functioning of the FTC.[116] To a large degree, other authority issues centered on the question of whether Congress, as the legislative branch of the national government, could constitutionally grant the FTC quasi-judicial powers. Many of the questions and arguments raised, both pro and con, mirrored those raised more than a quarter century before in the ICC debate.

The debate in Congress concerning the FTC was overwhelmingly centered on specific policy issues rather than authority questions—that is, whether Congress had the ability to create the agency under discussion. The debate on the floor of Congress was extensive. The Senate took up the bill twenty-nine times between June 13 and September 8, 1914; a total of fifty-two senators spoke on the issue, covering more than 500 pages of substantive debate in the *Congressional Record*. The House saw fifty-seven members speak on the issue on the six occasions between May 1 and September 10, 1914, that it took up the bill on the floor, covering 102 pages of substantive debate.

The most significant issue discussed was the definition of unfair trade practices; others included cross-ownership of stock between businesses in competition, whether the provisions of the bill regulated or prevented monopolies, business accounting practices, and the relationship of the Federal Trade Commission with antitrust policy generally. In a telling example of the sort of policy questions discussed, Sen. Frank Bandegee (R-CT) stated, "[N]obody will deny the right of Congress to regulate commerce among the States, no matter by whom conducted. The question is as to the wisdom of this Central Government here at Washington setting up a Federal tribunal . . . [and] the wisdom of the Federal Government here at Washington attempting to regulate all the attempts of the different corporations which are rivals for business to get business."[117]

To the extent that the members of Congress did discuss the authority of the new commission and whether Congress could grant such authority, they did so expressly acknowledging and asserting the independence of the commission from political forces, as well as the legislative and judicial nature of the proposed FTC. With regard to the commission's independence, Congress eliminated the Bureau of Corporations and transferred its powers to the FTC. This decision, however, was in large part born of public policy considerations that had an effect on presidential authority rather than being a direct attack on presidential authority itself. Specifically, the members of Congress decided that, as a matter of public policy, for the FTC to be most effective it needed to have the powers then held by the Bureau of Corporations; to enhance these powers;[118] and to be free to perform its functions at its discretion rather than the president's.[119]

The independence of the Federal Trade Commission from the political influence of the president and/or the president's executive officers was seen as a primary component that would lead to the success of the new commission. In fact, Rep. Andrew Montague (D-VA) claimed that first among the "salient features of the bill [is] . . . the transfer of the Bureau of Corporations and the Commissioner of Corporations, with all their authorities and duties as to the investigation, management, and control of corporations, with power to act in the discharge of these duties independently of the Cabinet or the President."[120] Rep. Dick Morgan (R-OK) added, "I believe it is unsafe for an administration in power, an administrative officer representing a great political party to hold the power of life and death over the great business interests of this country. . . . [W]e should . . . create a great, independent, non-partisan commission, independent of the President, independent of Cabinet officers, removed so far as possible from partisan politics, that would command the respect and confidence of all parties and of all the people of the Nation."[121]

Finally, Rep. J. Harry Covington (D-MD), in discussing the House bill that he sponsored, stated that "the great value to the American people of the [ICC] has been largely because of its independent power and authority. The dignity of the proposed commission and the respect in which its performance of its duties will be held by the people will also be largely because of its independent power and authority. Therefore the [House version of the FTC] bill removes entirely from the control of the President and the Secretary of Commerce the investigations conducted and the information acquired by the commission under the authority heretofore exercised by the Bureau of Corporations or the Commission of Corporations. All such investigations may hereafter be made upon the initiative of the commission, and the information obtained may be made public entirely at the discretion of the commission."[122]

Covington's last point regarding publicity of information reflects the most specific manner in which the Bureau of Corporations, as part of the Department of Commerce, could be utilized for political purposes.[123] As discussed previously, the provision written by President Roosevelt in the 1903 act that created the Bureau of Corporations dictated that the decision to make the information obtained by the bureau public rested with the president. Putting aside any presidential authority issues related to this provision, as a matter of policy it was too ad hoc to be an effective control of interstate commerce; it was described as a "failure" in that it did not "require the regular gathering of certain most important kinds of information through the medium of annual reports from industrial corporations engaged in interstate commerce."[124]

Although Congress sought to remove the presidency's direct control of the entity responsible for investigating unfair business practices, it did not eliminate the executive branch's influence outright. Section 6(d) of the Federal Trade Commission Act authorized the commission to undertake an investigation "Upon the direction of the President or either House of Congress to investigate and report the facts relating to any alleged violations of the antitrust Acts by any corporation." Section 6(e) provided the Attorney General with similar powers.

These specific provisions generated debate on the floor of Congress that brought to the forefront Congress's general concerns about undue political influences, particularly that of the president and the president's executive officers, upon the operation of the commission. As Senator Albert Cummins (R-IA) stated,

> I have always thought that a trade commission, as the Interstate Commerce Commission is, should be an independent tribunal attached to no department of the Government, owing allegiance to no officer of the Government. I think it should be clothed with adequate power of investigation. I think that it should be free to prosecute an investigation whenever it believes that it would serve the public welfare to do so, and if in the course of the investigation a violation of the antitrust law or any other law of the United States relating to this subject is developed, I think it ought to report the

result of its investigation to the Attorney General, whose duty it is to prosecute offenders; but I have never thought that we should put into the law a provision that would enable either the President or the Attorney General to command its activities.

The objection to it . . . is that, as the Senator from Idaho [William E. Borah] said the other day, there have been times when the antitrust law has been made the instrument, as is alleged, of promoting political fortunes. The President is a political officer; the Attorney General is a political officer connected with the policy of the administration and of the country. The trade commission should not be affected by those influences; and it is my judgment . . . that it will accomplish more—it will establish itself more firmly in the confidence of the people if it acts upon its own motion or acts upon a petition properly brought before it under certain provisions of the bill.[125]

Despite this lengthy statement, Senator Cummins balanced his opposition to sections 6(d) and 6(e) of the act against the overall benefit he believed the bill would provide. He concluded, "I do not think the commission should act upon the suggestion of the President . . . , but I have not believed that the presence of that provision was sufficiently important to change my general view of the proposed legislation."[126] In other words, the bill sufficiently achieved the goal to limit the president's direct influence over the new agency.

The second set of authority-related issues debated in Congress revolved around the legislative and judicial nature of the FTC. If one compares the ICC and FTC interactions, in the case of the former, the supporters of the legislation flatly denied that the commission was legislative and/or judicial in nature; it was an executive agency administering the law. Remember that the Senate even voted down an amendment that would have specifically stated this since it was "unnecessary." The FTC, however, was held up as having both legislative functions and judicial functions. Rep. Frederick Stevens (R-MN) compared the FTC's investigative functions to those of a congressional committee. He also referenced the judicial nature of the FTC—its "power to enforce the law against unfair methods of competition"—as "approaching no new subject . . . [where] the rules and limits seem well defined."[127]

Not all members, however, saw the authority granted to the FTC as beneficial or proper, particularly in relation to Congress's institutional authority. These critics raised points similar to those offered by opponents of the ICC's creation. For example, Sen. John Shields (D-TN) contended that "the provisions of this bill, in my opinion attempt to delegate to this commission legislative, judicial, and executive powers in clear contravention of our organic law."[128] Sen. George Sutherland (R-UT) argued vehemently against the powers delegated to the new commission: "[I]t is given a roving commission to investigate all the affairs of all the corporations of the country which may be engaged in interstate commerce; and that is the sole and only test of its jurisdiction, namely, to inquire whether or not a particular corporation is engaged in interstate commerce; and if it is, then the power is given to investigate all of its multiform and multifold activities, whether they relate to interstate commerce or not. . . . Now, I undertake to say, Mr. President, that that is a power which Congress can not devolve upon a commission; it is a power which Congress can not itself exercise; and, after all, that is the primary test of the power which we may devolve upon a commission— whether the Congress itself may exercise the power. If it can not, it is a power which can not be devolved upon a legislative commission."[129]

Moreover, Sen. James Reed (D-MO) maintained that "If we create a commission with power to prohibit all unfair practices in trade, then, in the name of goodness, what is the use of passing any more law? Why trouble ourselves further? Why not go home and go to rest and enjoy our sweet repose and say that the business of this country is in the hands of that commission, with full power to prohibit everything that is wrong and to promote everything that is right? That is the very question."[130]

The very question indeed—it was the one that Congress had to grapple with throughout this period when it came to questions of institutional authority in this area. How could Congress have balanced exercising its authority to address the issues raised by the changing economic environment with the need to create government agencies filled with the knowledge, singular focus, and authority to resolve such matters? Putting aside the constitutional question of delegating power and authority,[131] Congress resolved this subject largely for political, as compared to institutional, reasons but in doing so continually provided the presidency with authority either directly or indirectly. Sometimes the authority stemmed from the need to address new concerns, such as with the Department of Commerce and Labor; at other times, such as with the ICC and in this case the FTC, Congress delegated away its own existing authority.

Congress may have expanded its authority (or at least that of the national government generally) by providing a means for the government to legislate and regulate in new economic sectors. In doing so, however, Congress increased the authority of the presidency as well. Whereas Congress dominated the creation of the ICC, Wilson directed many of the important issues related to the creation of the FTC. The fact that his speech to Congress crystallized the efforts to create a trade commission just reaffirmed the view of the presidency as chief executive and the expectation that the president would shape the organizational structure of the government. As Representative Covington introduced his bill to the House, he directly attributed the measure to Wilson's efforts, calling it "the first legislative measure resulting from the message of the president read to Congress in January last on the subject of trusts and monopolies."[132]

Planting the seed was only part of the institutional authority that Wilson exercised in the creation of the Federal Trade Commission. He worked closely with the leaders in Congress, not simply urging the adoption of a specific provision or keeping abreast of unfolding matters but also working to craft many of the specifics of the legislation. For example, in one letter to Representative Covington, Wilson provided detailed comments on the language of one provision in the bill, to the extent of suggesting "striking out . . . the word 'the' on line seven and the insertion in line eight, after the word 'same,' of the word 'shall.' "[133] Wilson concluded the same letter with this observation: "I had yesterday a long talk with Senator Newlands and I think that if the House conferees will stand stoutly for Section V throughout, including the matter of the scope of the court review, they will win. I think I converted Senator Newlands to that view."

Wilson had similar interactions with Senator Newlands, who, after sending Wilson a copy of a tentative conference report, wrote, "It is hardly necessary for me to say that I welcome at any time any suggestion from you regarding the pending legislation."[134]

Possibly the most significant impact Wilson had on the legislative process was his assent to the strong commission approach, which may have been done for a number of politically motivated reasons. For example, the start of World War I abroad and the existence of a domestic economic depression forced Wilson "to seek a middle ground" with progressive Republicans.[135] In addition, Wilson sought "to forge a national electoral coalition of Democrats and Progressives" to expand the base of Democratic Party support.[136] His efforts were done in the face of strong criticism from Theodore Roosevelt, as some have argued, to "attract supporters of the decaying Progressive party organization by coopting a central component of the third party's platform."[137]

From a policy viewpoint, these political concerns led to the creation of a strong independent agency. From a partisan perspective, this switch helped reshape the Democratic Party. From an institutional approach, however, this change of position reflected the role that Wilson, as president, played in the interaction. Although he was unable to achieve his original policy preference, he was largely responsible for reconciling the differences that separated the House and Senate in order to clear the way for legislation to be passed. In other words, even with Wilson's change of position on the FTC, done for political expediency, the norm regarding the codified delegation of authority to the presidency did not alter. The presidency was still expected to have only a limited control over the ongoing functioning of the FTC. This interaction, however, highlighted that the presidency could also play a key role in the legislative process.

While Wilson's micromanagement of the legislative process may be in part due to his personal leadership style, just as Cleveland's and Roosevelt's involvement in this area was reflective of theirs, it is also indicative of the authority and role of the presidency in creating a new government organization. Wilson did not need to circumvent the standard policy-making process to get Congress to adopt the provisions he wanted, as Roosevelt did to obtain public support for the Bureau of Corporations. Instead, he merely provided and, possibly more importantly, was sought to provide his input on all components of the legislation to create the FTC. The leaders of Congress, who were working out the details of the legislation in conference committee, recognized and generally supported the role Wilson was playing.

Federal Trade Commission: Conclusion

The institutional interaction that resulted in the Federal Trade Commission involved both the presidency and Congress; it was one of coparticipation. Congress's actions, however, can be seen as an expected exercise of its legislative authority. The members drafted and negotiated the specific provisions of the legislation, including defining the manner in which it would be executed (namely, by delegating the power to determine what was an unfair business practice to the FTC). Congress also took it upon itself to reallocate to the FTC the powers it had previously delegated to the Bureau of Corporations, which was under the direct control of the presidency. Such reallocation can be seen within the scope of congressional authority. Therefore, the level of congressional involvement was simply what could be expected of any attempt to craft a major piece of legislation. The key component of this legislation was that it provided an additional safeguard to protect the new commission from undue outside influences (including the presidency) on its functioning.

President Wilson's participation in creating the Federal Trade Commission, however, went beyond strictly executive behavior and approached that expected of a legislator. One could expect Wilson, as chief executive, to be an important force in evaluating the need for a new administrative agency and requesting that Congress respond accordingly. He clearly did that in his January 20, 1914, message. His behavior, however, once the details of the bill were being fleshed out, was akin to that of an ex officio member of the conference committee and key legislator. Furthermore, the members of Congress accepted this behavior as appropriate — as something that was expected of him.

From this institutional interaction, we see two norms that have developed. First, Congress reinforced an understanding that it would readily delegate its authority to new entities. The extent of presidential control over the new entity was restricted primarily to the appointment of commissioners and requesting investigations; Congress ensured there would be no direct control over the functioning of the FTC as there was in the creation of the Bureau of Corporations. Second, the president gained more leeway in the process of establishing a new agency, particularly in terms of being involved in the detailed legislative work necessary to create it. In essence, there was a greater acceptance of presidential initiative while Congress continued to shield its surrogates from the direct control of the presidency.

CREATION OF ADMINISTRATIVE APPARATUS: CASE STUDIES CONCLUSION

The cases provide evidence that the president was involved in determining the need or general purpose of a new agency and that Congress was more involved with determining the exact responsibilities, powers, and structure of the new organization, with the specific exception of President Cleveland's role in creating the ICC.[138] Cleveland failed to exercise such authority. This can be explained, however, by the fact that the bill interaction in question was not over the creation of the ICC specifically but essentially involved the regulation of interstate commerce generally—an area, according to the Supreme Court, that is in the congressional domain. As for Roosevelt, he not only determined the need for a new entity but also was instrumental in the formation of a bureau to handle what he perceived as a threat to the growing economy. One could argue that Roosevelt actually exceeded what might have been expected of him by writing the section covering the responsibilities, powers, and structures of the Bureau of Corporations. As for Wilson, he too determined the need and general purpose for a new commission. Again like Roosevelt, he too went beyond what might be expected by actually having a hand in drafting parts of the eventual law creating the commission. For their part, the members of Congress generally exhibited behavior as anticipated. They were involved in determining the exact responsibilities, powers, and structure of the new organizations.

We also found that the president's role in creating administrative agencies grew throughout this era, while Congress was more responsive to presidential initiatives while maintaining a significant role for itself. What needs to be clarified is the type of growth exhibited. As one moves from the ICC case through the Department of Commerce and Labor/Bureau of Corporations case to the FTC, the role that the presidency played in the legislative process increased noticeably. Congress also appeared to be more responsive to presidential initiatives as demonstrated by its willingness to accept presidential advice on the crafting of the legislation and using the president's initial request as the basis on which to galvanize successful action. As might be expected, however, Congress retained the primary job of crafting the specifics of the legislation.

Although this evidence indicates that the president's legislative role became more extensive in the creation of administrative agencies, there does not appear to be a correlative increase in the formal delegation to the presidency of control over the functioning of those agencies. In fact, Congress can be seen as guarding against undue presidential influence in this respect.[139] Despite Roosevelt's efforts to bring the functioning of the Bureau of Corporations under the presidency's direction, Congress subsequently resisted establishing a new pathway in this manner by transferring the bureau's functions to the more independent Federal Trade Commission. By the end of this period, Congress and the presidency shared an expectation that both would contribute to the establishing of administrative agencies but that Congress would still retain greater authority over the functioning of its empowered surrogates.

The creation of the Interstate Commerce Commission, the Department of Commerce and Labor, and the Federal Trade Commission also demonstrates how easily coordinated scripting takes place within the policy-making process. Although instances such the Dominican Republic case (Chapter 2) may place the issue of presidential authority at the center of the policy debate, such critical events are not the only way in which coordinated scripts are developed. In the cases discussed in this chapter, authority issues may have been debated—at times contentiously. Nevertheless, the primary concern of many members of Congress was passing legislation necessary to address the political problems of the day. They were willing to accept the new coordinated scripts they helped create, as well as the increased presidential authority that resulted from it, in order to obtain resolutions to more pressing matters.

CHAPTER 4

Tariff

T he nation's economy during the period from 1881 to 1920 was adapting to an industrializing society. Political leaders sought to ensure economic growth without encouraging economic instability. Nevertheless, the industrializing national economy often resulted in periods marked by either large government surpluses or revenue shortfalls. One of the primary tools over which various political and economic interests fought to achieve the goal of growth without instability was the tariff.

Since a tariff is a tax on imported goods that provides revenue for the government to function, the need for tariff reform itself has often been tied to the then-current state of the government's revenue. Throughout history, evidence of falling revenue has been followed by the passage of high protective tariffs.[1] Conversely, when the government has had a surplus in revenue, it has generally tried to reduce the cost burden on its citizens associated with high tariff rates by reducing duties.[2]

THE CONTEXT: THE TARIFF DEBATE— PROTECTIONISM OR FREE TRADE

At the heart of the tariff question, from an economic viewpoint, is a debate between protectionism and free trade. The original basis of protectionism stemmed from the "infant industries argument," which maintains that a new industry in the nation cannot compete with older industries abroad.[3] Thus, such an industry is allowed to mature under the protection of legislation, which causes competing foreign products to cost more than similar domestic products. This argument can logically be extended so that tariffs can also be used to protect domestic industries from foreign industries with cheaper labor. The nation benefits from protectionist tariffs, according to this theory, by developing industrial independence and variety.[4] On the other hand, consumers are required to pay more for products than they otherwise would without the existence of the tariff.

One of free trade's goals, however, is to provide consumers with the lowest possible price for the products they seek. Promoters of free trade generally view protection as "a tariff which puts an obstruction in the way of exchange of goods between different countries," particularly when it is not applied to infant industries.[5] This obstruction provides an artificial increase in the cost of the articles affected. Further, opponents of protectionism link the development of monopolies with higher, protective tariffs. In fact, they charge, competition itself would deteriorate as protected industries would not have the incentive to operate efficiently.[6]

The debate between these two economic theories played out in the context of the tariff issue between 1881 and 1920.[7] As implied earlier, tariff policy generally ebbed and flowed with the level of government revenues. Thus, as the economy expanded and contracted throughout the period, there were often attempts to modify the existing general tariff policy in the perceived needed direction.

The nature of the nation's economy affected tariff issues during this period in another way as well. This connection between the economy and tariff policy generally linked people's economic interests with their position on the tariff. This linkage also reflected regional and sectional divisions. The most significant split was between the agriculturally based Midwest and the industrial regions in the East. The Midwestern farmers generally opposed protective tariffs,[8] whereas the Eastern industrialists favored it. Furthermore, "as industrialization moved westward, the protective doctrine took hold there."[9] Southerners generally opposed protective tariffs for more partisan reasons, although they had economic reasons as well.[10]

Although the tariff question was connected to economic and regional interests, the primary division regarding the tariff often split along partisan lines. Before the 1880s, the tariff issue was considered particularistic as tariff policies at any given time were shaped by specific interests.[11] As the period under study started, the nation was coming off the heels of the presidential election of 1880, during which the Republican Party grabbed the tariff issue as its own. More specifically during the election and after, the Republicans successfully transformed the issue from one of economic self-interest to one with a broader, more philosophical meaning. Playing upon themes of patriotism, the Republicans argued that a protective tariff would enhance America's greatness.[12] The Democrats, however, were unable to organize as quickly as the Republicans around this matter. Although party leaders favored a limited tariff for revenue only, certain key constituencies of the Democratic Party, such as labor and some agricultural interests, tended to favor protectionist tariffs at this time.[13] These tensions within the party did not initially bode well for the Democrats' ability to develop a coherent position on the tariff issue.

With the assassination of President Garfield, the Republican Party, under then President Arthur, suffered from a lack of presidential party leadership. This void was filled by the leaders in Congress, who in turn, caused the party to be both less coherent on the tariff issue and more vulnerable to electoral losses, which transpired in both the 1882 congressional and 1884 presidential elections.

During this time of incoherence, Congress nevertheless managed to pass one major piece of tariff legislation, the Tariff Act of 1883. In 1882 Congress authorized the appointment of a tariff commission to analyze and report to the next Congress any changes it thought were necessary to the existing tariff.[14] After receiving the commission's report, the House, where revenue bills must originate, was initially unable to agree on any legislation. Eventually, the House was able to pass a bill reducing some internal taxes, to which the Senate added an amendment that incorporated most of the tariff commission's recommendations. Through a legislative "maneuver" by protectionist forces in the House, the measure was referred to a conference committee, where changes were made mostly in a protectionist direction.[15]

The bill finally passed the Senate only by a "strict party vote of 32 to 31."[16] In the House, 23 Democrats voted with all but 5 Republicans in approving the conference report. In its final form, the bill contained fewer reductions than the proposed Senate bill and, in some cases, raised other rates. After all of the legislative wrangling, the tariff act changed the rates very little overall, helping it earn the nickname of the "mongrel tariff." In fact, the average rates on dutiable goods increased approximately 2 percent, for a rate of 45 percent, but were unchanged for free and dutiable goods, with a rate of 30 percent.[17]

Over the next several years there were efforts to amend the tariff, including several attempts by Grover Cleveland to achieve moderate tariff reform in the first few years of his presidency, but to no avail.[18]

The tariff issue was transformed once again in December 1887, when Pres. Grover Cleveland delivered his annual message, which he devoted entirely to the tariff issue. This decisive action served to make it a party issue and divided the Democratic-controlled House and Republican-controlled Senate.[19] The House passed the Mills bill, which followed Cleveland's call for a reduction in duties. In the Senate, though, the Republicans prepared a bill that attempted to change the tariff in a more protectionist direction. These efforts set the stage for the 1888 election, when the issue was placed directly before the people and was seemingly won by the Republicans, as Benjamin Harrison was elected president and the party gained majority control of both houses of Congress.

Since the tariff issue was at the center of the 1888 election, the election's results made it appear that a protectionist policy possessed a slight advantage in the electorate. This perception, however, provided a false sense of security as the Republicans would face the electoral wrath of a public dismayed by the passage of a highly protectionist tariff. The enactment of the McKinley Tariff in late 1890 led to the defeat of Republicans in the congressional elections of that year and the return of Grover Cleveland to the White House following the 1892 election.[20]

In terms of partisan politics during the 1890s, the tariff debate remained important but lost the centrality it once possessed. Even though other economic matters, such as the silver issue, came to the forefront of the policy agenda, the tariff still garnered attention in Washington. Following the 1892 election and a financial crisis in September 1893, Grover Cleveland and William L. Wilson (D-WV), chairman of the House Ways and Means Committee, coauthored a modest tariff-reducing bill that passed the House. After being substantially amended by the Senate, the resulting bill, the Wilson-Gorham Tariff Act, became law without President Cleveland's signature. Although the rate modifications the act made were for the most part in the direction of lowering the tariff, it by no means enacted very extensive changes.[21]

Once again in 1896 the silver question became a priority issue that played out in the electoral arena. Following that election, the Republicans did not have a controlling majority in the Senate without their pro-silver members, and the party leaders were unwilling to address the currency issue in such a situation. As a result, they used the tariff as a means to obtain a preferred policy position in at least one area of the economy, without jeopardizing their coalition of support.[22] During a special session, Congress passed the Dingley Tariff,[23] which would be the "longest-lived" general tariff in the United States.[24] It ushered in a period of economic prosperity, which the protectionists were quick to ascribe to the act itself.

Throughout the first decade of the twentieth century, the consensus within the Republican Party started to strain. Although some party members were pushing for additional protectionist measures, others, including President Theodore Roosevelt, were reluctant to pursue such a policy.[25] Throughout this decade, there was little significant policy activity on the tariff, but after twelve years the Dingley Tariff appeared unable to handle the growing changes in industry and the development of trusts that the act seemed to encourage. In 1908 the Republicans ran on a platform to usher in tariff revision, and William Howard Taft made tariff reform a central component of his campaign. Shortly after the elections[26] and then in a special session called by new President Taft,[27] the House took up a tariff bill, which became a battleground between protectionists and progressives in Congress.[28] The resulting act, the Payne-Aldrich Tariff, did not bring about significant changes in the tariff system, as it left an "extremely high scheme of rates, and still showed an extremely intolerant attitude on foreign trade."[29]

Following the passage of the Payne-Aldrich Tariff, however, the Republican Party splintered further, as progressive Republicans in Congress began to speak out and vote against the rest of the party. The election of Woodrow Wilson as president stemmed in part from this splintering in the Republican ranks.[30] After taking office, Wilson made tariff reduction a high priority. His efforts are reflected in the passage of the Underwood Tariff of 1913.[31] By the end of this period, the tariff matter was no longer the predominant issue or cohesive force that it once was for the parties. Although the Democrats were able to pass the tariff of 1913, they did not have the unanimous consent of their party members in Congress.[32]

Overall, the tariff issue played a significant role in the institutional interactions between the presidency and Congress between 1881 and 1920.[33] The significant number of bills and resolutions introduced into Congress evidences this fact (see Table A.5 in the Appendix). Between 1881 and 1893, 755 bills or resolutions relating to tariff rates and policy were introduced in Congress; of these, 14 became laws or joint resolutions approved by the president.[34] Between 1894 and 1907, 383 bills and resolutions relating to tariffs were introduced in Congress; 17 became law or were presidentially approved joint resolutions. (As an interesting aside, seven laws or resolutions related to products imported for exhibition purposes.) In the years between 1908 and 1920, 471 bills and resolutions were introduced in Congress, of which 16 became law or were resolutions approved by the president, including several private bills granting relief to specific individuals for certain duties. Also, for the first time in the 1881–1920 period, presidents vetoed tariff bills passed by Congress, as Taft vetoed 5 bills and Wilson rejected 2.[35] As Table A.6 in the Appendix shows, most of the bills or resolutions that became law or were presidentially approved were very specific, either relating to duties on certain items (e.g., coffee, tea, woolens, flax) or amending previous legislation. Further, many of the other specific proposals introduced through the years contained provisions that would later be incorporated into the large omnibus tariff revisions discussed earlier. The fact that there was so much activity on even the smallest of details speaks to the relevance this issue had for the institutions involved.

On its face, the issue of the tariff would seem not to present the presidency with many opportunity structures to expand the institution's authority, even during the period of 1881–1920. After all, the issue lies primarily within the scope of Congress's constitutional powers and thus its authority. The nature of opportunity structures, however, is that they are more likely to arise at times when the existing pathways are not allowing the political actors to satisfactorily address the pressing issues of the day. Further, the nature of the tariff issue is that the longer a tariff remained on the books, the more likely it would fail to satisfy its purpose—that is, at times the federal government may be collecting too much revenue from tariffs and at times not enough. This disjuncture between the purpose and the effect of an existing tariff would create a need for Congress to reassess the tariff and, in connection therewith, the potential for presidential opportunity structures.

CASE STUDIES

Of the three policy areas examined in this study, the interactions over the creation of comprehensive tariff policy were the most subject to partisan politics. The development of the McKinley, Dingley, and Underwood tariffs each followed a similar pattern: The partisan majority in Congress revised the tariff structure with only minimal, if any, opportunity for the minority to influence the legislation.[36] Although the members of Congress viewed the revision of the nation's tariff policy as an issue in its domain, presidential influence helped shape the process and final outcome of each tariff.

The history of the McKinley Tariff started in December 1887, when President Grover Cleveland utilized his annual message to Congress to highlight the need for reducing the nation's tariffs. Cleveland's effort to set the political agenda and provide the Democrats with a unifying issue, however, could not overcome the Republican majority in the Senate and failed to generate support in the electorate. As a result, in the 1888 election, the Republican Party gained control of both houses of Congress and the presidency, with the goal of increasing tariff rates as one of its top priorities.

With the political agenda already determined by the election, President Benjamin Harrison, who supported the efforts to establish a protectionist tariff, primarily left the issue to congressional Republicans headed by William McKinley, chairman of the House Ways and Means Committee. As Congress crafted the details of the tariff legislation, however, its decision to place sugar on the free list conflicted with the efforts of Secretary of State James Blaine to open Latin American countries for U.S. trade. This blending of foreign and domestic policy provided a segue for Blaine and Harrison to help shape the reciprocity provision of the McKinley Tariff that granted the presidency the authority to alter duties under certain conditions without any check by Congress.

The middle of this period saw the Republicans once again returning to control of Congress and the presidency. They sought to reestablish the protectionist duties and the reciprocity provisions of the McKinley Tariff, which the Democrats had eliminated under the 1894 Wilson-Gorman Tariff. William McKinley, now president, took an active role in setting the agenda and discourse of tariff revision and brought Congress together for a special session to address this issue. McKinley's efforts, however, for the most part stopped at this level as he left the work of determining new tariff schedules to Congress. In finalizing the details of the Dingley Tariff, Congress once again provided the presidency with the authority to alter duties. This time, however, the president would need to negotiate reciprocity treaties that would require ratification by the Senate. By including this specific provision, Congress displayed a willingness to grant the presidency additional authority, so long as it was exercised pursuant to the Constitution and in conjunction with Congress.

The final period saw a Democratic majority in Congress and Woodrow Wilson, a Democrat, in the White House. Policy issues related to presidential authority, such as reciprocity, were not as significant in the formation of the 1913 Underwood Tariff. Wilson, though, extended the proactive role played by his predecessor, McKinley; not only did he set the general discourse and call for a special session of Congress, but he also participated in recommending duties on specific items, keeping his party together, and generally pushing the legislative process. The Democrats in Congress supported Wilson's involvement in the legislative process, provided him opportunities to become involved, and defended him against Republican attacks.

McKinley Tariff: History

As mentioned previously, to understand the McKinley Tariff, one must start with President Cleveland's 1887 annual message, in which he focused exclusively on the tariff issue. In his speech, Cleveland argued that the "amount of money annually extracted . . . from the industries and necessities of the people, largely exceeds the sum necessary to meet the expenses of the government."[37] He called for a reduction in the tariff rates but clearly indicated that doing so was Congress's responsibility.

In handling the tariff as he did, Cleveland ran into several problems. First and foremost, although the Democrats were the majority party in the House, the Republicans held a two-seat majority in the Senate. Thus, after the House approved the Mills bill, a modest tariff-reduction bill that favored Southern economic interests, the Senate countered with another tariff bill and let them both die.[38] Second, Cleveland's emphasis on the tariff can be seen as a political ploy born of partisan and electoral politics. Cleveland hoped to provide the Democrats with an issue that would shift focus away from free silver and toward one that would provide the Democrats with electoral success in 1888. The Republicans, however, emphasized the nationalistic implications of Cleveland's speech—that the Republicans were seeking to protect and promote U.S. products while Cleveland's reduction would benefit only England. As a result, Cleveland provided the Republicans with an issue to rally around and which, in turn, enabled them to build a winning electoral coalition.

If the speech served one function for the political process of the day, it helped make the tariff a central issue of the 1888 elections. Both political parties made reference to the tariff in their 1888 platforms. The Democratic platform placed the issue in terms of the burden that "unnecessary taxation" placed on the American public, particularly labor: "Of all the industrious freemen of our land, an immense majority, including every tiller of the soil, gain no advantage from excessive tax laws; but the price of nearly everything they buy is increased by the favoritism of an unequal system of tax legislation. . . . All unnecessary taxation is unjust taxation. . . . It is repugnant to the creed of Democracy, that by such taxation the costs of necessaries of life should be justifiably increased to all our people. . . . Resolved, That this convention hereby indorses and recommends the early passage of the bill for the reduction of revenue now pending in the House of Representatives."[39]

The Republicans focused their platform language on the Democratic antiprotectionist efforts: "We are uncompromisingly in favor of the American system of protection; we protest against its destruction as proposed by the President and his party. They serve the interests of Europe; we will support the interests of America. We accept this issue, and confidently appeal to people for their judgment. The protective system must be maintained."[40]

Although Benjamin Harrison received fewer popular votes than Grover Cleveland, he won a majority in the electoral college.[41] In addition, the Republican Party obtained control of the House with a net gain of twenty-two seats and enlarged its majority in the Senate by eight seats. Harrison reiterated the Republicans' call for tariff revision on December 3, 1889, in his first annual message. With the issue and the Republican position already well defined, Harrison did not initially provide much guidance in the legislative process as the congressional Republicans, with their majority in hand, began consideration of the matter. As Sen. John Sherman (R-OH) wrote to President Harrison, "The President should 'touch elbows with Congress.' He should have no policy distinct from his party and that is better represented in Congress than in the Executive."[42]

By the time the legislative process was complete, the members of Congress had spent nearly ten months, nearly the entire first session of the Fifty-first Congress, crafting the McKinley Tariff. The Republicans in both houses controlled the legislative process; the Democrats were virtually shut out of every aspect of the bill's creation. As we will see later, they charged that the Republicans held important meetings drafting the bill in private, excluded the Democrats from the conference committee between the House and Senate, and did not provide sufficient or meaningful debate opportunities in which they could express their opposition to the bill.

Most of Congress's debate on the tariff focused on the policy specifics of the new tariff schedule (i.e., what the rate would be on specific items). Congress's treatment of woolens has been described as "the most important and most sharply debated part of the tariff system."[43] Congress retained the division of woolens into three classes (clothing, combing, and carpet wool) and slightly increased the tariff rates on the first two classes. It changed carpet wool from a specific duty to ad valorem, making "the duty adjust itself automatically to the quality and value of the wool."[44]

The policy issue that would come to hold the most significance for the institutional development of the presidency related to Congress's decision to place sugar on the duty-free list. Taken in isolation, this decision would seem to be a simple recognition of sugar as a necessity of life rather than a luxury. Secretary of State James Blaine, however, was concerned that this provision might undermine his efforts to open up trade in Latin American countries, which produced most of the sugar imported into the United States. By removing the duty, Blaine feared that Cuba and other Latin American countries would have no incentive to open up their markets to U.S. products and that the United States was providing these countries with a benefit without receiving anything in return.

Blaine set out to include a reciprocity provision in the tariff bill, meeting with members of Congress to promote the idea. On June 19, 1890, President Harrison sent a letter to Congress publicly supporting Blaine's efforts. Blaine drafted an amendment to the McKinley bill, which was introduced by Sen. Eugene Hale (R-ME) on the same day. This amendment read in part, "And the President of the United States is hereby authorized, without further legislation to declare the ports of the United States free and open to all the products of any nation of the American hemisphere upon which no export duties are imposed so long as such nation shall admit to its ports free of all . . . taxes . . ."[45]

In August, Sen. Nelson Aldrich (R-RI) introduced an amendment on which Harrison "worked behind the scenes" with Republican party leaders in Congress to develop compromise language.[46] The Aldrich amendment was approved by the Senate in early September 1890 and found its way into the final act.

After Republicans from the House and Senate resolved their differences on the McKinley bill in conference committee,[47] the two Houses took up final consideration of the bill, despite the fact that many members of Congress had already returned to their districts to campaign for the upcoming election and thus were not present for the voting.[48] On the conference report alone, there were 98 pages of debate in the *Congressional Record,* with 48 speakers in the House of Representatives and 40 pages of debate with 18 speakers in the Senate. The Senate passed the bill on September 30, 1890; the House approved it on September 27 and agreed to a technical correction on October 1, 1890. President Harrison signed the bill the same day.

McKinley Tariff: Analysis

As a matter of setting tariff policy, the McKinley Tariff Act largely represented a matter of congressional, as compared to presidential, control. Using the results of the 1888 election as a guide, the Republican members of Congress, led by McKinley, structured both the general policy and specific rates of the tariff. Presidential involvement was relatively limited, either providing general support for the Republican efforts or specifically trying to include some form of Blaine's reciprocity proposal in the final version of the bill.

Before addressing the McKinley Tariff specifically, we should consider the impact of Grover Cleveland's 1887 annual message on the McKinley Act from both a political and an institutional perspective. In focusing on the tariff, Cleveland was performing what he perceived as the proper role of the presidency: to identify areas that require legislative action. He referenced his constitutional duty to provide Congress with information on the State of the Union and proclaimed, "But I am so much impressed with the paramount importance of the subject to which this communication has thus far been devoted that I shall forego the addition of any other topic, and shall only urge upon your immediate consideration the 'state of the Union,' as shown in the present condition of our treasury and our general fiscal situation, upon which every element of our safety and prosperity depends."[49] Cleveland's role as president, however, did not extend much beyond this point, only to lend his support to the Mills bill.[50]

For Cleveland, Congress held the responsibility for putting his call for reductions into effect. He stated that Congress "alone can apply a remedy" to the problems the nation faced and that doing so required Congress to exert "great labor and care, and especially a broad and national contemplation of the subject."[51] Putting these institutional roles in perspective, Cleveland wrote to Congress: "I have deemed it my duty thus to bring to the knowledge of my countrymen, as well as to the attention of their representatives charged with the responsibility of legislative relief, the gravity of our financial situation. . . . If disaster results from the continued inaction of Congress, the responsibility must rest where it belongs."[52]

Cleveland attempted to exhibit leadership on the issue of the tariff, which in large part reflected his understanding of the presidency. While the presidency was expected to identify issues that should be addressed and suggest generally how the nation could best proceed, outside that narrow scope, the presidency was supposed to let Congress do what it deemed appropriate. His view of his role was not shared among the Republicans in Congress. Sen. John Sherman (R-OH) stated that "Cleveland made a cardinal mistake in [seeking to dictate] a tariff policy to Congress."[53] Cleveland's inability to get Congress to follow his lead primarily stemmed not from institutional concerns but from political and partisan motivations. In other words, Cleveland's lack of success came mostly as a result of supporting the wrong side of an issue at the wrong time. The likelihood of achieving a tariff reduction in the last few months of the Fiftieth Congress was small, given the Republican-controlled Senate and the partisan nature of the subject. Further, as an election issue, the tariff helped Harrison win in the North, a region that favored an increased tariff and gave him enough support to overcome Cleveland's advantage in the South. In addition, the Republican gains in Congress provided the party with a majority to implement such a policy in the next session.

From an institutional perspective, Cleveland's message provided two key insights. First, although Cleveland was unable to establish a new pathway by which he could successfully set the tariff agenda, he did reflect an understanding of the institutional roles of Congress and the presidency that can serve as a baseline by which to compare future behavior of presidents and members of Congress. Second, his message demonstrated the dominance of policy concerns and partisan divisions in this area. In other words, the politics of tariff revision were predominantly shaped by contextual factors rather than institutional concerns. That is not to say, however, that the politics of tariff revision did not have an impact on the institutional authority of the presidency and Congress.

With regard to the interaction that led to the McKinley Tariff, President Harrison's statement regarding the matter in his first annual message was in one way similar to Cleveland's message. It reflected not only his general support for a protective tariff but also the recognition that the issue was for Congress to consider. Harrison stated:

> I recommend a revision of our tariff law both in its administrative features and in the schedules. . . .
>
> The preparation of a new schedule of customs duties is a matter of great delicacy because of its direct effect upon the business of the country, and of great difficulty by reason of the wide divergence of opinion as to the objects that may properly be promoted by such legislation. Some disturbance of business may perhaps result from *the consideration of this subject by Congress,* but the temporary ill effect will be reduced to the minimum by prompt action and by the assurance which the country already enjoys that any necessary changes will be so made as not to impair the just and reasonable protection of our home industries. The inequalities of the law should be adjusted, but the protective principle should be maintained and fairly applied to the products of our farms as well as of our shops.[54]

Harrison, however, did not provide Congress with any significant directions as to how it should implement this recommendation.[55] This statement was the sole reference to the tariff in this address. Despite the prominence the issue played in his election, Harrison clearly left the matter in Congress's hands. Furthermore, throughout Congress's ten-month deliberation of the McKinley bill, Harrison generally maintained this position—that it was Congress's issue to craft and decide.

Harrison was in a position where he did not have to say anything else about the matter. If Harrison's role as president was to identify the need for and possible direction of legislative action, Cleveland's message and the 1888 election had already performed these tasks. The Republicans came into Congress with a clear agenda: to increase tariff rates. Therefore, the president was not required to provide leadership on this issue. Although Harrison's lack of activity may have been exacerbated by his conception of a limited presidency, the political context that surrounded the McKinley Tariff had already dictated a less proactive role for him.

President Harrison's only other formal statement to Congress as it was considering the McKinley bill was his June 19, 1890, letter supporting Secretary of State Blaine's efforts on reciprocity. Harrison wrote: "I transmit herewith, for your information, a letter from the Secretary of State, inclosing a report of the International American Conference, which recommends that reciprocal commercial treaties be entered into between the United States and the several other Republics of this hemisphere. . . . It has been so often and so persistently stated that our tariff laws offered an insurmountable barrier to a large exchange of products with the Latin-American nations that I deem it proper to call especial attention to the fact that more than 87 per cent of the products of those nations sent to our ports are now admitted free. . . . The real difficulty in the way of negotiating profitable treaties is that we have given freely so much that would have had value in mutual concessions which such treaties imply."[56]

Blaine expended a great deal of effort to get Congress to include the reciprocity provision in the McKinley Act. Harrison's personal efforts mainly consisted of interacting and corresponding with individual members of Congress. Much of this effort, however, was more informational in nature than persuasive.[57]

Blaine's and Harrison's actions and success regarding reciprocity indicate that the issue blurred the distinction between congressional control of tariff revisions and the presidency's dominance in shaping foreign relations. Since setting the nation's tariff policy was generally seen as a matter of taxation, the Constitution places the issue in the domain of Congress, specifically the House of Representatives, as Article I, Section 8 states, "The Congress shall have the power to lay and collect taxes, duties, imposts, and excises . . ." By putting sugar on the free list, however, Congress threatened to interfere with the Harrison administration's foreign policy. This also highlights the fact that the tariff is not solely a domestic issue. It is also an important matter for foreign commerce, which, although explicitly left in the Constitution for Congress to regulate, is an important component of foreign relations as well.[58] As a result, the tariff's impact on foreign affairs would generally fall within the presidency's institutional purview. Thus, by potentially hampering the secretary of state's efforts at negotiating trade relations, Congress provided Harrison and Blaine with both a reason and the justification by which they became involved in crafting this component of the bill.

The effect of the reciprocity provision on the institution of the presidency, however, was far greater than the efforts expended by Harrison. The final language of the McKinley Act provided that, upon the sole determination by the president of "reciprocally unequal and unreasonable" trade practices of countries producing specific items listed in the act (e.g., sugar, coffee, tea, hides), the president "shall have the power . . . to suspend, by proclamation to that effect, the provisions of the [McKinley] Act relating to the free introduction of such" items. With this provision, Congress allowed the president to "negotiate trade conventions and to modify tariff duties without congressional oversight."[59] In other words, the Republican majority in Congress granted the presidency the authority to change tariff duties without requiring any formal check by Congress. While this grant of authority was not universally supported and would be removed, reimplemented in a modified form, and eventually repealed over the next few decades, this initial grant is significant as a delegation by Congress to the presidency in a policy area of congressional dominance. Possibly the most significant long-term effect of the reciprocity provision, however, was that it provided the presidency with a formal, codified role in a policy area that was seen as existing predominantly in the congressional domain. Much like the way in which the creation of the ICC provided the presidency some degree of authority over interstate commerce through the power to appoint and remove commissioners, the reciprocity provision of the McKinley Act granted that institution authority that it otherwise did not have.

This grant of authority to the presidency did not escape the criticism of the Democratic minority in both houses of Congress. Rep. Henry G. Turner (D-GA) argued, "But I object to this reciprocity, because it inaugurates a principle in our Government that is contrary to the Constitution. This bill proposes to invest the President of the United States with the power to enact law, not simply execute it. It gives him the power when he thinks that these countries with which he desires reciprocity trade relations have been unfair to us. . . . Now, Mr. Speaker, I am opposed to giving the President any such power; in the first place, because the Constitution devolves that duty on Congress . . ."[60]

Rep. Hillary A. Herbert (D-AL) added that the reciprocity amendment "vests in the President authority which can be exercised only by Congress, the power to judge whether a law imposing duties on imports ought or ought not to be enacted. It is worthless for that reason. Congress has, and the President has not, the power to legislate."[61] Rep. Benton McMillin (D-TN), who managed the Democratic opposition in the House during the debate on the conference report, put the reciprocity provision in a philosophical light. After reading Section 3, the reciprocity section, of the McKinley bill, McMillin stated:

Do you see either reciprocity or good government in this?

Who ever heard of such extraordinary powers being surrendered by a free people to one man? When our fathers began this Government they wisely had revenue bills originate with the House of Representatives, because that body comes most directly and frequently from the people. But here the enemies of our institutions in this bill provide that they shall not originate in the House, nor in the Senate, but the President shall impose enormous taxes, remit them, and reimpose them at pleasure. . . .

A more cowardly and uncalled-for surrender of sovereign prerogatives was never made by the faithless representatives of a free people. Our ancestors, with more spirit and patriotism than we are evincing, rebelled against a smaller tax on less tea, imposed by the British Parliament and King George. Did we rebel against the Georges and a legislative annex only to go under the Harrisons without even a legislative annex?

If the founders of the Government had intended the President to exercise monarchical power they would have framed the Constitution differently. . . .

This amendment is not only a spiritless surrender of principle and power, but an overruling of the Constitution. If the people's representatives surrender this principle they should be relegated to the rear and representatives sent here more worthy the sires who bled for these liberties and the sages who toiled for this Constitution. . . .

Trust men that will give to the President of the United States more power than the Queen of England and the Empress of India has! Trust men who would vest in one man a power that is not exercised by the Czar of all the Russias! Before I would trust a Congress that would thus destroy the people's liberties, I would go and cradle my own child with a viper.[62]

The Democratic opposition in the Senate was primarily vented by Sen. John T. Morgan (D-AL) and Sen. John G. Carlisle (D-KY). Senator Morgan argued that the reciprocity provision represented "an authority that can only exist in the law-making power of this country" and that "No case will ever arise under this section of this bill which a court can settle. The President could not frame a proclamation upon its provisions that would not, on its face, violate the Constitution of the United States."[63] Senator Carlisle added, "All that Congress does in the matter is to prescribe the rate of duty, leaving all the circumstances, the entire question whether it ought or ought not to be imposed, to the judgment and discretion of the President himself."[64]

Sen. John Sherman (R-OH) defended the Republican majority's position against Morgan's and Carlisle's attacks. He argued that the power of Congress included "the absolute right not only to impose duties, but to leave to the President or to any other executive authority the determination of some fact upon the happening of which a duty may be either removed or may be levied" and that "in every stage of our history Congress has left a like discretion, similar in its nature, to the President of the United States."[65] In other words, the reciprocity provision merely represented the administration of a law as defined by Congress, in contrast to a delegation of legislative authority to the presidency.

Although the reciprocity provision was only one portion of the McKinley Tariff Act, the Democrats highlighted its importance for presidential authority. Regardless of how the Republicans tried to frame this grant of authority, it did at a minimum provide the presidency with a great deal of discretion without any formal check by Congress. As stated earlier, this grant was not permanent. Nevertheless, it reflected a coordinated script whereby Congress (or at least the Republican majority) was willing to allow more presidential leeway in legislative matters.

Reciprocity was not the only issue that the Democratic minority criticized the Republican majority for in framing the McKinley Tariff Act. The Democrats expressed their disapproval of what they perceived as limited meaningful debate time and their exclusion from the legislative process. For example, Rep. Theodore S. Wilkinson (D-LA) argued during the debate of the conference bill that, "[w]ith scarcely a pretense of deliberation, for a third time this House is called on to take such summary action on this measure as had been decreed by the little junta that control[s] with absolute sway all proceedings here. Time for sufficient argument, explanation, and amendment never has been permitted. The time to change a line or word among all its two hundred pages is gone forever now."[66]

Wilkinson concluded, "Go on Republicans; go on and pass by your united or your almost united vote your iniquitous, your sectional bill."[67] Sensing defeat, Wilkinson challenged the Republicans to let the bill face public opinion. William McKinley, concluding the House debate, accepted the challenge on behalf of Republicans by stating, "From here [the bill] goes to the people. Before that tribunal we invite you and invoke its deliberate and patriotic judgment, and to it all of us must yield."[68]

McKinley Tariff: Conclusion

Despite the focus here on reciprocity, in institutional terms the crafting of the McKinley Tariff Act was predominantly an exercise of congressional authority. The protectionist revision of the nation's tariff schedules was set by the Republican leaders in Congress, led by Rep. William McKinley. The overwhelming portion of the debate on the floor of Congress related to specific tariff levels. The interaction was largely defined by partisan politics and the setting of policy, not questions of institutional authority.

The extent to which authority issues were involved within the McKinley Tariff centered on the institutional interactions over the issue of reciprocity. Both the substance and process of these interactions enhanced presidential authority. The reciprocity provision of the legislation was a formal grant of authority by Congress to the presidency. It bestowed on the presidency the ability to set duties and tariff policy that the institution otherwise did not possess. Further, the blending of domestic tariff policy and foreign trade policy provided the means by which Harrison and Blaine shaped the reciprocity portion of the McKinley Act. Harrison's involvement in the legislative process, however, was limited and for the most part not in the plain view of the public.

Although the authority provided to the presidency was limited at the time, its long-term significance was much greater. Both Congress and

President Harrison (as well as President Cleveland) viewed the tariff revision as a matter in the congressional domain, once the president's role of highlighting the issue for consideration was fulfilled. However, they provided the means for greater presidential involvement in future tariff revisions. Through their interaction in this case, they laid a foundation that would tie tariff policy more to the presidency. Presidents could now be expected to play an increased role in revising the tariff, although the issue would still remain predominantly in the congressional domain.

Dingley Tariff: History

Much like the history of the McKinley Tariff, that of the Dingley Tariff started before the 1897 passage of that act. The path that led to the Dingley Tariff began shortly after the enactment of the McKinley Act. As both Republicans and Democrats wanted, the McKinley Act and its Republican authors were judged by the American people. To the Republicans' dismay, the American public elected a Democratic majority in the House in the 1890 election and in the Senate in 1892; Grover Cleveland, a Democrat, returned to the presidency in 1892 as well.

In 1894 President Cleveland worked with Rep. William L. Wilson (D-WV), chairman of the House Ways and Means Committee, to develop the general policy that the Wilson bill would reflect. After much revision by the Senate and in conference committee, the Democratic majorities moderately reduced the overall tariff rates as part of the Wilson-Gorman Tariff. Furthermore, the Democrats eliminated the reciprocity provision of the McKinley Act that they had protested four years previously.

Although the coinage of gold and silver dominated the 1896 election, both parties prominently mentioned the tariff in their platforms that year. Favoring a tariff-for-revenue-only policy, the Democrats "denounced as disturbing to business the Republican threat to restore the McKinley law, which has twice been condemned by the people in National elections."[69] The Republicans proclaimed that "Protection and Reciprocity are twin measures of American policy and go hand in hand. Democratic rule has recklessly struck down both, and both must be re-established."[70]

The Republicans regained control of both houses of Congress after the 1896 election, and William McKinley was elected president. The Republicans wanted to address the economy but were unable to form a majority consensus on coinage; thus they turned to the less divisive tariff issue. McKinley utilized his inaugural address to call for the reenactment of protectionism and reciprocity. In addition, he suggested the need for a special session of Congress to deal with the revenue deficits that the federal government had experienced each of the previous four years. Congress convened between March and July and passed the Dingley Tariff. On the conference report alone, the House had 49 pages of debates with 39 speakers in the *Congressional Record,* while the Senate had 131 pages with 41 speakers. The Dingley Tariff reestablished and even surpassed the protectionist duties set by the McKinley Tariff. Among the provisions of the Dingley Act, the Republicans placed duties back on wool, which the Democrats had repealed in 1894.

Although the House Ways and Means Committee initially proposed language similar to the McKinley Tariff's reciprocity provision, the Senate Republicans modified the provision. Unlike the McKinley Tariff, the Dingley Tariff did not allow the president to set tariff rates without congressional oversight. Instead, the president could negotiate a reciprocity treaty, subject to the advice and consent of the Senate, that "shall provide for the reduction . . . of the duties imposed by [the Dingley] Act, to the extent of not more than twenty per centum."[71]

Much like the McKinley Tariff (and the Wilson-Gorman Tariff as well), the legislative process establishing the Dingley Tariff was controlled by the majority party in Congress. The Democrats once again charged that they were largely excluded from significant decision-making processes and debate. Some members of Congress, however, expressed a desire to pass the Dingley Tariff regardless of the bill's provisions because they wanted the government to focus on what they viewed as the most significant issue facing the nation, currency, without the distraction of partisan-based tariff concerns.

Dingley Tariff: Analysis

Although fashioning the specifics of the Dingley Tariff was left to Congress, President McKinley helped establish the policy framework in which the interaction took place. In his inaugural address, McKinley stated, "There can be no misunderstanding, either, about the principle upon which this tariff taxation shall be levied. Nothing has ever been made plainer at a general election than that the controlling principle in the raising of revenue from duties on imports is zealous care for American interests and American labor. . . . To this policy we are all, of whatever party, firmly bound by the voice of the people—a power vastly more potential than the expression of any political platform. The paramount duty of Congress is to stop deficiencies by the restoration of that protective legislation."[72]

McKinley also argued that "especial attention should be given to the re-enactment and extension of the reciprocity principle of the law of 1890" and called for "a further experiment and additional discretionary power in the making of commercial treaties."[73] He also used this address to set the groundwork for a special session of Congress to revise the tariff:

> It has been the uniform practice of each President to avoid, as far as possible, the convening of Congress in an extraordinary session . . . . But a failure to convene the representatives of the people in Congress in extra session when it involves neglect of a public duty *places the responsibility of such neglect upon the Executive himself.* The condition of the public Treasury, as has been indicated, demands the immediate consideration of Congress. It alone has the power to provide revenues for the Government. Not to convene it under such circumstances I can view in no other sense than the neglect of a plain duty. . . . It has always seemed to me that the postponement of the meeting of Congress until more than a year after it has been chosen deprived Congress too often of the inspiration of the popular will and the country of the corresponding benefits. It is evident, there-fore, that to postpone action in the presence of so great a necessity would be unwise on the part of the Executive because unjust to the interests of the people. Our action now will be freer from mere partisan consideration than if the question of tariff revision was postponed until the regular session of Congress.[74]

McKinley followed up his inaugural address with a message dated March 15, 1897, to the reconvened Congress, specifically recommend-ing "that Congress . . . make every endeavor" to pass tariff legislation to raise "ample revenue."[75]

Although McKinley (as an individual) clearly had extensive knowl-edge of tariff politics and policy from his days in Congress, his behavior reflected an understanding that placed significant responsibility on the presidency. Although highlighting the importance of Congress's role in setting tariff policy and raising revenues, McKinley saw a necessary role for himself as president in addressing the government's revenue problems. Like Cleveland in his 1887 message, McKinley saw that, as president, his responsibility was to ensure that the nation's problems were addressed. While Cleveland assumed a certain level of responsibility for the presidency by dedicating his entire annual message to the issue, he placed the blame on Congress if the government did not respond. McKinley, on the other hand, contended that, if Congress did not return for the special session, that reflected poorly on him as president and not on Congress.

The congressional debate reflected the connection between the presidency and the nation's economic problems. By the 1896 election, the performance of the national economy was becoming tied to the presidency. Sometimes the Democrats used this connection to taunt their Republican colleagues. For example, Rep. Levin I. Handy (D-DE) stated, "I hear gentlemen declaring nowadays that they thought the good times would be immediate; but the talk was different last fall . . . and the wonder now is what has become of the men who talked so loud about the good times coming as soon as Mr. Bryan and the threat of free silver were out of the way. Mr. McKinley was elected, but the good times came not. . . . You could not expect good times to begin until the advance agent got the reins of power into his own hands; but the McKinley boom would surely begin its booming when he pronounced the magic words of the official oath. . . . The promise of prosperity has also been broken to our hope. . . . If this is McKinley's boom we have with us now, what will McKinley's panic be like when it comes along?"[76]

However, even some Republicans, such as Sen. John B. Allen (R-WA), stated, "We were promised prosperity when the present Chief Executive was elected to the Presidency? In fact, sir, the country was told that the moment he was elected, that moment prosperity would return to the country . . . And yet we have the most gigantic coal strike on hand now in this country or any other country has ever seen. A hundred per cent more men are engaged in striking for living wages to-day than ever struck in any industry in this country before."[77]

As we move through the years under study, we see responsibility for action start to shift from Congress to the presidency. In the beginning of the period, we saw a president who attempted to place the issue on the political agenda, only to meet with congressional reticence. By the time of the 1896 election and the interaction over the Dingley Tariff, the presidency's responsibility had come to include responding to and providing guidance and direction for the correction of the nation's economic problems. This understanding was held by the members of the Washington community—McKinley, congressional Republicans, and congressional Democrats alike. McKinley was not seeking simply to implement his party's platform and place the responsibility on Congress. Instead, as he stated, he sought to fulfill his "executive" responsibility to get Congress to address the issue. As a result, the performance of the national economy was becoming a political tool that could be used to attack the presidency, as well as Congress.

In his inaugural address and the message to Congress in March 1897, McKinley attempted to set the government's discourse and initiate the legislative process regarding tariff revision. Congress responded to the president's call, returning for the special session and reenacting a protectionist tariff with a reciprocity provision.

The reciprocity provision in the original draft of the Dingley Tariff presented by the House Republicans included language similar to that of the McKinley Tariff. The focus of the provision, however, was not Latin American countries but opening European markets. Rep. Albert J. Hopkins (R-IL), speaking on behalf of the Republican members of the House Ways and Means Committee, recognized the connection that Blaine pushed in 1890—the connection between tariff policy and foreign relations: "These [European] markets will remain closed until this bill becomes a law and our present Chief Executive is clothed with the authority that is contained in the reciprocity portion of this bill to enter into negotiations with all these countries and exact from them even-handed justice."[78]

Senate Republicans, however, were split over the appropriate language for the provision.[79] Although the tenets of the reciprocity provision of the McKinley Tariff were ruled constitutional by the Supreme Court,[80] the Senate Republicans were seeking to construct wording that Congress would approve. Sen. William Chandler (R-NH) primarily drafted the Senate reciprocity amendment, incorporating suggestions of Sen. George F. Edmunds (R-VT) and Sen. Orville Platt (R-CT).

Although the Senate reciprocity amendment represented a formal grant of authority to the presidency, it also served the more expedient purpose of deflecting the primary institutional criticism of the McKinley Tariff's reciprocity provision. Even the provision's most ardent critics admitted that the inclusion of the phrase "by and with the advice and consent of the Senate" "answer[ed] to some extent the objection" that the president had the "exclusive right to make treaties as to revenue without consulting the Senate," as the McKinley Tariff provided.[81]

With this leg taken out from under them, the Democratic minority focused its criticisms of the reciprocity provision on the usurpation of authority from the House of Representatives by *both* the presidency and the Senate. They viewed it as an "unconstitutional provision" that compelled "the House of Representatives, the Congress of the United States, . . . at the election of the President and the Senate, to abdicate their constitutional power to legislate upon the subject of taxation."[82] As Senator Edward W. Pettus (D-AL) argued:

> Now, what do you propose to do here? It is always best to simplify a law question in order to understand it clearly. I will illustrate what you propose to enact by an example. We levy a tax of 4 per cent ad valorem on hides imported into the United States, but we provide that whenever the President of the United States and the Senate shall see fit they may by treaty repeal that law and put hides on the free list. That is the sum and substance of this provision, except that it goes to all other things.
>
> But I am confining it now to hides merely for the purpose of illustration. You enact that the President and the Senate combined may make a contract by which that law is repealed, and instead of putting a duty of 4 per cent on hides, they shall put hides on the free list. They can not do it. The Constitution of the United States vests the President and the Senate with no such power. The Congress can do it, and nothing but the Congress. Do you propose to repeal a law by the will of anybody less than Congress? No, Mr. President, so long as the Constitution stands . . .[83]

For Senate Republicans, however, the reciprocity amendment merely represented the utilization of the presidency's and the Senate's treaty-making power "under the phraseology of the Constitution."[84] Furthermore, Sen. William B. Allison stated in response to the criticism that "it is not within the power of the President and the Senate to make

treaties which will change the law as to the rates of duty; that is a legislative power. We can do that certainly at one time as well as at another, and
we propose to do that now in this bill, so that when the treaty-making
power shall have been exerted, the legislative power gives the authority
to provide a change in these duties, which shall become operative when
the treaty is operative."[85]

Possibly the most significant aspect of the Senate's deliberation of
its reciprocity amendment was that it succeeded somewhat in breaking
down strict partisan divisions. In fact, some of the strongest support for
the presidency's and the Senate's institutional treaty-making powers and
their relationship to the reciprocity amendment was voiced by Democrats. For example, Sen. John T. Morgan argued, "I can not understand
why the President and the Senate, in the exercise of the treaty-making
power, may not put [the suspension of duties] upon the footing of an
agreement between the two countries, and why the act of Congress, if
now passed, would not operate in advance to ratify and confirm a treaty
and make it fully applicable to the subject."[86]

Sen. George Gray (D-DE), after mentioning that he had voted
against the reciprocity provision in the McKinley Tariff, added, "But in
this case we merely provide that when the treaty-making power of this
country is exercised in a certain direction by legislation we will accom-
modate ourselves to it. This is not conferring upon the President any
power. The treaty-making power resting in the president is conferred by
the Constitution . . . [s]o that the President and the Senate may make
a commercial treaty of any scope whatever; and although the Congress
of the United States may be unwilling to pass the legislation necessary
to carry into effect, the Congress of the United States can not limit or
qualify the power given by the Constitution to the President and the
Senate to make such treaties as in their judgment shall be wise and expedient."[87] The Senate amendment was later accepted by the House and
Senate conferees and included in the final text of the Dingley Act.

The Dingley Tariff's reciprocity provision held several implications
for presidential authority. The most basic one is simple: Congress once
again codified a grant of authority to the presidency in legislation,
thereby providing that institution with the ability to formally alter tariff
duties even though that ability falls squarely to Congress under the Constitution. In addition, the Senate Republicans' inclusion of the "advice
and consent" clause in this provision at first blush seems to be an institu-

tional check on the presidency—presidents cannot alter duties as freely as they could under the McKinley Tariff.

This provision, however, can also be seen as enhancing the presidency's institutional authority. First, it broadened congressional acceptance of the reciprocity provision's grant of authority to the presidency to include members of Congress who had opposed the McKinley Tariff's reciprocity provision. The grant under the Dingley Tariff was made consistent with the terms of the Constitution—the presidency already had the authority to negotiate treaties. Therefore, the reciprocity provision merely set into law a policy direction that presidents *and* the Senate could undertake, as well as the implications if they exercised their treaty-making powers in a specific manner. Second, the inclusion of this clause shifted the focus of the debate in the Senate, with the effect of dividing those who might oppose the provision on institutional grounds. The debate was not on presidential usurpation of congressional power but on the threat to the authority of the House of Representatives by the presidency *and* the Senate. This debate forced Democrats to choose: Either protect the institutional authority of the House or defend the powers of the Senate granted to it by the Constitution.

In its deliberations, Congress did not fully escape the "mere partisan consideration" of the bill that the president wanted to avoid. Certainly, as indicated earlier, not every issue pitted all of the Republicans against all of the Democrats. As Sen. William E. Chandler (R-NH) wrote to Sen. Edward O. Wolcott (R-CO), who was serving as a U.S. envoy engaged in bimetallism negotiations with France, "Everybody is good natured. I never knew such lack of party feeling and of bitterness of any sort. Even I am on good terms with everybody."[88]

Such "lack of party feeling," however, was not consistently maintained. For example, Rep. Nelson Dingley (R-ME) and Rep. Joseph W. Bailey (D-TX), the party leaders managing the floor debate of the House's consideration of the Dingley conference report, opened that debate with an exchange of partisan barbs:

DINGLEY: "[I]t was the earnest wish of the majority of the conferees, if possible, that the bill should be completed before the adjournment of the House tonight. [Applause on the Republican side] . . . The gentleman from Texas must be aware also of the fact that talk now is very expensive, involving as it does a loss to the Government of over $100,000 a day."

BAILEY: "But not so expensive as during the ten days that you have been trying to satisfy the greed of the sugar trust. [Applause on the Democratic side.]"

DINGLEY: "But the gentleman from Texas must be aware of the fact that never has a conference committee upon a tariff bill been enabled to complete their labors in so short a time as this. [Applause on the Republican side.] . . ."

BAILEY: "I'll grant that. I grant that you have completed it with considerable haste; because your work was well laid out for you before you begun. [Applause on the Democratic side.] You knew almost exactly what you were to do before you went into the conference room."

DINGLEY: "If my friends on the other side had been as well prepared in 1894, they would not have succeeded in making such a fiasco as they did. [Applause on the Republican side.]"[89]

Partisan interests still dictated much of the interaction over the Dingley Tariff as party lines remained the single most important division within the context of setting tariff policy.

As a final note about Congress's deliberations on the Dingley Tariff, several members recognized the need to move beyond the reworking of tariff legislation whenever shifting partisan tides altered the party composition of the presidency and Congress. For example, Sen. Richard F. Pettigrew, a Silver Republican from South Dakota, opposed the act but refrained from voting on final passage, wished that the next election would be decided "upon the real questions" of economic prosperity, and "desire[d] no further sham battle over schedules in a tariff."[90] Sen. William Allen, a Populist from Nebraska, who also refrained from voting on the conference report, concluded that "The tariff must no longer be an issue in American politics and it will be if this bill should be defeated."[91] While their wishes were somewhat realized, as the Dingley Tariff survived twelve years as the nation's tariff policy, tariff politics itself did not disappear from the U.S. political scene.

Dingley Tariff: Conclusion

The Dingley Tariff, like the McKinley Tariff before it, was largely an exercise in congressional policy-making authority—deliberating tariff schedules, setting new rates, and so on. Furthermore, like the McKinley Act, Dingley contained a reciprocity provision that related directly to issues of presidential authority. Not only did the Dingley Act codify a formal grant of authority to the presidency similar to the McKinley Tariff, but it also did so in a manner that drew support from a wider breadth of members of Congress.

The express grants of authority to the presidency under the McKinley and Dingley tariffs were not vastly different. The primary difference was Dingley's retention of a formal role for Congress. From this, one sees that unchecked grants of authority were not acceptable to congressional Democrats; grants of authority that acknowledged the Senate's institutional authority were less problematic (although still far from universally accepted).

In terms of presidential authority in the legislative process, McKinley more clearly defined and expanded the role of the presidency in tariff politics. Whereas Cleveland consistently emphasized and Harrison publicly exercised only limited presidential authority, McKinley held out a specific role, albeit a still fairly limited one, for the presidency in tariff politics. While tariff issues still needed to be resolved by Congress, McKinley sought to establish the preliminary framework within which Congress would act. Further, McKinley was willing to accept the blame if the national government proved unable to address what he perceived as the need for tariff revision. McKinley's rhetoric reflects that, although not formalized into law, the presidency was becoming responsible for leading the government's efforts to address the nation's economic ills. The behavior of McKinley and the members of Congress during the deliberations of the Dingley Tariff both reflected and enhanced such a shared understanding. Although McKinley neither recommended nor was asked to recommend (at least publicly) specific points on the tariff legislation, he helped set the policy direction of the new act.

Underwood Tariff: History

The nation operated under the Dingley Tariff's protectionist duties for a dozen years, until the passage of the Payne-Aldrich Tariff in 1909. While slightly reducing the overall rate of taxation on imports, this tariff primarily adapted the Republicans' protectionist policies to the then-current economic situation. Congress eliminated the reciprocity provision of the Dingley Tariff "as these reciprocity agreements never had been of any significance, except as indicative of the disappearance of any intention to deal with tariff questions in this way."[92] Finally, the Payne-

Aldrich Tariff provided for the utilization of maximum and minimum principal and created a tariff board that determined when maximum duties should be applied.

With the fissure in the Republican Party and the advent of the Bull Moose Progressive Party, the 1912 election added a new twist to the standard partisan debate that surrounded any tariff issue. Each party staked out a position on the potential tariff reform. The Democrats placed tariff reform as the first item on its platform, stating "We declare it to be a fundamental principle of the Democratic party that the Federal government, under the Constitution, has no right or power to impose or collect tariff duties, except for the purpose of revenue. . . . The high Republican tariff is the principal cause of the unequal distribution of wealth; it is a system of taxation which makes the rich richer and the poor poorer. . . . We favor an immediate downward revision of the existing high and in many case prohibitive tariff duties."[93]

The Republicans "reaffirm[ed] our belief in a protective tariff. . . . The protective tariff is so woven into the fabric of our industrial and agricultural life that to substitute it for a tariff for revenue only would destroy many industries and throw millions of people out of work."[94] Finally, the position of Theodore Roosevelt's Progressive Party was: "We believe in a protective tariff. . . . We demand tariff revision because the present tariff is unjust to the people of the United States. . . . We condemn the Payne-Aldrich bill as unjust to the people. The Republican organization is in the hands of those who have broken, and cannot again be trusted to keep, the promise of necessary downward revision. . . . The Democratic party is committed to the destruction of the protective system through a tariff for revenue only—a policy which would inevitably produce widespread industrial and commercial disaster."[95]

The Democrats, already with a majority in the House following the 1910 election, benefited from the division within the Republican ranks and gained majority control of the Senate and the presidency in 1912. Much like William McKinley before him, President Woodrow Wilson cited the need for tariff reform in his inaugural address in 1913. Also like McKinley, Wilson called a special session of Congress for the express purpose of revising the nation's tariff policy. Wilson, however, played a more proactive role in getting the Underwood Tariff passed than McKinley played in the Dingley Tariff. Whereas McKinley let the legislative process move forward after setting the initial discourse, Wilson worked with Oscar Underwood and Democratic party leaders to shape the legislation both before and while Congress considered the bill during the special session.

Also unlike his predecessors, Wilson publicly involved himself in passing the legislation. Previous presidents—Cleveland, Harrison, McKinley, Taft—generally monitored and pushed the passage of tariff legislation in an informal, behind-the-scenes manner. Extending the presidency's role to shape the discourse on the topic, Wilson worked openly with Congress, including making precedent-setting speeches and conferring with legislators on Capitol Hill. Although Republicans criticized him for such behavior, Democrats supported his overt exercise of presidential authority.

Congress deliberated the Underwood Tariff throughout the spring and summer of 1913. On the conference report alone, the House had 64 pages of debates with 43 speakers in the *Congressional Record*, while the Senate had 42 pages with 26 speakers. The Underwood Tariff finally became law on October 3, 1913. Among its primary features were:

- considerable additions to the free list (including raw wool)
- abolition of compensatory duties corresponding with the old rates on raw materials
- replacement of specific duties by ad valorem rates in many cases
- taxation of plain kinds of goods less than fancy kinds—luxuries higher than necessities
- reduction of rates generally
- application of the so-called competitive principle to rates intended to be protective[96]

The Underwood Act did not include reciprocity provisions similar to those of the McKinley or Dingley tariffs. Section IV.A of the act, however, provided simply "That for the purpose of readjusting the present duties on importations into the United States and at the same time to encourage the export trade of this country, the President of the United States is authorized and empowered to negotiate trade agreements with foreign nations wherein mutual concessions are made looking toward freer trade relations and further reciprocal expansion of trade and commerce: Provided, however, That said trade agreements before becoming operative shall be submitted to the Congress of the United States for ratification or rejection."

Underwood Tariff: Analysis

Wilson's behavior in the Underwood Tariff interaction was not vastly different from that exhibited by his presidential predecessors; it was, however, different in degree. Wilson displayed an understanding of the presidency that called for greater activity in the legislative process. While still recognizing certain institutional limits, he not only set the discourse and initiated the legislative process publicly like McKinley but also helped develop the legislation before it was introduced, made recommendations for specific tariff rates, and worked with Congress to get the legislation passed.

In his inaugural address, Wilson listed altering the tariff as his administration's number one priority. He elaborated on his tariff ideas in a speech delivered at a joint session of Congress in the chamber of the House of Representatives on April 8, 1913:

> I have called the Congress together in extraordinary session because a duty was laid upon the party now in power at the recent elections which it ought to perform promptly, in order that the burden carried by the people under existing law be lightened as soon as possible. . . . It is clear to the whole country that the tariff duties must be altered. . . .
>
> We have seen tariff legislation wander very far afield in our day—very far indeed from the field in which our prosperity might have had a normal growth and stimulation. . . . We long ago passed beyond the modest notion of "protecting" the industries of the country and move boldly forward to the idea that they were entitled to the direct patronage of the Government. . . .
>
> It is plain what those [new tariff] principles must be. We must abolish everything that bears even the semblance of privilege or of any kind of artificial advantage, and put our business men and producers under the stimulation of a constant necessity to be efficient, economical, and enterprising, masters of competitive supremacy, better workers and merchants than any in the world. . . . [T]he object of the tariff duties henceforth laid must be effective competition, the whetting of American wits by contest with the wits of the rest of the world.[97]

Wilson's rhetoric is similar to that of McKinley more than two decades before: the necessity of immediate action, the need for the special session, and the responsibility to address the economic problem.

Although this speech opened the special session and Congress's deliberation of tariff reform, Underwood and the other members of the Ways and Means Committee had already drafted the Underwood bill; they had done so in conjunction with President Wilson. As early as January 8, 1913, Wilson and Underwood met to discuss the timing of the special session.[98] Wilson and Underwood kept in contact throughout the first few months of the year, discussing things such as competitive conditions and whether the bill should be introduced as separate measures or as omnibus legislation.[99]

Wilson continued his proactive behavior after the special session began. He followed up his speech to Congress opening the session by visiting the members of the Senate Finance Committee at the Capitol building. In regard to this meeting, Wilson stated, "This conference was to discuss the tariff. I am glad I had it and I hope the Senators will let me come and consult them frequently. The net result of this meeting is that we don't see any sort of difficulty about standing firmly on our party programme."[100]

Over the course of the next few months, Wilson maintained contact with the members of Congress who expressed their positions and requested any personal assistance the president might provide. For example, on April 18, 1913, Rep. Elsworth Raymond Bathrick (D-OH) wrote to Wilson regarding the tariffs on cloth and ready-made clothing, which he considered "prohibitive."[101] Wilson turned around the next day and wrote to Oscar Underwood about this issue: "I beg your pardon for calling your attention to this so late in the game, but I write chiefly to inquire if this were a deliberate arrangement, the consequences of which with regard to the price of the cheaper sort of clothing were analyzed. . . . I know that you will pardon my calling these matters to your attention as they come up."[102]

After reviewing the tariff revisions on these items, Underwood responded to Wilson on April 22: "I think it would be dangerous to make a reduction below the value of the cloth and I believe that the bill has reduced the tax on the cloth as low as it is safe to go at this time. It gave me pleasure to receive your suggestion."[103]

Wilson used opportunities such as this to try to maintain party solidarity on the tariff legislation. For example, on July 15, 1913, he wrote to Sen. John Randolph Thornton (D-LA):

> Let me say that I fully recognize the difficulty of your position in the matter of the sugar schedule and do not wish to minimize it any degree. . . . Undoubtedly, you should have felt yourself perfectly free in the caucus to make every effort to carry out the promises you had made to your own people, but when it comes to the final action, my own judgment is perfectly clear. No party can ever for any length of time control the Government or serve the people which can not command the allegiance of its own minority. I feel that there are times, after every argument has been given full consideration and men of equal public conscience have conferred together, when those who are overruled should accept the principle of party government and act with the colleagues through whom they expect to see the country best and most permanently well served.
>
> I felt that I owed it to you that I should express my own judgment as frankly as you have done me the honor of expressing yours.[104]

As this illustrates, Wilson, like his predecessors, worked behind the scenes to push along the legislative process. He worked to moderate intraparty differences and to shape the final outcome of the legislation.

Despite these efforts to direct the government's tariff policy generally and to serve as his party's leader, possibly the most significant aspect of Wilson's behavior in shaping the Underwood Tariff was his *public* recommendation on two items that had been the source of much debate in previous tariff revisions: sugar and wool. As Representative Underwood was quoted in the *New York World* and the *New York Times* on April 17, 1913, "Out of the four thousand and more items in the bill, the President only made two suggestions, those affecting the sugar and wool schedules. It seems to me that *we should accept those suggestions from the President of the United States.*"[105]

The importance of both Wilson's suggestions themselves and Congress's acceptance of them transcended just changing the tariff schedules on sugar and wool; they held larger implications for presidential authority. Wilson went beyond the understanding of the presidency displayed by his predecessors as a general overseer of policy who worked behind the scenes to develop legislation. Here, the president was becoming publicly involved with the setting of tariff rates. Just as important, such a coordinated script permitting his behavior was accepted by the members of Congress—or at least the Democratic majority.

Congressional Republicans criticized Wilson for his behavior, as well as congressional Democrats for following him. The harshest attack came from Rep. Hampton J. Moore (R-PA): "Mr. Speaker, it may or may not be true that the President is dictating the passage of this tariff bill. He informed us in person last March that he desired legislation . . . [and] followed up his recommendations by sundry personal visits to 'the other side of the Capitol,' more, as it was explained, for tariff legislation. Since these precedent-breaking visitations the newspapers have told us of return visits by Senators and Representatives to the White House 'to confer' upon tariff matters, and occasionally it has been announced that the President at these conferences has 'given expression to his views,' and in some instances has 'spoken plainly' and in some others 'stood firmly' for these things which he wished to find in any bill presented for his signature."[106]

Representative Moore continued, "[T]he procession of 'conferences' at the White House and 'caucuses' at the Capitol attested the eagerness of the representatives of 'a free and untrammeled Democracy' to do their master's bidding. . . . [Congressional Democrats were] still professing an undying love for the people, but keeping a weather eye on the White House plum tree, lest the slightest variation in your marching order shall cause a loss of your political pickings."[107]

Moore even used the words of Representative Underwood against him and his party colleagues. Moore cited Underwood's response on the floor of Congress on May 17, 1910, to a recommendation made by President William Howard Taft for an appropriation for the creation of a tariff board. Underwood had argued at the time that, "From the beginning of the Government down to the present time we have written every tariff bill that this country has lived under without the intervention or the dictation of the President of the United States. The Congress up to this time has been able to exercise sufficient intelligence and sufficient energy to gather the facts themselves and put their findings into law."

Moore's point was clear: The Democrats had forsaken their previous defense of the institution of Congress for a new script premised on the partisan expediency of supporting President Wilson.

Congressional Democrats, however, defended Wilson and themselves against these attacks. Rep. Andrew J. Montague (D-VA) countered: "I must observe that public pressure works no injury to American institutions; it is secret and silent pressure which occasions anxiety and alarm. The exercise by the President of this plain constitutional prerogative has loosened upon him a flood of abuse. His action is called federalistic and kingly, gentleman forgetting that this somewhat similar performance of the crown is almost the one democratic action of royalty. But there must be some coordination between the legislative and executive branches of our Government, and I submit that it is better to have this coordination in the open than in secret; better to have the Executive voice resounding through this Chamber than in charmed whispers around the banquet table."[108]

Rep. I. S. Pepper (D-IA) argued: "Surprising as it may seem, there are some who, during the course of debate upon the bill, have felt called upon to criticize the President of the United States for the part he has taken in the legislation. It is particularly noticeable, however, that such criticism has found little response of approbation among the people at large. . . . For my part, I glory in the fact that we have a President with the courage and the patriotism to take his part in the battle against special interest and privilege and protected monopoly."[109]

Finally, Rep. Champ Clark (D-MO) added this: "There has been a good deal of talk first and last about President Wilson's action with reference to this bill. I congratulate him for the part that he has taken in this legislation. [Applause on the Democratic side.] If I had been elected president I would have gotten a good tariff bill through this House sure as you are alive. He has simply discharged his duty in the open. [Applause on the Democratic side]."[110]

This understanding of the presidency supports greater public presidential involvement in the legislative process. It encourages—in fact requires—the presidency to coordinate legislation with Congress since it was "the president's part" or "the president's duty" to do so. Although many of the issues related to the tariff were still under congressional control, the president was becoming a more integral part of crafting tariff policy.

The key to this understanding is that the president's role is closely connected to Congress in its exercise of its institutional authority. Congress was recognizing a greater role for the presidency in forming tariff policy and setting duty rates. The primary requirement was that this role be exercised in collaboration with Congress and not in lieu of it. In other words, Congress would be willing to work with the president, but it was not disposed to let the president work alone.

Underwood Tariff: Conclusion

The institutional interaction that resulted in the Underwood Tariff was still a congressionally dominated issue. Underwood and the members of the Ways and Means Committee shaped many of the legislation's details prior to the special session, and Congress spent a great deal of the session finalizing them. However, Congress opened the door to greater presidential involvement—an opportunity that Wilson fostered.

Wilson's behavior was the most proactive of any president under review here in revising a tariff. He exhibited many characteristics similar to those of his predecessors. He worked with party leaders behind the scene to mollify differences within his party; he called for a tariff revision and shaped the general framework in which Congress worked. His actions, however, also extended beyond what had been seen before by presidents. Although still not a full coparticipant in shaping tariff policy, he nevertheless moved the presidency in that direction.

Congress, or at least the Democratic majority, supported this expanded role for the presidency. Although this growth was housed within the context of partisan bickering, a phenomenon that shaped the formation of most tariff legislation, the net result was greater presidential influence in this policy area. Most significantly, the members of Congress essentially told the president that he was welcome to work within their territory as long as he worked with them. By doing so, Congress provided the presidency with the authority to help craft tariff policy—one that had originally rested solidly in the congressional domain. Though this authority was not codified by law, the practice provided a potentially more expansive role for the presidency.

TARIFF: CASE STUDIES CONCLUSION

In the tariff policy area, we have seen an increased role for the presidency in terms of developing the discourse and, by the end, the actual legislation.[111] We saw a similar phenomenon in the creation of administrative agencies as well. As was the case in that area, Congress was reluctant to grant sole control over the operation of the tariff once passed. Congressional members, however, supported greater presidential authority as long as it was wielded in conjunction with Congress.

The tariff presents a more limited growth area for the presidency than did either of the two previous policy areas. Tariff debates centered on policy questions decided on the floor of Congress throughout the entire period under study. What formal powers the presidency appeared to gain, for example in terms of treaty negotiation, were primarily a restatement of what the Constitution already provided.

However, an informal institution of authority was emerging. By the time the Underwood Tariff became law, tariff politics were not exclusively controlled by Congress. Although Congress maintained its dominance in terms of setting tariff rates, the presidency was becoming more involved in the policy-making process, which the members of Congress supported and fostered. Furthermore, Wilson displayed his involvement in the issue publicly—letting the members of Congress and the nation know that he was working on passing tariff reform. Thus, although there was movement away from what may be termed exclusive congressional control over the tariff, the presidency had not yet reached a point where it could be said to be a coequal partner in crafting tariff revisions.

Although Wilson was not a coequal, his behavior was much like that of a chief legislator. More importantly, similar behavior can be traced back to McKinley and, to a lesser degree, Harrison and Cleveland. Each president identified a legislative need, encouraged Congress to respond to it, and (setting aside Cleveland for the moment) then facilitated the development of a partisan-based coalition that passed the legislation. Moreover, Congress responded favorably to this leadership exhibited by each of these presidents. Each of them achieved a degree of legislative success and extended those of his predecessors. Although the members of Congress may not have acquiesced in presidential initiatives (as they did, for example, in the Haitian intervention in 1915), they did support and in fact provided a basis for presidential forays into the legislative arena.

In the other two policy areas, questions of institutional authority were often at the heart of the interactions. Congress and the presidency had to face these questions directly to resolve the issues before them. Such was not the case in the setting of tariff policy. Instead, the issues focused on specific policy questions, such as what items should be on the free list or what constituted an appropriate tariff on wool, sugar, or cloth. Within the multitude of pages of *Congressional Record* debate, questions of institutional authority would arise, and Congress would address them accordingly.

The aspect of this issue area that seems most crucial to the development of the presidency is that a shift occurred in the understanding of presidential leadership. We see a greater correlation between economic performance and presidential responsibility; with this comes the expectation that the presidency should steer the nation toward economic prosperity. To borrow the words of President William McKinley, this was becoming the "Executive's duty" to the nation.

Although this duty, as it were, is part of a larger trend, at least with respect to the tariff, it emerged out of the partisan dynamics on the issue. It called for a broader, more public role for the president in setting the agenda on the tariff and in being more involved in the details of tariff legislation. The emergence of this duty serves as a lesson on how coordinated scripting and long-term institutional development is often the residue of short-term political forces. The appropriateness of a president trying to exercise any sort of leadership on the tariff was often tied to the partisan alignment of the presidency and Congress. Whereas Cleveland's efforts to lead fell silent on the Republican Senate, McKinley helped set the tariff agenda with a Republican Congress. Although Oscar Underwood rebuffed the leadership of William Howard Taft, he embraced Woodrow Wilson's active role in passing tariff legislation. But in each case, the more that any one president was able to do with respect to the tariff, the better able his successors, regardless of party affiliation, were able to command authority to lead on this issue.

CHAPTER 5

Continued Scripting of the Presidency

lthough the presidency was underspecified at the founding, it was provided with an incentive structure for the defining and crafting of a role for the institution vis-à-vis the other institutions—a role premised not on specifically defined powers but on the authority of the institution. Along the lines of what James Madison predicted, the individual self-interests of the occupants of the office would lead them to desire a more defined role for the presidency.[1] This development, however, took some time to come to full fruition, for (1) the incentive structure set forth at the founding placed a premium on retaining the congressionally driven focus of national government, and (2) the limited role for the national government left little opportunity to break from legislative dominance. Certainly when incentives and opportunities did present themselves some redefinition took place, such as early expansion of the presidency's ability to commit troops;[2] however, little changed in the nation's early years with respect to the overall role of the presidency.

The context of a growing national government, however, created opportunity structures that were conducive to the aspiration of a more refined role for the presidency. We have seen that a context such as this occurred in the post-Reconstruction, pre-Progressive era, when the shared understandings guiding action were called into question or were found inadequate to address the contemporary problems the growing national government faced. Within this dynamic environment, we find evidence of pathways for redefining or crafting new roles. As coordinated scripts developed during the resolution of short-term imperatives and were reaffirmed in subsequent interactions, the shared understandings became informal institutions of authority that adhered to the fabric of the original, constitutionally defined presidency. The institutionalization process we have uncovered is one of ongoing scripting in which new pathways emerge, including perhaps ones previously considered but discarded when the original pathway leading to the operative shared understanding becomes too rigid and too costly to follow. This possibility of continual reflection on the pathways chosen does not dismiss, however, the potency of the residue left by the crafting of these coordinated scripts. For the institutions are the repositories of this residue—of the shared understandings—and use it as the basis to wield expanded authority.

It is important then, before discussing what all of this might mean for the presidency today, to reflect on the theory of institutionalization provided here (including the concepts of coordinated scripting, norms/shared understandings, and informal institutions of authority) and what has been uncovered about this theory within the historical contexts and case studies examined. After doing so, we will be in a position to look at what this theory of institutionalization means for the contemporary presidency and onward.

COORDINATED SCRIPTING, SHARED UNDERSTANDINGS, AND INSTITUTIONALIZATION

Over the forty-year period of this study, a total of nine cases in three policy areas have been examined, specifically considering five presidents and thirteen different sessions of Congress. The number of pages of congressional debate ranged from none to hundreds; presidential activity spanned a full range as well. Despite the focus on the presidency and Congress, the impact of the judiciary, partisan interests, the media, and public opinion were all apparent in the cases examined. Although these factors are not the direct focus of this study, they provided the environmental context that often fed into the motivations of the actors.

These cases provide insight into the concept of coordinated scripting and how it leads to shared understandings of expected behavior (i.e., norms). First and foremost, they provide strong evidence to support the existence of norms and the patterned behavior associated with them. The coordinated scripting between the presidency and Congress evidenced in the cases provided the basis for the patterned behavior exhibited in each policy area during this era. One example involves presidents committing troops abroad without significant congressional checks when the threat of intervention by European powers put U.S. economic interests at risk. Another example lies in the administrative area, when Congress allowed the president to participate fully and even to direct the creation of administrative agencies. Patterned behavior was also exhibited in other, less distinct, ways (e.g., presidential recognition that Congress should be involved to some degree in making policy decisions after the president committed troops to a potentially hostile area or Congress's attempts to limit the president's influence over the functioning of administrative agencies once created). Furthermore, the cases show that patterned behavior that did not exist at the start of the era could be established during it. Examples of this include the development of an "executive's role" in addressing the need for tariff reform.

Other theories could be considered, but none would seem to have the ability to provide as much order as the theory developed in this work to the randomness across the three policy areas, nine cases, and forty years. For example, a theory based on changing partisanship would fail, as the patterned behavior exhibited did not always change with the partisan composition within Congress and the presidency. To the contrary, patterned behavior was exhibited often *in spite of* partisan changes. A theory that links the behavior of members of Congress to the institution's structure and organization might also prove to be unsatisfactory because the members of Congress exhibited patterned behavior across Congress's different institutional structures between 1881 and 1920, including both the pre- and postrevolt against Speaker Cannon in 1910. In addition, a theory of patterned behavior exhibited during this era based on the realignment of 1896 would have less explanatory power because the realigning issues associated with that election were generally limited to economic concerns and would have limited explanatory power in the foreign policy area. Also, many of the foundations for the patterned behavior in the post-1896 period can be found in the pre-1896 era. Given all this, since the case studies provide evidence of patterned behaviors in the midst of the random variables that cannot be controlled and since no rival theory seems able to explain such behavior as well as the theory developed here, we have a basis upon which to support the arguments made herein.

Now that the existence of presidential norms has been established, we can consider the type of shared understandings of the behavior that presidents were expected to exhibit. At the beginning of each case study there is an initial understanding of the presidency's level of authority. As one moves through the forty-year time period, one can begin to establish the process by which these understandings not only affect the original interaction but also continue to affect subsequent ones. Therefore, each case taken together as part of a connected stream demonstrates a growth in the areas in which the presidency can act and the expectation of a greater presidential role in each area. Further, it is important to keep in mind that this growth was not consistent across policy areas but was often correlated with the level of constitutional authority the presidency initially has vis-à-vis Congress.

Within the cases, we can see the impact of both institutions' presumed authority on the interactions between the presidency and Congress. For example, the presidency was expected to have greater authority in the area of foreign affairs, an expectation that was supported with the commitment-of-troops cases. In each case, Congress allowed the president to commit troops prior to any involvement on its part and supported such commitment subsequently, either through its action or inaction. On the other hand, Congress was presumed to have greater authority in addressing domestic issues. This was exemplified in that institution's continued prominence throughout the period in crafting tariff legislation. Finally, the Constitution provides both the president, as head of the executive branch, and Congress, as overseer of the implementation of legislation, with presumed authority with regard to establishing administrative agencies. The cases demonstrated increased presidential prominence in the creation process while Congress maintained control of the functioning of the agencies once created. Further, the evidence from the cases shows that the behavior expected of the president at any time was not simply derived from the institution's constitutionally granted authority. Instead, within each area, a different set of norms emerged and became part of the institution.

We are now in a position to ask how this patterned behavior and set of expectations became institutionalized. More generally, we are seeking to understand the dynamics that foster institutional change under any given set of contextual circumstances. Based on the cases, we can develop a fuller conception of how shared understandings develop generally, become part of what defines a political institution, and help shape behavior and decisions in future interactions regardless of the occupants of the institutions at that time.

When the president and members of Congress, whoever they may be, interact over a public policy issue, they are working to solve a political problem facing the nation. This fact was born out in the cases examined in this work. In each one, a political problem arose that was seen as requiring the federal government to respond to it, whether it was a threat by European nations to U.S. interests in specific countries, the need to create a government agency to address the growing and changing U.S. economy, or the problems associated with tariffs that were either too high or too low (depending on one's view).

As the actors in the political institutions attempt to resolve the problem, they must do so with incomplete information. They may or may not be aware of the full implications that any policy process or decision may have in the long run. In addition, these actors' decisions can be shaped by a number of different factors. One such factor of direct importance to this work is considering previous actions—that is, looking to the past to see what was successful. In doing so, each action becomes part of an ongoing, connected process. Perhaps the best example of this is Wilson's intervention in Haiti and his consideration of both the pros and cons of utilizing an approach based on Theodore Roosevelt's strategy in the Dominican Republic.

The president and members of Congress, however, face many outside imperatives that force them to respond to political problems in certain ways. For example, public pressure and demands for action may cause political actors to accept resolutions to a problem that they might not accept absent such demands, as we saw with the creation of the ICC. Furthermore, the outcome of a policy interaction may be subject to partisan and electoral forces. Presidents and members of Congress alike may pursue campaign positions set forth by their political parties in platforms, or they may seek to implement a policy long advocated by the parties, as we saw in the three tariff cases. In addition, international issues not directly tied to those at hand in any interaction may also figure into the decision-making process. Such a case is best seen in the U.S. intervention in Haiti, where Congress was, some have argued, too preoccupied with the war in Europe and troubles with Mexico to focus on Wilson's actions.

Further, these influences do not rule out other factors, such as individual personality or quests to assert one's authority. Such factors often test the established boundaries of prescribed behavior, although not always with the same outcome. One only has to consider Theodore Roosevelt's successful challenge of the Senate over the Dominican Republic treaty compared with Grover Cleveland's attempt to place tariff reductions on the political agenda. Whereas the eventual outcome of the Dominican interaction led to increased presidential leeway, Cleveland was unable to establish new pathways for presidential activity.

While these contextual factors make a difference in directing the substance and process of policy development, they tell us little about—and at times even mask—the larger process that is of interest in this work. Further, they tell us little about the lasting implications that the interaction holds for the institutions. For long after any particular interaction is forgotten, what is retained is the understanding of the roles each institution is expected to play in future interactions. While the theory herein seeks neither to explain the origins of policy nor to understand the reasons for the adoption of a specific policy alternative,[3] it does attempt to incorporate these factors and to ask a much broader question, one designed to help us understand who in the political system is able at any given time to direct the system in response to any political problem and, in turn, what facilitates institutional change and development.

The answer to the latter question, as demonstrated by the coordinated scripting and behavior throughout the cases, is changing understandings of expected behavior. As has been shown, norms may indeed arise and be layered upon the institutional framework in existence at that given time to create informal institutions of authority. This can occur as new problems arise and need to be addressed, as actors realize that certain understandings no longer fit the problems of the day or when an actor manages to push the boundaries of the institutions. The critical component of any change, however, is whether enough actors in the political system accept a new understanding as appropriate.

A minority certainly may express resistance to a change, as was the case of Southern Democrats like Hernando Money or John Morgan, who were suspicious of presidential authority. The essential factor, however, in any institutional change is the eventual, majority-based outcome of any interaction. The motivations for that outcome might be affected by contextual, power considerations—for example, who controls the agenda, how persuasive a president is, or what party holds the majority in Congress. The substantive issue agenda and the vision of government that any given individual may hold might also impact the roles ascribed to the institutions. Most important for understanding institutional development, however, regardless of the motivations behind the majority's behavior, is the outcome of any given interaction, which can have lasting implications for both the presidency and Congress as institutions.

The institutional implications of any interaction may be by design, such as the discretion Congress provided the presidency in the wake of the Samoan intervention. The implications that an interaction may hold for the institutions may be known, but (a) not pose a significant change at the time, (b) be of secondary importance to other considerations, and/or (c) be ignored. For example, the creation of the Bureau of Corporations within the Department of Commerce and Labor raised many institutional concerns in Congress that were left unaddressed due to the public pressure to create the new agency. Further, because of the incomplete information they possess, the political actors may not fully realize the scope of the action they decide to pursue; for example, providing the presidency with the power (however controlled) to appoint ICC commissioners served to grant it authority in an area where it previously had none. The result of all this is that when actors—presidents and members of Congress—become embroiled in incremental policy making, they may fail to rise above the imperatives of "real politics" to consider the full implications of their actions. The institutional changes that result may merely be residual by-products of the institutional interactions. Despite this fact, however, they become the lasting understandings of the institutions and the roles they play—the roles that will shape the behavior of future actors.

CASE STUDIES RECONSIDERED

A review of the cases will demonstrate how the concepts of coordinated scripting, shared understandings of expected behavior, and the institutionalization process play out within them. Starting with the commitment of troops, in the case of Samoa, the problem that needed to be addressed was how to protect U.S. interests against the threat of the German ships already at the islands. By the time of this interaction, the presidency already possessed the authority to commit troops to an area of potential hostility where U.S. interests were threatened. Thus, President Cleveland, acting as commander in chief and not in conjunction with Congress, decided how to respond to the situation: commit U.S.

ships to the area. The outcome of this interaction solidified the response as an acceptable exercise of presidential authority.

On the other hand, the answer to the question of who should determine the nation's long-range policy was not so clear. Both the president and Congress essentially pointed to one another and said, "Tell me what you want to do." However, if anything, the grant of authority to the presidency, as reflected in the $600,000 in appropriations to be used under presidential discretion, favored the presidency for future interactions. The understanding that seemed to emerge was that the president had greater authority in this area as long as Congress was involved in the process. Under these conditions, Congress was quite willing to delegate additional authority to the presidency.

In the next case, Pres. Theodore Roosevelt put the understandings that had developed to the test. Although he followed the previously established norm by committing troops to protect U.S. interests, his behavior was seen (by some) as violating the norm regarding working with Congress to establish long-term policy. The concern that many congressional Democrats and some Republicans had was not so much that the president would primarily decide the details of U.S. policy but that he would do so without Congress's input. Roosevelt explicitly challenged the norm regarding congressional involvement by implementing the modus vivendi after the Senate failed to ratify the treaty he placed before it.

Congress, despite the arguments to preserve its role in foreign affairs, lost authority to the presidency, both through its general inaction for two years while the modus vivendi was in effect and by ultimately supporting a modified version of Roosevelt's policy. As a result, the case of the Dominican Republic intervention further institutionalized the norm that the president should direct the government's response when U.S. interests abroad were threatened. Not only did this case demonstrate that the president had the authority to commit troops, but the outcome of the interaction also reflected an increase in presidential authority in unilaterally deciding long-term policy details.

With the intervention in Haiti, the norms supporting broader presidential authority had apparently become institutionalized. Despite his initial concerns regarding presidential authority, Woodrow Wilson followed the lessons that the Dominican Republic interaction had left for him. With ten years' perspective on Roosevelt's efforts, Wilson understood that the presidency had the authority to intervene in the affairs of other countries under certain conditions, and a policy such as Roosevelt's would be seen as necessary and effective. As a result, Wilson cautiously decided that his institutional authority was sufficient for him to proceed without prior congressional input into or approval of his policy.

In pursuing such a course, Wilson was able to accomplish virtually everything that Roosevelt had wanted a decade earlier. Due in large part to Roosevelt's efforts and the success of his policy in the Dominican Republic, however, Wilson was never challenged in the exercise of his authority. The norm that the president could commit troops to protect U.S. economic interests remained unchanged. The norm that the president would consult with Congress regarding the long-term policy, however, seemed to be relaxed as Congress left the issues associated with the continued intervention to the president's discretion.

In starting to examine presidential authority in creating administrative agencies, the role of the presidency in establishing the ICC was clearly understood—it was virtually nothing. The Supreme Court had already declared that the regulation of interstate commerce was a congressional matter. Therefore, in providing for such regulation Congress created the ICC as a tool for its implementation, with only presidential assent. This process was dependent solely on the members of Congress. Members such as Rep. John Reagan and Sen. Shelby Cullom provided the leadership necessary to see that the problems facing the nation—the economic burdens associated with unfair railroad practices—were addressed. The members of Congress also made the necessary policy decisions to put the solution into effect.

The outcome of the interaction did not affect the presidency's authority to direct the government since Cleveland did nothing to address the problem, except for a brief comment of lukewarm support near the end of the process. For the most part, the outcome of the interaction did little for the presidency's authority to implement the details, except to the extent that one of the policy decisions made by Congress was to codify a grant of authority to the presidency. The key lesson drawn from this interaction for future ones lay in Congress's delegation of authority, both in terms of its general delegation to the ICC and its specific delegation to the presidency through its appointment power. The actors who would be involved in creating other agencies subsequent to the ICC would draw on the norm of delegating authority established by Congress.

In the interaction regarding the Department of Commerce and Labor, the informal norms regarding presidential behavior as understood by the members of Congress and President Roosevelt provided for greater presidential involvement. Unlike with the ICC, the leadership behind creating this department came from the presidency and not Congress. Roosevelt's call for such an agency served as the catalytic event for its passage, whereas similar efforts had fallen short in the past. As a result, Congress responded to presidential leadership, approving the new department and the Bureau of Corporations within it partly because the president emphasized their necessity.

We can detect a norm regarding the expectation that the presidency will direct the process of creating new agencies. This interaction reflects an understanding that the president has the authority to shape the structure of the executive branch, of which the president serves as head. In addition, Congress not only exercised its authority to shape and pass the legislation needed to create the new department but also provided the presidency with the authority to participate in that process as well. Here we see an emerging norm that accepted presidential involvement in the process of crafting the details of the new agency, its jurisdiction, and its powers as evidenced by the general (although not universal) acceptance by congressional members of Roosevelt's "legislative behavior" (i.e., writing the Nelson amendment establishing the Bureau of Corporations). Further, presidential authority formally expanded as specific grants to the presidency were codified in the legislation, which provided the presidency with the authority to influence the functioning of the new apparatus.

In the Federal Trade Commission interaction, the norms regarding presidential behavior in this policy area were reinforced and layered upon the understandings already in place. In fact, they had become more ingrained, as the president was fully expected to both direct the government's response to the issue and to guide the legislative process. Congress not only accepted the president's dual roles but also sought his input on issues when none might have been forthcoming. These norms regarding the dual roles were fairly clear and understood by actors in both institutions.

Wilson, like Roosevelt before him, fueled the FTC's passage as the members of Congress responded to the president's request for a trade commission. In addition, again like Roosevelt, Wilson became involved in crafting the specifics of the legislation. However, the understanding held by many members of Congress of what the president should be doing exceeded the view of the presidency's role that existed in 1903, when the Department of Commerce and Labor was established. Wilson both acted and was requested to act like a "chief legislator," working to draft parts of the bill and to see that the measure would pass over the legislative hurdles it faced.

The most uncertain area regarding presidential authority in this policy realm rested in formal grants of authority codified in legislation. Specifically, the members of Congress can be seen as having a general concern that the president should have only limited influence over the ongoing functioning of the newly established agencies, which were congressional surrogates with certain powers delegated to them. The formal authority granted to the presidency throughout the three cases, however, did not reflect a consistent application or understanding of this position. For example, Congress limited presidential influence over the ICC to the appointment of its members. This influence codified a grant of authority in a policy area in which the presidency previously had no such authority. With the Department of Commerce and Labor, Congress supported an extensive grant of authority to the presidency over the functioning of the new department, specifically by linking the Bureau of Corporations and its powers of publicity directly to the president. Congress subsequently retreated from this position by transferring those powers to the Federal Trade Commission and away from the direct control of the presidency. In doing so, it indicated that there was no clear norm or institutionalized understanding regarding presidential control of the functioning of administrative agencies created as surrogates for Congress.

In the tariff realm, the development of presidential norms is somewhat similar to those in the creation of administrative agencies. The presidency started the era with little authority in this area, given the constitutional authority of Congress in domestic affairs generally and matters of taxation specifically. Although the presidency experienced additional layering of informal norms with respect to the tariff, Congress expressed concern about the formal grants of authority as codified in legislation.

Within this realm, Congress started with the authority both to direct the government's response to calls for tariff revision and to decide all of the details of the resulting legislation. Although Grover Cleveland tried to stake out the former role for the presidency, such an understanding was not shared. The presidency's role was minimal, as the members of Congress and even President Harrison expected the president to do little. Even though Harrison had supported tariff revision, he left it for Congress to address the problems that many Republicans associated with tariffs that were too low.

Congress exercised its authority fully under the direction of Rep. William McKinley. If not for the fact that the proposed tariff legislation encroached on presidential authority in foreign affairs, Harrison would have had little need to become involved in the crafting of the legislation. Congress provided the opportunity for the president and, more specifically, his surrogate (the secretary of state) to do so. As a result, though, the outcome of this interaction had little effect on the presidency as an institution—only to the extent that the door for greater presidential involvement was left ajar.

By the time Representative McKinley became President McKinley, the presidency's responsibility had come to include responding to and providing guidance and direction for correcting the nation's economic problems. Unlike President Cleveland before him, who placed the responsibility for tariff revision squarely on Congress, President McKinley proclaimed that his role as executive was to direct the government's response to the nation's problems. His actions reflected this assumption; just as important (if not more so), the behavior of the members of Congress reflected McKinley's statement as well. Indeed, both McKinley and the members of Congress understood that the presidency's role was to help identify the need for revision and to set the discourse for the change in policy.

The members of Congress heeded the challenge handed down by McKinley and set forth the many different tariff rate schedules defined in the Dingley Tariff. In other words, they retained the authority to craft the details of the tariff legislation, an understanding that the president shared. As a result, these understandings of the roles of Congress and the presidency provided a basis upon which subsequent interactions could be shaped.

These expected behaviors were institutionalized by the time of the Underwood Tariff. The presidency maintained its position to direct the government's response, as President Wilson acted like McKinley before him in calling attention to the need to revise the tariff and to set the discourse for doing so. Congress, for its part, retained most of the authority to shape the policy. Its members continued to exercise their substantial authority to write the legislation necessary to revise the tariff.

President Wilson's involvement, however, extended beyond simply identifying and directing the problem. He delved into the legislative component of crafting the tariff, and Congress accepted this behavior; as a result, a new norm may have begun to emerge. Wilson helped establish a new norm that provided a role, albeit a relatively limited one, akin to the chief legislator role seen in the administrative agency cases. Thus, the outcome of the interaction solidified presidential authority in some areas and expanded it in others.

The most contentious area within the tariff cases regarding presidential authority stemmed from codified grants of authority. Congress went back and forth on the issue of reciprocity and the grant of authority to the presidency associated with it. Despite these changes and ultimate removal of the reciprocity provision from tariff legislation, the presidency's authority in the tariff area grew significantly during the era from 1881 to 1920. It went from an area in which the presidency had a limited role in the process to one in which it had the authority to identify the need for and to affect the outcome of any tariff legislation.

Through the three policy areas, we see several different models of institutionalization occurring. In the commitment of troops, presidential authority to direct the government's response to foreign problems was high throughout the entire era. As such, the president possessed the authority to use the military to address certain problems abroad and was expected to do so. In terms of the presidency's ability to craft and implement policy decisions, the presidency's authority started at a more moderate level, constrained somewhat more by the president's own understanding of his institutional authority than by that held by many members of Congress. Over the cases, however, a more expanded notion of presidential authority was accepted among various actors, thus leading to certain informal institutions of authority and providing for a wide range of acceptable presidential behavior.

In the creation of administrative agencies, presidential authority to direct the government's response to certain political problems, as well as its authority to craft policy, started virtually at zero, again in large part due to the policy issue at hand and the Supreme Court's decision regarding who controlled the regulation of interstate commerce. The presidency's authority to direct the government's response to the problems associated with needing a new government agency increased dramatically with the subsequent two interactions. The presidency could thus be expected to do things such as identify the need for new agencies and the general issues that would fall under its jurisdiction. Similarly, the presidency's authority to craft the details of the response also increased dramatically throughout the era, but not quite at the same rate as its authority to direct the response. By the end of the era, the expectation that the president would be involved in the legislative process creating new agencies had become institutionalized as well.

As in the case of administrative agencies, the presidency's authority in the area of the tariff was initially minimal. However, its authority to identify problems, set the general discourse, and direct the response grew through the subsequent cases. Although this increase in authority is significant, the presidency's authority to be active in the details of tariff legislation grew, but at a much slower rate. By the end of the era, the shared understandings of expected presidential behavior provided for some degree of participation by the presidency in the legislative process, but the issue remained primarily in Congress's domain.

The evidence within each case and the preceding discussion demonstrates *how* norms of presidential behavior become institutionalized—through the interactions over policy, the creation of coordinated scripts, and the adaptation of the members of Congress and the presidency to all that had preceded them. The question remains, though, of *why* they become institutionalized. Based on the theory developed and the evidence drawn from the cases, we can see that Congress lies at the heart of many of the institutionalization processes of the presidency between 1881 and 1920. By looking at the interactions involved, Congress can be seen as responsible for much of the authority the presidency acquired during the forty-year era: It granted authority to the presidency when the president had been silent on the issue; it provided additional authority to the presidency when only a little may have been needed; it approved presidential efforts to assert institutional authority, and so on. This does not rule out the fact that individual presidents such as Roosevelt and Wilson pushed the boundaries of presidential action; after all, as chapter 1 points out, presidents have a vested interest in building the institution's authority.[4] What is key to understanding the process of development, however, is that although such attempts to expand the boundaries of presidential action were important turning points for the presidency, they constitute only half of the story of why the institution's authority expanded. It is through the ongoing coordinated scripting focused on achieving short-term goals and in which Congress agreed to certain understandings that resulted in additional authority for the presidency. The question remains as to why Congress would agree to such understandings that resulted in significant grants of authority to the presidency.

The answer to this question lies in part in the context that surrounded the interactions throughout the entire forty-year period under consideration. America's nationalizing political and economic systems provided many new challenges; they created new *national* problems that could effectively be addressed only by the *national* government. As a result, the national government faced not only a greater number of political problems but also a growth in terms of the scope and types of issues it was required to be resolve. If we assume that the president and members of Congress at any given time sought to address or solve a problem facing the country, then this nationalization placed a great deal of work at the feet of the political actors in Washington.

The members of Congress were thus faced with a multitude of issues upon which they had to decide how to proceed. On one hand, they could act in such a way as to maximize, or at least maintain, their institution's authority. That would require, however, that Congress not only craft the legislation needed to address the nation's problems but also exercise the institution's authority so as to direct the government's response to the problems. On the other hand, Congress could transfer its authority or grant new authority to other actors to address the problems. By the Constitution, Congress had to retain the formal authority to enact legislation. It could delegate, however, much of its informal authority and a great deal of its other formal authority to various surrogates, including the presidency and administrative agencies.

Thus, the answer to why the presidency institutionalized around a set of shared understandings of expected behavior stems in part from Congress's need to address the problems of the day expediently. Congress and the president had to focus on the nation's short-term political needs, which often left the long-term institutional ramifications as a secondary concern. In some instances, initiatives by the president offered an acceptable pathway toward an expedient resolution. Some of the norms regarding presidential behavior, however, were established by the members of Congress, even when the president at the time may not have been pursuing the associated authority. The residual by-product of this short-term-focused, public policy-making process was the establishment of agreed-upon methods—both in terms of process and substance—for addressing the problems of the day. Even when institutional concerns were addressed, the potential and actual long-term costs associated with increased presidential authority did not outweigh the benefits of resolving the immediate problem and having an approach for quickly resolving similar ones that might subsequently arise.

LESSONS DRAWN FROM THE CASE STUDIES

This research provides a number of important findings for our understanding of the presidency, its developmental process, and its role in the U.S. political system. This work is premised on the view that the presidency, as a political institution, is more than just the formal rules or organizational structures within it. The first key finding of this work, therefore, has been to demonstrate that the presidency can rightfully be conceived in terms of informal shared understandings of the behavior that presidents are expected to exhibit—in other words, norms. Although only one component of the political institution, presidential norms have been shown to continue and become part of the informal institution of authority of the presidency and the institutional memory that lasts beyond one or two officeholders. Moreover, such norms are continually refined as further expectations and additional authority are layered upon the institution.

Closely related to this point is the idea that the institutionalization of the presidency—that is, the process by which these informal understandings are developed and become part of the institution—is ongoing. It starts with the Constitution and the prescribed boundaries set forth therein. As problems arise, the need to respond to them necessitates the development of new understandings and sets of expectations that go along with them. Although for the most part these expectations begin informally, they are the standard by which other actors judge job performance—that is, is the president doing what we expect our chief executive to do? However, the developmental process of the institution described in this work is not linear in nature, nor should it be seen as moving toward any specific equilibrium point. Instead, the institution is constantly changing, albeit often very slowly, and the understanding of the presidency can expand or contract with any given interaction and may do so differently across policy areas.

What an ongoing understanding of the development of the institution provides is a way to connect different time periods. By having enough of a continuum of understanding—that is, a range of time in which one knows what the presidential norms are—one should be able to predict what should happen in future interactions. This allows one to transcend periodicity and to connect various time periods. In doing so, one sees that the presidency, through its institutional interactions with Congress, has gained additional authority, which was subsequently layered on top and became part of the institution; it did not suddenly develop such authority without the building blocks of the past.

Through this new way of understanding the presidency we can better know who is expected to affect change at any given time and who is perceived to have the right to do so—in other words, who possesses the authority to lead the political system. As a result, this research demonstrates that its authority-based theory can address questions regarding the presidency that a personal, power-based approach cannot. Although a president's personal power may affect the outcome of a specific interaction, it is transitory. At a maximum, any given president's personal power is relevant for as long as that individual is in office. Authority, on the other hand, transcends the individual. While it too can ebb and flow, it generally survives transitions of personnel, partisanship, and so on. Furthermore, presidential authority provides the parameters and serves as a predictor of presidential behavior.

Possibly the best examples that indicate the benefits of considering presidential authority and the limitations of focusing on power are those cases in which presidential authority grew, even slightly, with only minimal or no presidential involvement (i.e., the ICC and, to a lesser degree, the McKinley Tariff). Under a power-based conception of the presidency, the institution should not have benefited from the interaction. Given the level of presidential activity and the resulting lack of exercise of either Cleveland's or Harrison's personal influence, Congress should have been able to address the problem the nation faced as it pleased, even if doing so meant limiting the presidency in some fashion. Under the authority-based theory derived here, however, we understand why Congress acted in the manner in which it did and, further, the implications of those interactions for future presidents.

This authority-based view also reorients us to look at the conditions under which presidents can affect change (e.g., how presidents act differently and are expected to do so in different policy areas). In other words, the behavior that a president is expected to exhibit is dictated in part by that person's position rather than by any personal traits. Although the president may be expected to lead the government's response to a problem in one policy area, the president may not be expected to do so in another.

From this, we can see that leadership is a trait not only of individuals but also of institutions and that individuals are placed in leadership roles simply by their position within an institution. For example, Cleveland exhibited "leadership" in resolving the Samoan affair because he was commander in chief and needed to respond to the threat to U.S. interests, not solely because of his personal characteristics. William McKinley exhibited two types of leadership in tariff legislation depending on his institutional roles. As chairman of the House Ways and Means Committee, he worked to craft the legislation that bears his name and saw that it was passed. His role was one of legislative leadership. As president, however, McKinley believed that the "executive's role" was to direct the government to address the problems associated with the then-current tariff levels. Given that leadership can rest in institutions, the institutions can in turn set the parameters of leadership behavior for the individuals in them. This is not to say that presidents cannot extend beyond or reshape the parameters of institutional leadership, only that institutional leadership can pressure presidents, regardless of who they are, to act in a certain manner, both in terms of exhibiting a minimum level of leadership or constraining the president so that the "leadership" of the chief executive does not exceed the authority placed in the institution at that time.

This research also reorients us to examine the presidency vis-à-vis Congress and in the larger political system generally, rather than centering our focus as scholars on the presidency alone. In doing so, we see that the interactions between the two institutions can lead to a variety of outcomes for each one's authority. With the theory developed in this work, we begin to understand the reasons why Congress delegated away its own authority—namely, to find expedient resolutions to short-term policy imperatives—and what that delegation eventually meant, in a cumulative sense, for the widening of the boundaries of executive action.

In addition, the theory developed here and the cases examined demonstrate that that the U.S. political system is not a presidency-centered one. Although any given president may seem to test the boundaries of presidential authority, that person's ultimate success is based on whether other actors in the system share the understanding of that role and perceive that the president has the right to act in such a manner. Without other actors sharing that understanding, the presidency would be seen as conflicting with the system and often be checked by the other institutions. For example, Theodore Roosevelt was considered to be pushing the limitations of the institution by forcing Congress to accept the Bureau of Corporations as he envisioned it. Congress later took it upon itself to check the presidency by preventing direct presidential control through the transfer of the bureau's power to the FTC, an independent regulatory agency.

INSIGHTS FOR THE CONTINUED SCRIPTING OF THE PRESIDENCY

The story of institutionalization in this book, built upon a notion of coordinated scripting and the growth of informal institutions of authority, requires us to ask what all of this means for the continued coordinated scripting and the institutionalization of the presidency. First, this analysis allows us to build a better comprehension of the ongoing dynamic relations between the policy-making branches, the way in which change occurs, and the reasons that understanding the original design and the rich layering of informal institutions of authority, as well as individual and institutional actions, matters. Second, the cases we have discussed are instructive in that the institutionalization process is conditional on the policy area, the actors involved, the prior understandings of the institutions, and the idea that change is fluid and not unidirectional. Furthermore, the cases reveal that short-term motivations to reach compromised solutions drive the creation of coordinated scripts that lead to the development of informal institutions of authority or, in other words, an institutional memory with long-term effects on how that authority can be wielded. Further, we see a vision emerging of the energetic president that was central to the Hamiltonian view of the presidency, and we gain an appreciation of the fact that the emergence of this vision is predicated upon the Madisonian structure and the subsequent adaptations it set into motion.

From this analysis, we realize that presidents have an interest in developing and then codifying shared understandings conducive to fleshing out their vaguely defined constitutional role in the separated system. Due to the institutionalization of authority, however, the contemporary presidency is caught in a situation where the expectations that go along with the institutionalized authority demand bolder action by the president; nevertheless, this action may be limited since the president must still operate within the system of separation of powers. Presidents who might try to defer to the constitutionally prescribed role of Congress and not exercise the additional understandings of authority that have been institutionalized over time would, at a minimum, be seen as adversely affecting the role of the presidency and more likely as a failure. Furthermore, the likelihood of Congress supporting this course of action would be minimal at best.

Although seemingly counterintuitive that it would not be pleased with such deference, Congress has participated in the crafting of such shared understandings and has a vested interest in retaining them. The members of Congress have a political motivation in wanting to maintain the status quo. Although Congress, as the original first branch of government, may retain the ultimate constitutional power to affect change, the demand for presidential action provides Congress and its members with political cover so they do not have to play the leadership role. In fact, there is a disincentive to take such initiative since the costs of failure in the eyes of the public (and therefore each member's reelection constituency) can be fully born by the presidency in the wake of congressional silence or acquiescence to presidential initiative. Scholars of presidential-congressional relations sometimes lament the passivity of Congress in allowing the ceding of authority to the presidency in such a manner and call for congressional reassertion and resolve; members of Congress have at times even tried to reassert the institution's authority. Nevertheless, the incentive to take such action carries little weight in light of the potential pitfalls that Congress might face with such change.

Therefore, contemporary presidents are faced with a continuum of pathways for leadership in the current institutional environment (moving from the easiest to the hardest option):

1. Presidents can wield the authority derived from the residue of past shared understandings and do so with the full knowledge that the weight and inertia of the status quo are with them. Congress would be less likely to challenge this precedent since it not only is in their interests but would also be difficult to challenge in the wake of the expectations that accompany such authority.

2. Presidents can attempt to take advantage (or, depending on one's view, exploit) opportunity structures that allow for modifications to the existing scripts. This pathway may often be employed in that it is not that costly and offers a means for any president who wants to leave a personal mark on the institution.

3. Presidents can seek to shape the context to be conducive to change (i.e., to create new shared understandings) favorable to the presidency. One mechanism often employed here, for example, is "going public."[5] The increasingly frequent use of this mechanism is made more understandable by the fact that the expectations for achieving success are measured by how well the outcome achieves the president's objective. The public can therefore be an ally to use against the Congress to make the costs of pursuing a new shared understanding less than those associated with retaining the old.

4. Presidents can attempt to craft new shared understandings by exhibiting or exercising authority that goes beyond the institutionalized shared understandings. On one hand, the payoff in terms of the precedent for authority that might be wielded by the presidency in the future is vast; on the other hand, the risk not only to the presidency but also (in the most extreme cases) to the separation of powers system (e.g., constitutional crises, institutional stalemates) makes this pathway risky for any president. Furthermore, in order to be successful in pursing this strategy, a combination of the right personal skill, institutional cooperation, and context are required. Although a president might think the conditions are conducive to crafting a new shared understanding, those that fail are rated as less successful, while those select few who judge right are the "great" leaders in our nation's history.

Each of these pathways is premised, to varying degrees, on presidential leadership. Leadership, however, while requiring individual action is a cooperative enterprise. No matter which pathway enumerated above a president chooses to pursue, the ultimate success of these choices will be dependent upon Congress and other actors in the political system agreeing to walk the same pathway.

The lesson here is that the Hamiltonian-style presidency that has emerged, one that is energetic and is required in order for a chief executive to lead successfully, is still moored in the Madisonian structure. Although the accumulation of the residue of authority has allowed more leeway for presidents to be "energetic," they are nonetheless ultimately constrained by and can be tamped down by the original constitutional allocation of authority. This leeway, however, reflects a false consciousness that develops among governmental actors and within the broader political context and that adheres to the shared understanding with the justification that "this is how we have always done it" without grasping the fact that things may not have always been done that way or that the pathway chosen can be changed. Although more discriminating eyes may see the shared understanding for what it really is—a more efficient means for resolving political issues that has grown out of the residue of previous interactions—to actors mired in the process, these shared understandings provide a standard operating procedure that reduces uncertainty and decreases the costs of reaching a resolution. These understandings and this authority derived from them, if not codified through law or other mechanisms, are precarious warrants for leadership or action subject to challenge.

To understand how established shared understandings can be challenged, both successfully and unsuccessfully, consider, for example, certain 1970s-era reforms, which represented a time in which Congress declared it was reestablishing its authority and taking it back from the imperial presidency. Not unlike the era studied in the present book, this period too provided a key context for the institutions by calling into question the authority of the presidency and the coordinated scripting that underpinned its growth.[6] However, a closer look at three examples— the Congressional Budget and Impoundment Control Act of 1974, the Independent Counsel Act (formally known as the Ethics in Government Act of 1978), and the War Powers Resolution of 1973—reveals both Congress's ability to successfully challenge certain understandings and the difficulty in challenging others. Although Congress articulated this goal of reestablishing its authority, it did not always attack the issues that it was seeking to reform from a position of strength based on its own constitutional powers. Instead, Congress at times sought to implement reforms employing the coordinated scripting that led to the appearance of the imperial presidency in the first place.

The Congressional Budget and Impoundment Control Act of 1974 sought to prevent presidents from dictating what appropriations would be spent. Congress pursued this reform based upon the reasoning that it, not the presidency, controlled the power of the purse. This was by far the most successful reform action because Congress pitted its constitutionally derived power against the presidency's informal institutions of authority. Despite the coordinated scripting that had previously developed and that allowed the presidency to dictate control of the use of funds, Congress delved below the layers of understandings that had built up and undercut them using its own constitutional powers—a far stronger foundation for action than the presidency's informal institution of authority with respect to this issue. This demonstrates how precarious the informal institutions of authority can be when challenged by raw constitutional power.

With respect to the Independent Counsel Act, Congress attempted to remove from the control of the presidency the ability to hire and fire investigators—an issue that touches upon Congress's implied constitutional power of oversight.[7] Despite the fact that Congress has this implied power, it did not try to implement a reform by exerting it. Instead, Congress sought reform based upon the creation of an independent counsel. Although this approach proved to be a good short-term compromise that allowed Congress to appear as if it were putting its investigatory power above politics, it did not reestablish Congress's authority in this area. Congress continued the shared understanding (reflected even in the case studies in Chapter 3) of delegating its authority to another actor in the name of achieving a short-term goal, thus not necessarily strengthening its institutional position vis-à-vis the presidency.

With the War Powers Resolution, Congress may have believed it was asserting its constitutional powers, but it failed to break free of the coordinated scripting that had developed around this issue—coordinated scripting that had already allowed the transfer of authority to the presidency. Congress even went so far as to codify what had previously been an informal understanding, namely the president's ability to initiate short-term engagements. In addition, the vague language of the resolution did not modify the coordinated scripting on the issue of the war power. Presidents since the resolution's passage have interpreted its vague language along the lines of the existing coordinated scripting that supports presidential authority. Congress has continued to behave as if it is adhering to the understandings of presidential and congressional behavior associated with the previous scripting it tried to reform. This continued adherence results from certain incentives—incentives regarding political responsibility, expediency, and partisan control of the presidency—that do not encourage the members of Congress to act differently. As a result, the War Powers Resolution has not provided any meaningful check on the informal institutions of authority for the presidency on this issue.[8]

These examples show that the original intent of the separation of powers system—that individual action is conditioned on institutional action—is still intact. They also reflect that the costs of challenging shared understandings can be significant—in some ways, requiring the institutions to reverse more than two hundred years of development in order to strictly adhere to the original constitutional allocation of authority. Furthermore, these examples demonstrate that there has indeed been an intertwining of what was constitutionally provided and what has been created through coordinated scripting—that the presidency has a better-defined role and leeway to act based on the accumulations of informal institutions of authority.

These informal institutions allow the presidency to appear more capable than Congress, even though Congress remains fundamentally the more powerful institution as prescribed by the Constitution. When Congress acts upon the authority of the presidency built within the established coordinated scripts, it is buying into a more institutionalized notion of that office. Moreover, Congress, by doing so, actually reinforces the informal institutions of authority and the right of the presidency to affect change—and, perhaps more importantly, the right of the presidency to lead in the U.S. political system.

In the happenstance of everyday policy making, collective decision making allows for the unintended development of informal institutions of authority that, with their ongoing use, become ingrained and harder for the institutions (as well as other actors in the political system) to distinguish what was a part of the original fabric of the institution from what has been created over the years of coordinated action. This work lays bare such discrepancies and provides an explanation for institutional stalemates that may arise and that leave even the most institutionally sensitive actors asking "how did we get here?" and "can anything possibly be done?" So we know why we have this false consciousness regarding presidential authority wherein the president is expected to resolve political problems of the day despite not necessarily having the powers to do so, but why does this false consciousness persist? Certainly, presidents of today lend credence to this misperception of authority by claiming credit for all things (e.g., the economy). As a result, they are subsequently held accountable by other actors within and outside of government for such despite the fact that these claims by presidents are not grounded in the original constitutional design, but instead in informal understandings that arose out of interactions over other policy matters and that are subject to change if conditions for doing so are ripe.

The institutionalization process defined by this work provides some hint that any changes need to be ongoing, incremental ones fostered by the vigilance of each institution to its own interests and not its short-term policy decisions. There is little call, however, for even this sort of institutional reform. Presidents do not seek reforms to free the presidency from the pressures of the sometimes unattainable expectations that come with the buildup of authority because the president and the presidency would pay a much greater price by losing the ability to lead. Members of Congress have incentives to not seek any such reforms. Even when they do attempt to rein in the presidency, however, the changes sought are not always based upon Congress's constitutional power but instead are defined by the shared understandings that have developed.

This study, while not recommending specific reforms, does shed light on the microprocesses that drive institutional change and the necessity for understanding their ramifications for the U.S. political system. Furthermore, by shedding light on these microprocesses, we can better appreciate the delicate balance that was set into motion by the Founders and the fact that a lack of attention to the long-term position of the institutions begins a cascade of subtle changes that can trap the institutions into what may ultimately be a pathway with undesirable consequences for their respective institutional interests. This cascade, as we have seen, is created through the coordinated scriptings that contain shared understandings of expected behavior that are the basis for the creation of informal institutions of authority.

So what are we to make of this institutionalization process? As narrated herein, the story of change in the U.S. political context is hidden in the ongoing scripting. The consequences of understanding this idea is that what is "modern" is really just a logical sequence of the pathways of ongoing change, that punctuated change is in fact the alteration of these coordinated scripts at key contexts, and that the precedents these coordinated scripts provide are the ingredients of the institutionalization process and the subsequent relaying of behavioral guidance from one administration to the next. The ramification of comprehending such an institutionalization process is an appreciation that, although the Founders worried about the "vortex" the legislative branch might become, this story of the institutionalization of the presidency invokes John F. Kennedy's proclamation that "The presidential office is the vortex into which all the laments of national decision are irresistibly drawn."[9]

Appendix

- Did an initial survey of several volumes throughout the time period covered in this research to develop an initial working list of key words to locate as subject headings in the *Congressional Record* Index.
- Systematically reviewed each volume in the time period (vols. 13–60) page by page for all relevant titles related to the issue areas under study and compiled a larger working list of key words as I went through the volumes.
- Developed the short list of key words based on the working list shown below. The short list eliminated words that may initially have been related to the topics but turned out not to be necessary, as well as words that simply referred the reader to another word in the subject index.
- Compared the short list with secondary sources to ensure that relevant examples of military commitments were included in the database (most were listed in the index under the names of specific countries or another heading).
- Photocopied pages of the subject index in each *Congressional Record* index that contained one of the key words from the short list and highlighted the key words.
- Created the database housing information on each bill introduced in Congress related to the areas under study based on the subject title found in the index.
- After developing the set of potential institutional interactions housed in the database, obtained the disposition of each bill and resolution (i.e., did it die, did it pass one or both houses, was it approved by the president?) and checked them with presidential requests.

SHORT LIST OF KEY WORDS

Economic

1. Relation of Economy
   Regulation
   Trusts
   Commerce
   Interstate Commerce
2. Tariff
   Tariffs
   Import Duties

Military (Commitment of Troops)

1. Actual Troop Commitment
   Military
      Intervention
      Usage
   Troops
   War
   National Defense
   Treaty
      (Specific countries/specific events)

Operation of Executive Branch

1. Creation/Functioning
   Executive Department
      Create/establish
      Restructure/reorganize
   Bureau
      Create/establish
      Restructure/reorganize
   Department
      Create/establish
      Restructure/reorganize

General Terms

1. President of the United States
2. Federal
3. National

Note: The database also includes information on coinage and personnel that was not utilized in this research.

Table A.1. Treaties and Executive Agreements, 1881–1920

President	Year	Agreements	Treaties
Garfield/Arthur	1881	1	4
Arthur	1882	4	10
	1883	4	2
	1884	3	8
Cleveland	1885	5	2
	1886	1	7
	1887	3	4
	1888	2	6
Harrison	1889	1	2
	1890	2	2
	1891	6	5
	1892	2	7
Cleveland	1893	0	2
	Subtotal	34	61
	Total	95	
	Annual Average	7.31	

President	Year	Agreements	Treaties
Cleveland	1894	2	3
	1895	2	2
	1896	2	4
McKinley	1897	2	3
	1898	7	4
	1899	9	9
	1900	7	8
McKinley Roosevelt	1901	6	9
Roosevelt	1902	9	11
	1903	1	11
	1904	7	13
	1905	10	7
	1906	7	13
	1907	15	10
	Subtotal	86	107
	Total	193	
	Annual Average	13.79	

President	Year	Agreements	Treaties
Roosevelt	1908	4	35
Taft	1909	7	4
	1910	5	12
	1911	2	8
	1912	3	4
Wilson	1913	4	15
	1914	7	23
	1915	13	1
	1916	7	2
	1917	4	1
	1918	9	12
	1919	7	11
	1920	3	3
	Subtotal	75	131
	Total	206	
	Annual Average	15.85	

Source: Based on Gary King and Lyn Ragsdale, *The Elusive Executive: Discovering Statistical Patterns in the Presidency* (Washington, D.C.: CQ Press, 1988).

Table A.2. Events of Commitment of Troops

Date	President	Location	Region	Reason	Size	Duration	Prior Congressional Authorization
1873–1882	Garfield/Arthur	Mexico	Latin America	Pursue bandits	Unknown	More than 1 year	No
1882	Arthur	Egypt	Other	Protect lives/interests	100–1,000	0–2 mos.	No
1885	Cleveland-1	Colombia (Panama)	Latin America	Protect lives/interests	Unknown	3–12 mos.	Yes
1888	Cleveland-1	Korea	East Asia	Protect lives/interests	Fewer than 100	0–2 mos.	No
1888–1889	Cleveland-1/Harrison	Samoan Islands	Pacific Islands	Protect lives/interests	Unknown	3–12 mos.	Yes
1888	Cleveland-1	Haiti	Caribbean	Protect lives/interests	Unknown	0–2 mos.	No
1889	Harrison	Hawaii	Pacific Islands	Protect lives/interests	Unknown	0–2 mos.	No
1890	Harrison	Argentina	Latin America	Protect lives/interests	Unknown	0–2 mos.	No
1891	Harrison	Haiti	Caribbean	Protect lives/interests	Unknown	0–2 mos.	Yes
1891	Harrison	Bering Sea	Other	Protect lives/interests	Unknown	3–12 mos.	No
1891	Harrison	Chile	Latin America	Protect lives/interests	100–1,000	0–2 mos.	No
1894	Cleveland-2	Brazil	Latin America	Protect lives/interests	Unknown	0–2 mos.	Yes

Date	President	Location	Region	Reason	Size	Duration	Prior Congressional Authorization
1894	Cleveland-2	Nicaragua	Latin America	Protect lives/ interests	Unknown	0–2 mos.	No
1894–1896	Cleveland-2	Korea	East Asia	Protect lives/ interests	Fewer than 100	More than 1 year	No
1894–1895	Cleveland-2	China	East Asia	Protect lives/ interests	Unknown	More than 1 year	No
1895	Cleveland-2	Colombia (Panama)	Latin America	Protect lives/ interests	Unknown	0–2 mos.	Yes
1895–1896	Cleveland-2	Korea	East Asia	Protect lives/ interests	Unknown	3–12 mos.	No
1896	Cleveland-2	Nicaragua	Latin America	Protect lives/ interests	Unknown	0–2 mos.	No
1898	McKinley	Nicaragua	Latin America	Protect lives/ interests	Unknown	0–2 mos.	No
1898–1899	McKinley	China	East Asia	Protect lives/ interests	Unknown	3–12 mos.	No
1899	McKinley	Nicaragua	Latin America	Protect lives/ interests	Unknown	0–2 mos.	No
1899	McKinley	Samoan Islands	Pacific Islands	Suppress rebellion	Fewer than 100	0–2 mos.	Yes
1899–1901	McKinley	Philippine Islands	Pacific Islands	Suppress rebellion	More than 10,000	More than 1 year	Yes
1900–1901	McKinley	China	East Asia	Int'l 3rd party	1,000– 10,000	More than 1 year	No
1901	T. Roosevelt	Colombia (Panama)	Latin America	Protect lives/ interests	Unknown	0–2 mos.	Yes

Year	President	Country	Region	Purpose	Forces	Duration	
1902	T. Roosevelt	Colombia (Panama)	Latin America	Protect lives/interests	Unknown	3–12 mos.	No
1903	T. Roosevelt	Honduras	Latin America	Protect lives/interests	Unknown	0–2 mos.	No
1903	T. Roosevelt	Dominican Rep.	Latin America	Protect lives/interests	Fewer than 100	0–2 mos.	No
1903–1904	T. Roosevelt	Syria	Other	Protect lives/interests	Unknown	0–2 mos.	No
1903	T. Roosevelt	Panama	Latin America	Protect lives/interests	Unknown	0–2 mos.	Yes
1903–1904	T. Roosevelt	Abyssinia	Other	Protect lives/interests	Fewer than 100	0–2 mos.	No
1904	T. Roosevelt	Dominican Rep.	Latin America	Protect lives/interests	100–1,000	0–2 mos.	No
1904	T. Roosevelt	Morocco	Other	Protect lives/interests	Unknown	0–2 mos.	No
1904	T. Roosevelt	Panama	Latin America	Protect lives/interests	Unknown	0–2 mos.	Yes
1904–1905	T. Roosevelt	Korea	East Asia	Protect lives/interests	100–1,000	More than 1 year	No
1905–1907	T. Roosevelt	Dominican Rep.	Latin America	Control/protectorate	Unknown	More than 1 year	No
1906–1909	T. Roosevelt/Taft	Cuba	Caribbean	Protect lives/interests	Unknown	More than 1 year	Yes
1907	T. Roosevelt	Honduras	Latin America	Protect lives/interests	Fewer than 100	0–2 mos.	No
1910	Taft	Nicaragua	Latin America	Protect lives/interests	100–1,000	0–2 mos.	No

Date	President	Location	Region	Reason	Size	Duration	Prior Congressional Authorization
1911	Taft	Honduras	Latin America	Protect lives/interests	Fewer than 100	0–2 mos.	No
1911–1912	Taft	China	East Asia	Protect lives/interests	Unknown	More than 1 year	Yes
1912	Taft	Panama	Latin America	Int'l 3rd party	Unknown	0–2 mos.	Yes
1912	Taft	Cuba	Caribbean	Protect lives/interests	Unknown	3–12 mos.	Yes
1912	Taft	Turkey	Other	Protect lives/interests	Unknown	0–2 mos.	No
1912	Taft	Nicaragua	Latin America	Protect lives/interests	Unknown	More than 1 year	No
1913	Wilson	China	East Asia	Protect lives/interests	1,000–10,000	More than 1 year	Yes
1913	Wilson	Mexico	Latin America	Protect lives/interests	Fewer than 100	0–2 mos.	No
1914	Wilson	Haiti	Caribbean	Protect lives/interests	Unknown	3–12 mos.	No
1914	Wilson	Dominican Rep.	Caribbean	Suppress rebellion	Unknown	0–2 mos.	No

Year	President	Location	Region	Purpose	Troops	Duration	
1914	Wilson	Mexico	Latin America	Other	Unknown	3–12 mos.	No
1915	Wilson	Dominican Rep.	Caribbean	Protect lives/interests	Unknown	0–2 mos.	No
1915–1934	Wilson	Haiti	Caribbean	Control/protectorate	Unknown	More than 1 year	No
1916–1924	Wilson	Dominican Rep.	Caribbean	Control/protectorate	1,000–10,000	More than 1 year	Yes
1916	Wilson	China	East Asia	Protect lives/interests	Unknown	0–2 mos.	Yes
1916–1917	Wilson	Mexico	Latin America	Pursue bandits	1,000–10,000	More than 1 year	No
1917	Wilson	Atlantic Ocean	Other	Other	Unknown	0–2 mos.	No
1917	Wilson	Cuba	Caribbean	Protect lives/interests	Unknown	More than 1 year	Yes
1917	Wilson	China	East Asia	Protect lives/interests	Unknown	0–2 mos.	Yes
1918–1919	Wilson	Mexico	Latin America	Pursue bandits	Unknown	More than 1 year	No
1918–1920	Wilson	Russia	Other	Int'l 3rd party	1,000–10,000	More than 1 year	No
1919	Wilson	Dalmatia	Other	Int'l 3rd party	Unknown	0–2 mos.	No
1919	Wilson	Turkey	Other	Protect lives/interests	Unknown	0–2 mos.	No

Date	President	Location	Region	Reason	Size	Duration	Prior Congressional Authorization
1918–1920	Wilson	Panama	Latin America	Int'l 3rd party	Unknown	More than 1 year	Yes
1920	Wilson	China	East Asia	Protect lives/interests	Unknown	3–12 mos.	Yes
1920	Wilson	Guatemala	Latin America	Protect lives/interests	Fewer than 100	0–2 mos.	No
1920–1922	Wilson	Siberia	Other	Protect lives/interests	Fewer than 100	More than 1 year	No

Source: Based on J. Terry Emerson, "War Powers Legislation," West Virginia Law Review 74 (1972): 53–119.

Table A.3. Breakdown of Commitment of Troops

	1881–1893		*1894–1907*		*1908–1920*		*Total*	
President	Garfield/Arthur	2	Cleveland-2	7	T. Roosevelt	0		
	Cleveland-1	4	McKinley	6	Taft	7		
	Harrison	5	T. Roosevelt	14	Wilson	22		
	Cleveland-2	0						
Region	Latin America	4	Latin America	15	Latin America	11	Latin America	30
	Caribbean Islands	2	Caribbean Islands	1	Caribbean Islands	7	Caribbean Islands	10
	Pacific Islands	2	Pacific Islands	2	Pacific Islands	0	Pacific Islands	4
	East Asia	1	East Asia	6	East Asia	5	East Asia	12
	Other	2	Other	3	Other	6	Other	11
Reason	Protect lives/interests	10	Protect lives/interests	23	Protect lives/interests	17	Protect lives/interests	50
	Pursue Mexican bandits	1	Pursue Mexican bandits	0	Pursue Mexican bandits	2	Pursue Mexican bandits	3
	Suppress rebellion	0	Suppress rebellion	2	Suppress rebellion	1	Suppress rebellion	3
	Int'l 3rd party	0	Int'l 3rd party	1	Int'l 3rd party	5	Int'l 3rd party	6
	Control/protectorate	0	Control/protectorate	1	Control/protectorate	2	Control/protectorate	3
	Other	0	Other	0	Other	2	Other	2
Size	Fewer than 100	1	Fewer than 100	4	Fewer than 100	4	Fewer than 100	9
	100–1,000	2	100–1,000	2	100–1,000	1	100–1,000	5
	1,000–10,000	0	1,000–10,000	2	1,000–10,000	4	1,000–10,000	6
	More than 10,000	0	More than 10,000	1	More than 10,000	0	More than 10,000	1
	Unknown	8	Unknown	18	Unknown	20	Unknown	46
Duration	0–2 Months	7	0–2 Months	17	0–2 Months	14	0–2 Months	38
	3–12 Months	3	3–12 Months	3	3–12 Months	4	3–12 Months	10
	More than 1 year	1	More than 1 year	7	More than 1 year	11	More than 1 year	19
Prior Congressional Authorization	Yes	3	Yes	9	Yes	10	Yes	22
	No	8	No	18	No	19	No	45
	N = 11		N = 27		N = 29		N = 67	

Source: Based on J. Terry Emerson, "War Powers Legislation," *West Virginia Law Review 74* (1972): 53–119.

Table A.4. Administrative Organizations Created or
Elevated by Law, 1881–1920

Year	President	Agency	Created/Elevated
1882	Arthur	Secret Service	C
1883	Arthur	Civil Service Commission	C
1884	Arthur	Bureau of Animal Industry	C
1884	Arthur	Bureau of Labor	C
1884	Arthur	Bureau of Navigation	C
1884	Arthur	Division of Island Waterways	C
1887	Cleveland	Division of Ornithology and Entomology	C
1887	Cleveland	Interstate Commerce Commission	C
1888	Cleveland	Board of Ordnance and Fortification	C
1888	Cleveland	Department of Labor	E
1889	Harrison	Bureau of Appointments	C
1889	Harrison	Department of Agriculture	E
1890	Harrison	Division of Publications	E
1890	Harrison	United States Weather Bureau	C
1891	Harrison	Bureau of Immigration	C
1892	Cleveland	Record and Pension Office	E
1893	Cleveland	Office of Road Inquiries	C
1897	McKinley	Copyright Office	C
1898	McKinley	Industrial Commission	C
1901	Roosevelt	Bureau of Chemistry	E
1901	Roosevelt	Bureau of Forestry	E
1901	Roosevelt	Bureau of Plant Industry	C
1901	Roosevelt	Bureau of Soils	E
1901	Roosevelt	National Bureau of Standards	E
1902	Roosevelt	Bureau of Insular Affairs	E
1902	Roosevelt	Bureau of the Census	E

Year	President	Agency	Created/ Elevated*
1902	Roosevelt	Bureau on Insular and Territorial Affairs	C
1902	Roosevelt	Reclamation Service	C
1903	Roosevelt	Bureau of Corporations	C
1903	Roosevelt	Bureau of Entomology	E
1903	Roosevelt	Bureau of Fisheries	E
1903	Roosevelt	Bureau of Manufactures	C
1903	Roosevelt	Bureau of Statistics	E
1903	Roosevelt	Bureau of Trade Relations	C
1903	Roosevelt	Department of Commerce and Labor	C
1903	Roosevelt	Passport Bureau	E
1905	Roosevelt	Bureau of Biological Survey	E
1907	Roosevelt	Bureau of Reclamation	E
1908	Roosevelt	Bureau of Investigation	C
1910	Taft	Bureau of Lighthouses	C
1910	Taft	Bureau of Mines	C
1910	Taft	Commission on Fine Arts	C
1910	Taft	Division of Far Eastern Affairs	C
1910	Taft	Division of Information	C
1910	Taft	Division of Latin American Affairs	C
1910	Taft	Division of Near Eastern Affairs	C
1910	Taft	Division of Western Affairs	C
1910	Taft	Workmen's Compensation Commission	C
1911	Taft	National Forest Regulation Commission	C
1911	Taft	President's Commission on Economy and Efficiency	C
1912	Taft	Children's Bureau	C
1912	Taft	Commission on Industrial Relations	C

Year	President	Agency	Created/Elevated*
1913	Wilson	Board of Mediation and Conciliation	C
1913	Wilson	Department of Commerce	C
1913	Wilson	Department of Labor	C
1913	Wilson	Federal Reserve Board	C
1913	Wilson	Rock Creek and Potomac Parkway Commission	C
1914	Wilson	Bureau of War Risk Management	C
1914	Wilson	Federal Trade Commission	C
1915	Wilson	Coast Guard	C
1915	Wilson	Naval Advisory Committee for Aeronautics	C
1916	Wilson	Council of National Defense	C
1916	Wilson	Bureau of Efficiency	E
1916	Wilson	Federal Farm Loan Board	C
1916	Wilson	Federal Farm Loan Bureau	C
1916	Wilson	Militia Bureau	C
1916	Wilson	National Park Service	E
1916	Wilson	Shipping Board	C
1916	Wilson	Tariff Commission	C
1916	Wilson	U.S. Employees' Compensation Commission	C
1917	Wilson	Aircraft Production Board	C
1917	Wilson	Federal Board for Vocational Education	C
1917	Wilson	General Munitions Board	C
1917	Wilson	War Industries Board	C
1918	Wilson	Air Service	E
1918	Wilson	Interdepartmental Social Hygiene Board	C

Year	President	Agency	Created/Elevated*
1918	Wilson	Commission for Standardization of Screw Threads	C
1918	Wilson	War Finance Corporation	C
1918	Wilson	War Labor Administration	C
1919	Wilson	Public Buildings Commission	C
1920	Wilson	Federal Power Commission	C
1920	Wilson	Railroad Labor Board	C
1920	Wilson	Women's Bureau	C

Source: Compiled from Lloyd M. Short, The Development of National Administrative Organization in the United States; Donald R. Whitney, ed, Government Agencies; and the author's own research.

* "C" means that the administrative agency was created. "E" means that the agency was elevated.

Table A.5. Congressional Activity on the Tariff, 1881–1920

President	Congress	Laws and Resolutions	Senate Bills	Senate Resolutions	House Bills	House Resolutions	Concurrent Resolutions	Senate Joint Resolution	House Joint Resolution	HR Report
Garfield/ Arthur	47	3	16	0	79	5	1			
Arthur	48	0	12	1	86	2				1
Cleveland	49	3	14	11	87	5				
Cleveland	50	1	14	1	99	8				
Harrison	51	5	8	7	72	7				
Harrison	52	2	6	0	151	7				
Cleveland	53	4	9	4	87	2				
Cleveland	54	1	3	2	5	1				
McKinley	55	5	9	4	23	5				
McKinley	56	2	5	1	34	0			4	
Roosevelt	57	3	12	3	70	1			4	
Roosevelt	58	3	10	0	57	2				
Roosevelt	59	0	5	0	77	0				
Roosevelt	60	1	10	3	119	5			1	
Taft	61	4	8	0	62	0		2	4	
Taft	62	3	8	0	99	0				
Wilson	63	2	10	0	29	0		1	1	
Wilson	64	6	10	0	25	0				
Wilson	65	0	4	0	8	0				
Wilson	66	0	7	0	52	0			3	
		48	180	37	1321	50	1	3	17	1

Source: Compiled by author from *Congressional Record*.

Table A.6. Tariff Laws and Resolutions, 1881–1920

President	Congress	Session	Bill Number	Law #	Bill Title	Additional Notes
Arthur	47	1	H.R. 4680	Public law Ch. 120	To repeal discriminating duties on tea and coffee, the products of the possessions of the Netherlands	
Arthur	47	2	H.R. 6187	Public law Ch. 6	To amend the act titled "An act to repeal discriminating duties on goods produced east of the Cape of Good Hope," approved May 4, 1882	Amended act is H.R. 4680 (listed above)
Arthur	47	2	H.R. 5538	Public law Ch. 121	To reduce internal taxation	
Cleveland	49	2	H.R. 7860	Public law Ch. 215	To amend an act titled "An act to amend the statutes in relation to the immediate transportation of dutiable goods, and for other purposes," approved June 10, 1880	
Cleveland	49	2	H.R. 8923	Public law Ch. 123	To amend an act in relation to the immediate transportation of dutiable goods, and for other purposes, approved June 10, 1880	
Cleveland	49	2	H.R. 9653	Public law Ch. 221	To amend section 3058 of the Revised Statutes	
Cleveland	50	1	S. 1564	Public law Ch. 56	For the relief of importers of animals for breeding purposes in certain cases	
Harrison	51	1	H.R. 9416	Public law Ch. 1244	To reduce the revenue and equalize duties on imports, and for other purposes	
Harrison	51	1	H.R. 4970	Public law Ch. 407	To simplify the laws in relation to the collection of revenues	
Harrison	51	1	H.R. 584	Public law Ch. 13	To modify existing laws relating to duties on imports and the collection of revenue	

President	Congress	Session	Bill Number	Law #	Bill Title	Additional Notes
Harrison	51	1	H.R. 9548	Public law Ch. 200	Providing for the classification of worsted cloths as woolens	
Harrison	51	2	H.Res. 251	Res. 11	To correct an error of punctuation in the tariff act of 1890	House Joint Resolution
Harrison	52	2	S. 1831	Public law Ch. 29	To admit free of duty the wreckage of the ships USS *Trenton* and USS *Vandalia*, presented by the United States to the king of Samoa	
Harrison	52	2	H.R. 10351	Public law Ch. 216	To continue the duties on certain manufactures of flax at the rate now provided by law	
Cleveland	53	1	H.Res. 22	Res. 14	To amend the act approved April 25, 1890, relating to the admission of articles intended for the World's Columbian Exposition	House Joint Resolution; purpose of original act was to provide for exposition
Cleveland	53	2	H.R. 4864	Public law Ch. 349	An act to reduce taxation, to provide revenue for the government, and for other purposes	Bill became law without president's signature
Cleveland	53	2	H.R. 7753	Public law Ch. 201	To exempt articles of foreign exhibitors at the interstate commerce fair at Tacoma, Wash., from payment of duties	
Cleveland	53	3	S. 2353	Public law Ch. 20	To exempt articles of foreign exhibitors at the Portland Universal Exposition, at Portland, Ore., from payment of duties	

Cleveland	54	H.Res. 239	2	Res. 18	Admitting free of duty needlework and similar articles imported by the New York Association of Sewing Schools for exhibition purposes	House Joint Resolution
McKinley	55	H.R. 379	1	Public law Ch. 11	To provide revenue for the government and to encourage the industries of the United States	
McKinley	55	H.R. 3941	1	Public law Ch. 3	To authorize the president to suspend discriminating duties imposed on foreign vessels and commerce	
McKinley	55	H.Res. 182	2	Res. 19	Providing the temporary admission free of duty of naval and military supplies procured abroad	House Joint Resolution
McKinley	55	H.R. 7271	3	Public law Ch. 454	Amending the act titled "An act to allow the return free of duty certain articles exported from the United States for exhibition purposes," approved May 18, 1896	Purpose of original act was to provide for exposition
McKinley	55	H.R. 10398	3	Public law Ch. 157	Providing for the entry, free of customs duties, of certain bells presented by Edwin M. Stanton to the Iowa Agricultural College, Ames, Iowa	
McKinley	56	H.R. 3334	1	Public law Ch. 487	To amend section 3005 of the Revised Statutes of the United States	
McKinley	56	H. Joint Res. 74	2	Res. 11	Authorizing articles imported from foreign countries for the sole purpose of exhibition at the San Antonio International Fair and at the Texas State Fair and Dallas Exposition, to be held in the cities of San Antonio, Tex., and Dallas, Tex., to be imported free of duty, under regulations prescribed by the secretary of the treasury	House Joint Resolution

President	Congress	Session	Bill Number	Law #	Bill Title	Additional Notes
Roosevelt	57	2	H.R. 16649	Public law Ch. 189	To provide rebate of duties on coal, and for other purposes	
Roosevelt	57	2	H.R. 15155	Public law Ch. 1016	To refund the amount of duties paid on merchandise brought into the United States from Porto Rico between April 11, 1899, and May 1, 1900, and also on merchandise brought into the United States from the Philippine Islands between April 11, 1899, and March 8, 1902, and for other purposes	
Roosevelt	57	2	H.R. 15794	Public law Ch. 1	To amend section 20 of an act titled "An act to simplify the laws in relation to the collection of the revenues," approved June 10, 1890	
Roosevelt	58	2	H.R. 9658	Public law Ch. 949	To provide for the withdrawal, free of duty under bond, from the Louisiana Purchase Exposition of any duty articles and materials donated to incorporated institutions established for religious, philosophical, educational, scientific, or literary purposes, or to any state or municipal corporation	
Roosevelt	58	2	H.R. 11135	Public law Ch. 1818	Amending an act approved March 3, 1901, titled "An act to provide for celebrating the one-hundredth anniversary of the purchase of the Louisiana Territory by the United States, by holding an international exhibition of arts, industries, manufactures, and the products of the soil, mine, forest, and sea in the city of St. Louis, in the State of Missouri	Purpose of original act was to provide for exhibition

President	Congress	Session	Bill	Public law	Description
Roosevelt	58	3	H.R. 17102	Public law #180	To extend the time within which action for the recovery of duties paid in Porto Rico may be brought in the Court of Claims under the act of April 29, 1902
Roosevelt	60	1	H.R. 17506	Public law #146	To amend an act titled "An act to simplify the laws in relation to the collection of the revenues," approved June 10, 1890, as amended by the act titled "An act to provide revenues for the government and to encourage the industries of the United States," approved July 24, 1897
Taft	61	1	H.R. 1438	Public law #5	To provide revenue, equalize duties, and encourage the industries of the United States, and for other purposes
Taft	61	2	S. 4639	Public law #78	Concerning tonnage duties on vessels entering otherwise than by sea
Taft	61	3	H.R. 30570	Public law #440	To authorize the receipt of certified checks drawn on national and state banks for duties on imports and internal taxes, and for other purposes
Taft	61	3	H.R. 30281	Public law #514	To provide for the entry under bond of exhibits or arts, sciences, and industries
Taft	62	1	H.R. 13679	Public law #4	To amend an act titled "An act to authorize the receipt of certified checks drawn on national and state banks for duties on imports and internal taxes, and for other purposes," approved March 2, 1911

President	Congress	Session	Bill Number	Law #	Bill Title	Additional Notes
Taft	62	3	H.R. 24703	Public law #421	To extend the authority to receive certified checks drawn on national and state banks and trust companies in payment for duties on imports and internal taxes and all public dues	
Taft	62	3	H.R. 12813	Public law #362	To refund duties collected on lace-making and other machines and parts or accessories thereof imported after August 5, 1909, and before January 1, 1911	
Wilson	63	1	H.R. 3321	Public law #16	To reduce tariff duties and to provide revenue for the government, and for other purposes	
Wilson	63	1	H.R. 7595	Public law #14	Providing for the free importation of articles intended for foreign buildings and exhibits at the Panama-Pacific International Exposition, and for the protection of foreign exhibitors	
Wilson	64	1	H.R. 16763	Public law #271	To increase the revenue, and for other purposes	
Wilson	64	1	H.R. 2184	Private law #68	Providing for the refund of certain additional duties collected on pineapples	Private law

Wilson	64	1	H.R. 11471	Public law #61	To amend paragraphs 177 and 178 of an act titled "An act to reduce tariff duties and to provide revenue for the Government, and for other purposes," approved October 3, 1913, relating to the duty of sugar, molasses, and other articles
Wilson	64	1	H.R. 7256	Private law #57	Providing for the refund of duties collected on certain tobacco cuttings
Wilson	64	2	H.R. 9288	Private law #203	Providing for the refund of certain duties illegally levied and collected on acetate of lime
Wilson	64	2	S. 4384	Private law #216	Providing for the refund of duties collected on flax-preparatory machines, parts, and accessories imported after August 5, 1909, and before January 1, 1911

Source: Compiled by author from *Congressional Record*.

Notes

CHAPTER 1

1. Jefferson's statement recognizing the need for institutional development, inscribed in one of the walls at the Jefferson Memorial, is originally from a letter to Samuel Kercheval dated July 12, 1816. In Merrill D. Peterson, ed., *Thomas Jefferson: Writings,* 559.

2. See Corwin, *The President: Office and Powers, 1787–1957: History and Analysis of Practice and Opinion.*

3. See Thurber, "An Introduction to Presidential-congressional Rivalry."

4. The concept of coordinated scripts used here is akin to the idea of framing as used in a sociological perspective. Under this approach, a frame can be defined as "[a]n interpretive schemata [*sic*] that simplifies and condenses the 'world out there' by selectively punctuating and encoding objects, situations, events, experiences, and sequences of actions within one's present or past environment. . . . [T]hey also function simultaneously as modes of attribution and articulation" (Snow and Benford, "Master Frames and Cycles of Protest," 137). For an example of a work that employs framing in this manner, see Pellow, "Framing Emerging Environmental Movement Tactics: Mobilizing Consensus, Demobilizing Conflict."

5. For a review of the "Grammar of Institutions" see Sue E. S. Crawford and Elinor Ostrom, "A Grammar of Institutions." They base their grammar on a "view that institutions are enduring regularities of human action in situations structured by rules, norms, and shared strategies, as well as by the physical world. The rules, norms, and shared strategies are constituted and reconstituted by human interaction in frequently occurring or repetitive situations" (582).

6. One recognition of this change is found in the words of Herbert Storing, who said in 1974, "the presidency is a creature of the Constitution, it is an office established by the Constitution; yet today's presidency is—or seems to be—a threat to that Constitution" (in Joseph M. Bessette, ed., *Toward a More Perfect Union: Essays by Herbert J. Storing,* 377).

7. For an elaboration of this line of argument, see "The Federalist No. 48," in Clinton Rossiter, ed., *The Federalist Papers.*

8. "Energy in the Executive is a leading character in the definition of good government. . . . A feeble Executive implies a feeble execution of the government. A feeble execution is but another phrase for a bad execution; and a

government ill executed, whatever it may be in theory, must be, in practice, a bad government" (ibid., "The Federalist No. 70").

9. See ibid., "The Federalist No. 48."

10. As Hamilton wrote, "The ingredients which constitute energy in the Executive are, first, unity; secondly, duration; thirdly, an adequate provision for its support; fourthly, competent powers" (ibid., "The Federalist No. 70").

11. By looking deeper at the formal institutional structure set forth in Article II, one would see that the enacting clause in the article leaves the presidency the ability to grow beyond what the Constitution states. This growth potential becomes even more apparent when this language is contrasted with the enacting clause for Congress in Article I, which states that "all legislative power *herein granted* shall be vested in a Congress of the United States" (emphasis added). Such language made Congress not only the more fully developed and powerful institution at the founding by explicitly enumerating its powers but also the more constrained for growth vis-à-vis the presidency. Scholars have noted how the institution of the presidency was granted limited powers when created (see, e.g., Genovese, *The Presidential Dilemma: Leadership in the American System,* 28), yet has transformed into what has been called the most powerful office in the world (see, e.g., McDonald, *The American Presidency: An Intellectual History,* 1).

12. See, for example, Neustadt's classic work, *Presidential Power and the Modern Presidents: The Politics of Leadership from Roosevelt to Reagan,* in which his primary concern is power relationships between presidents and other political actors. He has expressed his interest in presidential influence and what the president can "accomplish to improve the prospect that he will have influence when he wants it" (4). His perspective of presidential power has become nearly synonymous with the "personal presidency."

13. Theodore J. Lowi, "Foreword: Political History and Political Science," ix.

14. Scholars of political development have utilized numerous approaches to political change, including the functional, cultural, decision-making, and leadership approaches. See Almond, "Approaches to a Developmental Causation."

15. Periodization refers to "a constructive or a postulated definition of the society-type in question, the system of its social relations, with its historically evolving requirements, capacities, patterns of authority, and structures of power, in its general historical formation and in its more historically specific circumstances and stage of evolution" (Martin J. Sklar, *The United States as a Developing Country: Studies in U.S. History in the Progressive Era and the 1920s,* 2). See chapter 1, "Periodization and Historiography," generally. See also Jillson, "Patterns and Periodicity in American National Politics."

16. See, for example, Sidney M. Milkis, *The President and the Parties.*

17. See Stephen Skowronek, *The Politics Presidents Make: Leadership from John Adams to George Bush.* He notes that "this repeated pairing of dismal failure with stunning success is one of the more striking patterns in presidential history" (8).

18. Examples of prominent studies that have sought to examine the president's power relationships in different settings include Fred I. Greenstein's analysis of President Eisenhower's "hidden-hand" leadership (a "style that explicitly departed from the emphasis of most presidents since Franklin D. Roosevelt on establishing what Neustadt calls professional reputation"), which examines the president's personal influence, which stemmed from this style (Greenstein, *The Hidden-hand Presidency: Eisenhower as Leader,* 5). William Grover has studied the Carter and Reagan presidencies within a structural setting based on a political-economic theory (Grover, *The President as Prisoner: A Structural Critique of the Carter and Reagan Years*). In *Going Public: New Strategies of Presidential Leadership,* Samuel Kernell developed an institutional setting in which a president can enhance his power and achieve success by going outside those institutions. Finally, Paul Light has examined presidential behavior in a structural setting based upon electoral cycles and the president's learning curve (Light, *The President's Agenda: Domestic Policy Choice from Kennedy to Reagan*). For a different approach in utilizing power relationships while analyzing the presidency, see, for example, Moe, "The Politicized Presidency."

19. For additional discussion regarding informal powers, see, for example, Neustadt, *Presidential Power,* and Tulis's discussion in *The Rhetorical Presidency,* 9–11.

20. For example, Skowronek *(The Politics Presidents Make)* defines power as the "resources, both *formal and informal,* that presidents in a given period have at their disposal to get things done" (18; emphasis added).

21. See Clinton Rossiter, *The American Presidency,* 2. As the editor's preface for this edition states, for Rossiter, "one way of recognizing authority is to ask who gets blamed if things go wrong" (xi). See also Corwin, *The President, Office and Powers, 1787–1957,* and Pyle and Pious, *The President, Congress, and the Constitution: Power and Legitimacy in American Politics.* The formal, constitutional approach was later abandoned by those who focused on political power and used authority as their foil.

22. See Skowronek, *The Politics Presidents Make;* March and Olsen, *Rediscovering Institutions: The Organizational Basis of Politics.*

23. This example does not eliminate the ability of other actors to initiate this process of institutionalization. Congress or the courts, for example, may place certain obligations on the president. Subsequently, the president could then assert that this institutionalized shared understanding justifies the president's acting in a similar manner in the future.

24. Scholars have categorized types of leadership in a variety of ways. Perhaps the most famous is James MacGregor Burns's distinction between transactional leadership (in which "leaders approach followers with an eye to exchanging one thing for another") and transforming leadership (in which the "transforming leader looks for potential motives in followers, seeks to satisfy higher needs and engages the full person of the follower"; Burns, *Leadership,* 4). Similarly, George C. Edwards III characterizes one type of leader as a facilitator of change, who "exploits opportunities to help others go where they want to

go anyway," and a second type as a director of change, who "creates opportunities to move in new directions, leading others where they otherwise would not go" ("Presidential Leadership of Congress: The Role of Legislative Skills," 214). Bruce Miroff sets out four types of leadership: aristocratic, democratic, heroic, and dissenting (*Icons of Democracy: American Leaders as Heroes, Aristocrats, Dissenters, and Democrats*).

25. For an argument that political change "arises out of 'friction' among mismatched institutional and ideational patterns," see Robert C. Lieberman, "Ideas, Institutions, and Political Order: Explaining Political Change."

26. Under a strictly constitutional view of authority, the Founders can be considered the most politically important people in the nation at any time because they are the ones who defined "what constitutes a legitimate exercise of governmental authority" (Pyle and Pious, *The President, Congress, and the Constitution*, xx). Such a conception of authority, however, neither incorporates nor explains the growth of the informal institutions of authority discussed here.

27. For a discussion of sequencing and the interaction between rigid, embedded structures and the more fluid elements of politics, see Robert Jervis, *System Effects: Complexity in Political and Social Life*.

28. Karen Orren and Stephen Skowronek, "Beyond the Iconography of Order: Notes for a 'New Institutionalism.'"

29. For the importance of understanding informal institutions, see Helmke and Levitsky, "Informal Institutions and Comparative Politics."

30. Opportunity structures were also available for Congress, as mentioned elsewhere in this text.

31. Peri Arnold discusses the "interplay between the behavior of individual incumbents and the routines of institutionalization" ("The Institutionalized Presidency and the American Regime," 216).

32. Norms have been defined as "problem-solving devices for dealing with the recurrent issues of social life: conflict and cooperation" (Kratochwil, *Rules, Norms, and Decisions: On the Conditions of Practical and Legal Reasoning in International Relations and Domestic Affairs*, 69). With this definition, norms can be considered devoid of any moral, prescriptive component, which is sometimes associated with the concept. Instead, norms are predictions of current and future behavior. "Institutionalized norms express a world view that influences behavior not only directly, by setting standards of appropriateness for behavior, but also indirectly, through selective prefabricated links between values that individuals or collectivities habitually rely upon to address specific problems" (Katzenstein, "Coping with Terrorism: Norms and Internal Security in Germany and Japan," 267). Furthermore, Katzenstein argues that institutionalized norms become part of the collective consciousness that "creates habits of interpretation and repertoires of action" and that they "can be violated by behavior; but they cannot be invalidated" (ibid., 268).

33. Norms reflect the pattern of actions or behaviors "that will be reproduced, without requiring recurrent mobilization to secure such reproduction"

(Jepperson, "Institutions, Institutional Effects, and Institutionalism," 145). For a review of the larger debate surrounding the use and definition of norms in political science, sociology, and psychology, see authors such as Robert Axelrod ("An Evolutionary Approach to Norms"); Barry R. Weingast ("A Rational Choice Perspective of Congressional Norms"); Herbert B. Asher ("The Learning of Legislative Norms"); David W. Rohde, Norman J. Ornstein, and Robert L. Peabody ("Political Change and Legislative Norms in the U.S. Senate, 1957–1974"); Jon Elster *(The Cement of Society: A Study of Social Order);* Richard DeRidder and Rama C. Tripathi, eds. *(Norm Violation and Intergroup Relations);* and Jack Bilmes *(Discourse and Behavior).*

34. This idea is similar to Arthur L. Stinchcombe's "historical causes" or, in his words, "a historicist explanation . . . is one in which an *effect* created by causes at some previous period *becomes a cause of that same effect* in succeeding periods (Stinchcombe, *Constructing Social Theories,* 103; emphasis in the original). See also John C. Harsanyi, "Explanation and Comparative Dynamics in Social Science"; Robert Jervis, "Timing and Interaction in Politics: A Comment on Pierson"; and Stanley Lieberson, *Making It Count: The Improvement of Social Research and Theory.*

35. See Elisabeth Clemens and James M. Cook for a discussion of "Institutions as Eliminating Alternatives" ("Politics and Institutionalism: Explaining Durability and Change," 458–59).

36. In Douglass C. North's words, "At every step along the way there were choices—political and economic—that provided real alternatives. Path dependence is a way to narrow conceptually the choice set and link decision making through time. It is not a story of inevitability in which the past neatly predicts the future" (*Institutions, Institutional Change, and Economic Performance,* 98–99).

37. Paul Pierson states, "Long movement down a particular path will have increased the costs of switching to some previously foregone alternative" (*Politics in Time: History, Institutions, and Social Analysis,* 41).

38. Presidents may push against these boundaries but must be careful not to break outside them. Such parameters surrounding leadership are important for the U.S. political system, for the system "need[s] leadership, but if [it is] to remain constitutional [it] also need[s] limits on leadership" (Bert A. Rockman, *The Leadership Question: The Presidency and the American System,* 1).

39. For relevant works exploring related issues or themes during parts or all of this time period, see, for example, Stephen Skowronek, *Building a New American State: The Expansion of National Administrative Capacities, 1877–1920;* Morton Keller, *Affairs of State: Public Life in Late Nineteenth-century America;* Joel H. Silbey, *The American Political Nation, 1838–1893;* Pamela S. Tolbert and Lynne G. Zucker, "Institutional Sources of Change in the Formal Structure of Organizations: The Diffusion of Civil Service Reform, 1880–1935"; and Alexander Keyssar, *The Right to Vote: The Contested History of Democracy in the United States.*

40. Woodrow Wilson called the 1880s a time of congressional government (Wilson, *Congressional Government: A Study in American Politics*).

41. See Nelson C. Polsby, "The Institutionalization of the House of Representatives"; and Schickler, *Disjointed Pluralism: Institutional Innovation and the Development of the U.S. Congress*.

42. See Skowronek, *Building a New American State*.

43. See Michael E. McGerr, *The Decline of Popular Politics: The American North, 1865–1928*.

44. See Sidney M. Milkis and Michael Nelson, who state that "what marked the twentieth-century transformation of the executive was the emergence of the president, rather than Congress or the party organizations, as the leading instrument of popular rule" (*The American Presidency: Origins and Development, 1776–1990*, 259).

45. "The ingredients which constitute energy in the Executive are, first, unity; secondly, duration; thirdly, an adequate provision for its support; fourthly, competent powers" (Rossiter, ed., *Federalist Papers*, "The Federalist No. 70," 392).

46. Note that authority within each policy area does not lie exclusively with one institution (e.g., authority in the domestic realm does not lie exclusively with Congress); instead, authority within each policy area can be seen as tending toward one institution rather than another.

47. Robert Zevin, "An Interpretation of American Imperialism."

48. Morton Keller, *Regulating a New Economy: Public Policy and Economic Change in America, 1900–1933*.

49. Skowronek, *Building a New American State*.

50. These potential interactions were identified by doing a subject search of each policy area within the *Congressional Record* index, James D. Richardson's *Compilation of the Messages and Papers of the Presidents*, a collection of executive orders, as well as supplemental information compiled from secondary sources.

51. Another example of a behavioral norm (outside the legislative arena) that developed during the first part of the twentieth century that still exists today is what may seem to be the insignificant practice of the president's throwing out the first pitch on opening day of each baseball season. William Howard Taft, a big fan of baseball, started this practice, and through the years it has come to be expected that the incumbent president will continue to do so. President Clinton's refusal to throw out the first pitch on opening day of the 1995 season if the baseball club owners used replacement players in lieu of the striking major leaguers shows the significance that has developed around this practice. What may seem to be a small gesture can be viewed as the president's purposely violating a behavioral norm of the institution to sanction the baseball club owners for making a business decision with which he disagreed. Given that the president had no authority to otherwise intervene in the strike (see *Youngstown Sheet and Tubing Co. v. Sawyer*), Clinton utilized the most effective tool he had to reflect his position. Only when the baseball players ended their strike did Clinton back off his stance as well.

52. The codification of such shared understandings, like public policies generally, "place[s] extensive, legally binding constraints on behavior." Moreover, "public policies represent very substantial extensions of political authority that further the incentives and resources of political actors—often dramatically (Pierson, *Politics in Time*, 34 and 150, respectively).

53. Single case studies are ill suited for demonstrating change and typically show little variation within the case (Dietrich Rueschemeyer, Evelyne Huber Stephens, and John D. Stephens, *Capitalist Development and Democracy*).

54. "If two or more cases are shown to support the same theory, replication may be claimed. The empirical results may be considered yet more potent if two or more cases support the same theory but do not support an equally plausible, rival theory" (Robert K. Yin, *Case Study Research: Design and Methods*, 38).

55. My reasoning here is similar to Stinchcombe's argument, in which he states that "the central operation for building theories of history is seeking causally significant analogies between instances" (Arthur L. Stinchcombe, *Theoretical Methods in Social History*, 7).

56. For example, a decision that would maximize the comparability of a set of cases but that limited their significance and/or sustained nature would be inappropriate for this study. In other words, the goal is to develop a set of cases that is strongly rooted in all of the criteria, which will result in improving the analytic generalization that can be drawn from the cases.

57. Related to the issue of other possible cases for study is the question of potential rival hypotheses. As Yin states, to have the strongest possible findings from the case studies, one needs to be able to show that another theory could not explain them. Another benefit of the established case selection process is that it can be used as a means of controlling for randomness and can thus enhance the chance that a rival theory does not explain the cases better. To extend this point, rival theories could be based on other factors such as the changes in the president, members of Congress, and institutional factors of Congress. Another possibility may be that patterned behavior based on coordinated scripting is not exhibited during this era. If the empirical results of the case studies, however, provide evidence of patterned behaviors in the midst of the random variables that cannot be controlled, then that would provide substantial support for the theory developed earlier.

58. See, for example, *Bas v. Tingy,* which dealt with Pres. John Adams's committing troops without a declaration of war; *Talbot v. Seeman,* in which the Supreme Court decided that Congress may authorize general hostilities or a partial war; *Martin v. Mott;* the Prize Cases; and the Protector.

CHAPTER 2

1. The avoidance of entangling alliances refers to this as the United States' "traditional insistence upon complete freedom of action that rigidly barred any

international commitments binding for the future." See Foster Rhea Dulles, *The Imperial Years,* viii. Dulles also refers to this era as a struggle between "isolationism and internationalism" (ibid.). This dichotomy, however, misses the point that the United States pursued expansionist policies throughout much of the nineteenth century (e.g., the Mexican War). The nation was "isolationist" in the sense that it avoided conflict or alliances with major European powers.

2. Richardson, ed., *A Compilation,* 4886.

3. William Appleman Williams, *The Tragedy of American Diplomacy,* 16. For more on the "white man's burden," as this responsibility has been called, see the speech made by Sen. Henry Cabot Lodge (R-MA) in the Senate on Mar. 7, 1900 (U.S. Congress, *Congressional Record,* 56th Cong., 1st sess., 2617–30); and Fred Harvey Harrington, "The New World Power." See also Ernest R. May, *Imperial Democracy: The Emergence of America as a Great Power,* 8–9.

4. Harrington, "New World Power," 500.

5. U.S. Congress, *Congressional Record,* 56th Congress, 1st sess., Mar. 7, 1900, 2629.

6. See Harrington, "New World Power," 491.

7. Williams, *Tragedy of American Diplomacy,* 29. Williams also notes that "the generalization about the relationship between expansion, democracy, and prosperity became well-known as the frontier thesis advanced by Frederick Jackson Turner in 1893" (ibid., 28). He also states that similar theories were put forth by people such as Brooks Adams and William Graham Sumner.

8. Harrington, "New World Power," 508.

9. Consider, for example, one of the most significant efforts by the government to promote and protect trade: the desire to build an interoceanic canal to improve shipping. A shortcut from the Atlantic to the Pacific Ocean could have reduced shipping time by a third, as compared to a trip around the southern tip of South America. The primary obstacle to the nation's desire to build a canal, however, was the Clayton-Bulwer Treaty between the United States and Britain. This treaty, signed in 1850, provided that neither country could exercise exclusive control over a canal route through Latin America.

Those who wished to see a canal built viewed Clayton-Bulwer as contrary to the Monroe Doctrine. Finally, in December 1884, Chester Arthur's secretary of state, Frederick Frelinghuysen, disregarded Clayton-Bulwer and signed a treaty with Nicaragua that provided the United States the exclusive right to build a canal jointly owned with Nicaragua. This agreement also established a permanent alliance and a guarantee of protection of Nicaragua by the United States. The Senate narrowly rejected the treaty in January 1885 but then moved to reconsider it shortly thereafter. When Grover Cleveland took office in March 1885, however, he withdrew the agreement on the grounds that no one nation should hold the power that would be imparted by the canal and the treaty. The development of an interoceanic canal, however, remained on the political agenda into the time when Theodore Roosevelt became president. When a carefully planned revolution broke out in Panama against Colombian rule, it reportedly had the implicit support of Roosevelt, who saw it as a means to obtain canal rights through Panama. The involvement of the United States in the revolution saw U.S. troops both seizing the Panamanian railroad in an effort to keep transit free and keeping Colombian troops from landing in the country. The subsequent treaty that was negotiated provided for the United States to receive control over a ten-mile-wide canal zone and to guarantee Panamanian independence.

10. As one example of the connection between economic expansion and U.S. foreign policy, President Taft undertook a policy known as Dollar Diplomacy, which sought to open China for U.S. investments. Although the policy promoted economic expansionism, it did not involve the use of the military in any significant way. However, when Dollar Diplomacy was implemented in Latin America and the Caribbean, where the interests and role of the United States were more defined, it at times included a military component. In this region, Dollar Diplomacy added to previous policies that would block European intervention and provide stability to the region, while also providing opportunities for U.S. investors.

The most significant incident involving U.S. intervention in Latin America pursuant to Dollar Diplomacy occurred in Nicaragua. After a revolution led to the resignation of dictator José Santos Zelaya, who was anti-American and had financed the country's debt through a European syndicate, Secretary of State Knox negotiated a convention with the new Nicaraguan president that would have made Nicaragua a protectorate. This convention, however, was never brought to a final vote in the U.S. Senate. The Committee on Foreign Relations failed to report the treaty to the full body. The terms of the agreement, however, were implemented before the Senate acted on it (See W. Stull Holt, *Treaties Defeated by the Senate: A Study of the Struggle between President and Senate over the Conduct of Foreign Relations,* 238). After another revolt broke out in 1912, the United States, at the request of the Nicaraguan president, intervened militarily to protect U.S. interests. Another treaty that would have assisted Nicaragua financially was also not considered by the Senate (see Robert D. Schulzinger, *American Diplomacy in the Twentieth Century,* 45–49). Taft experienced similar difficulties with the Senate's refusal to consider a treaty providing a loan to Honduras to protect it from British creditors. One problem with Dollar Diplomacy was its lack of support within both the United States and Latin America. Although Dollar Diplomacy was not supported as a policy, Taft's behavior (i.e., the financial and military intervention) was not widely questioned.

When Woodrow Wilson took office, he denounced Dollar Diplomacy, at least verbally. His policy toward Latin America and the Caribbean was one along the lines of missionary diplomacy, in which the United States, out of a sense of moral superiority, sought to build a spiritual union in Pan America (see Alexander DeConde, *A History of American Foreign Policy,* vol. 1: *Growth to World Power (1700–1914),* 383; Julius W. Pratt, *Challenge and Rejection:*

The United States and World Leadership, 1900–1921, 85; and Williams, *Tragedy of American Diplomacy,* 53). Although different in motivation from Dollar Diplomacy, Wilson, under the guise of missionary diplomacy, incorporated and moved beyond Taft's behavior. For example, Wilson, through Secretary of State Bryan, negotiated another treaty with Nicaragua, which eliminated a provision that would have allowed U.S. intervention in Nicaraguan affairs. Even though the Senate agreed to the new treaty, Wilson continued to intervene virtually at will.

Decaying financial conditions and internal revolutions in the Dominican Republic and Haiti provided additional opportunities for Wilson to intervene. In both countries, a U.S. military government was established. Furthermore, in Haiti, the United States forced the Haitians to sign a treaty that gave the United States control of virtually every governmental function. This treaty passed the Senate unanimously.

11. For example, the role of the United States in establishing its interests in the Hawaiian Islands—at the expense of the native queen—emphasizes the growing influence of the expansionist and internationalist views that were becoming predominant within the United States (see May, 13–14, and DeConde, *A History of American Foreign Policy,* vol. 1, 296–302). In January 1893, the U.S. minister in Honolulu, John L. Stevens, agreed to support a small group of Americans who wished to have Hawaii annexed by the United States in their revolution attempt. Through the use of U.S. troops and threats of American strength, Stevens and the revolutionary group were able to intimidate Hawaii's Queen Liliuokalani into relinquishing control to them. Although Stevens was later criticized for his role by Harrison's secretary of state, John W. Foster; James H. Blount, whom Cleveland appointed to investigate the incident; and President Cleveland himself, Cleveland was unable to restore Hawaiian rule to the native Hawaiians. By then, U.S. expansionist interests had led the nation toward a growing international role.

The resolution of the situation with Hawaii favored those who wanted control over the islands. In 1894 the Republic of Hawaii was established, and the Cleveland administration recognized it. Making use of a clause in the 1896 Republican Party platform, McKinley pursued the annexation of Hawaii, sending a treaty to the Senate in June 1897. Hawaiian annexation received opposition internationally from Japan and domestically from those people, mostly Democrats, who opposed expansionism. The Japanese eventually backed off from their position after receiving a $75,000 payment. The antiexpansionist Democrats, however, were able initially to block the ratification of the annexation treaty. A year later, however, the United States was embroiled in the Spanish-American War, and McKinley was prepared to issue an executive decree annexing Hawaii as a war measure. Congress, "spurred on by manifest destiny and war fever," passed a joint resolution of annexation, which McKinley later approved (DeConde, *A History of American Foreign Policy,* vol. 1, 302). Similarly, McKinley reportedly declared that "We need Hawaii just as much and a great deal more than we did California. It is manifest destiny" (Charles S. Olcott, *William McKinley,* 379). The annexation provided the nation with its first major acquisition off the North American continent.

12. The six defeated treaties were with Nicaragua (1885), Mexico (1886), and Great Britain (1888, 1889, and 1897) and included the Treaty of Versailles, which ended World War I. See *Congressional Quarterly's Guide to Congress,* 293. The other treaties that the Senate caused to not be perfected were often either not voted upon at all or changed in such a way that the president did not renegotiate the new terms with the other parties. See Holt, *Treaties Defeated by the Senate.* Holt's chapter titles provide another sense of the institutional relationship between the presidency and Congress during this time. He refers to the period preceding the Spanish-American War as "A Period of Senatorial Domination" and to that between the Spanish-American War and 1920 as the Senate having "Bitter Contests with Presidents."

13. The United States and Britain negotiated an arbitration treaty, the Olney-Pauncefote Convention, in the wake of the Venezuelan boundary dispute in the 1890s. In 1899 the first Hague peace conference established a permanent court of arbitration. Theodore Roosevelt's secretary of state, John Hay, negotiated a set of ten bilateral treaties obligating the United States to utilize the Hague arbitration court under certain conditions. Yet all of these efforts met with resistance within the United States, particularly the Senate, for one or both of two reasons. First, implicit in its consideration of the Olney-Pauncefote Convention and explicit in its consideration of the Hague conference treaties, the Senate did not want the United States to forsake a policy of nonentanglement, particularly when it meant being locked into agreements with countries of which it was wary. Second, the Senate asserted that the arbitration treaties, which provided that the president would negotiate the terms and scope of an arbitration, allowed the president to bind the nation internationally without congressional approval. Thus, these agreements would force the Senate to lose what it saw as its proper control over foreign policy. As a result of the Senate's positions, the Olney-Pauncefote Convention was defeated, and the others were substantially weakened. Roosevelt, in fact, withdrew the original set of arbitration treaties. Hay's successor as secretary of state, Elihu Root, with Roosevelt's agreement, negotiated twenty-four new arbitration treaties, which included a provision that required the Senate to approve the scope of any arbitration. William Howard Taft continued Roosevelt's efforts to establish arbitration treaties and experienced a similar result. Taft's secretary of state, Philander C. Knox, negotiated broad arbitration treaties with both Britain and France that were designed to resolve disputes, even those of "national honor," through arbitration and without the use of troops. The Senate, again not wanting to forego its claim to control foreign policy, amended the agreements so as to move the decision of what was a proper, justiciable issue for arbitration from the presidency to the Senate. Taft believed that this amendment so undermined the accord that he never completed its ratification.

14. Between 1913 and 1914, Wilson's secretary of state, William Jennings Bryan, negotiated thirty "cooling-off" treaties, so named because of the provision that neither of the parties who signed a treaty and were involved in a dispute would begin military hostilities while the dispute was under investigation by an international commission. Unlike some of the arbitration treaties that preceded them, the cooling-off treaties were approved in the Senate, primarily because the United States was neither bound to the investigation committees' recommendations nor prevented from exercising any powers (merely only agreeing up front to delay any exercise of power during the cooling-off period). In other words, these treaties neither forced the United States to become entangled with another country nor required the Senate, in its view, to forsake its power and prerogative.

15. The Pan American Trade Conference was an effort to promote trade and peace within the Americas. The conference stemmed from Garfield's and Arthur's secretary of state, James Blaine. After Blaine persuaded Arthur to hold the conference and sent out invitations, Arthur replaced Blaine with Frederick Frelinghuysen, who withdrew them. In 1888, however, Congress requested that President Cleveland hold such a meeting and that he call for, among other things, uniform trade regulations to provide for free trade in the Western Hemisphere. Ironically, by the time the conference was held in 1889, Blaine had returned to the office of secretary of state under Benjamin Harrison and was elected president of the conference. Although the final work of the gathering did not result in anything significant, the underlying purpose of the conference—to design government policies and international relationships to promote a set of economic interests—reflected the expansionist interests that were becoming dominant.

16. Although Woodrow Wilson pursued interventionist policies throughout Latin America, he also promoted the idea of a Pan American league that would bring the nations in the Western Hemisphere together.

17. This also compares to an annual average of 5.85 treaties and executive agreements during the thirteen-year period that preceded the period under consideration.

18. These cases were first published in J. Terry Emerson, "War Powers Legislation." Emerson wrote that "the list includes only actual battles, landings, or evacuations. Deployments to maintain an American presence, or alerts bringing an advance state of readiness are not included, except for seven or eight incidents when the risk of war was unusually grave. No military operations known to have been subsequently disavowed or repudiated have been included. The list was prepared with the direction of U.S. Senator Barry Goldwater and is published with his consent" (ibid., Appendix, n1, 88). This list was subsequently used in the 1973 hearings of the War Powers Subcommittee of the Committee on Foreign Affairs. This list was supplemented with a database of institutional interactions as described in chapter 1.

19. Following the war, the United States occupied Cuba, with the imperial-

ist forces calling for the annexation of Cuba and the anti-imperialists pushing for a withdrawal from the island. McKinley balanced these viewpoints by seeking to establish an independent Cuba—but on American terms, which were codified in the Platt Amendment (a modification of an army appropriation bill) passed in March 1901. These terms, which were required to be embodied in a treaty between Cuba and the United States, allowed for, among other things, the withdrawal of U.S. troops. It reserved the right, however, for the United States to intervene in Cuban affairs in the future, which the United States did somewhat reluctantly in 1906. The terms set forth in the Platt Amendment were very one sided but do serve to provide an example of the United States starting to assert itself over weaker countries in the Western Hemisphere to protect and extend its interests.

20. McKinley placed Guam under the control of the U.S. Navy Department and ordered the secretary of the navy to take the necessary steps for the protection and government of the island through the issuance of Executive Order 108-A on December 23, 1898.

21. Although the possession of the Philippines appealed to the imperialist viewpoint, it also provided the basis for a significant anti-imperialist backlash. In February 1899 the Filipinos revolted against U.S. rule. The United States invested substantial resources in the conflict, including committing more than 125,000 troops. Although the United States was able to suppress the rebellion, the uprising provided a warning for those that may have been wary of increased involvement internationally; it led many to question whether the continued expansion of U.S. interests was worthwhile.

Despite this backlash, the United States maintained a presence in East Asia. For example, in 1900 McKinley contributed more than five thousand troops to an international effort to protect foreign legations in China during the Boxer Rebellion. The U.S. involvement in East Asian affairs, however, was not offensive or expansive in nature. Instead, U.S. involvement was related to protecting its limited interests in the region. In fact, of the six instances in which U.S. troops were committed to an East Asian country during the middle period from 1894 to 1907, all involved protecting American lives and property during a time of unrest. Also indicative of the United States' view toward the region, the Taft-Katsura Agreement was an informal accord in which the United States consented to stay out of Korea if Japan stayed out of the Philippines. Also relevant to the discussion of U.S. interests in the Far East is the United States' relationship with Japan as it related to their respective interests in East Asia. Throughout 1906 and 1907, tensions between the United States and Japan increased, due in part to anti-Japanese discrimination in the United States, to the point that a war between the two seemed quite probable. Theodore Roosevelt took a two-pronged course to prevent an outbreak of fighting. First, he sent a large battleship fleet on a cruise as a demonstration of U.S. military strength.

Second, Roosevelt, through Elihu Root, negotiated a very limited, five-year arbitration treaty with Japan that had the practical effect of being little more than a peace gesture. Of more importance was the Root-Takahira Agreement signed on November 30, 1908, in which the two countries agreed to respect each other's possessions in the Pacific and preserved the status quo. For the United States, the agreement was considered a diplomatic victory because, even though it appeared to have made concessions to Japan, it decreased the chance that matters of secondary importance would result in a war between the two countries.

The importance of this agreement is twofold. First, the pact was framed in such a way that the issue was not normative (i.e., whether the United States could or should have any claim to interest in East Asia) but instead portrayed as a practical consideration, in which any limited gain the United States might receive by pursuing its interests would be outweighed by an increased risk of hostilities with Japan. Second, unlike the arbitration treaties, for example, Congress was relatively quiet on the subject; the issue was resolved primarily through the president and his appointed delegate.

22. Although this opposition is sometimes considered "isolationist," another interpretation of the motives of its leaders, such as Henry Cabot Lodge, is that they did not want the League of Nations to restrict the United States' ability to intervene in the affairs of other countries.

23. See DeConde, *A History of American Foreign Policy*, vol. 2: *Global Power (1900 to the present)*, 74–75.

24. The "reasons" refer to those given by the actors involved, as reflected in Emerson's article. Even "defensive" uses of force, however, could be used more aggressively. For example, during the 1880s, U.S. forces seized Canadian ships that were capturing seals in the Bering Sea, outside the United States' traditional three-mile territorial limit. The argument was that, since the seals' breeding grounds were on U.S. territory, they were U.S. property, even if they swam beyond the three-mile territorial limit (see DeConde, *A History of American Foreign Policy*, vol. 1, 284–87). The United States later agreed to settle this dispute with Britain through arbitration. Although the United States lost its arbitration hearing, this incident reflects the fact that the government was willing to be more aggressive in pursuing the nation's perceived interests.

25. Navassa Island, Haiti, in 1891.

26. In addition to these incidents in which troops were committed, several disputes occurred in which military hostilities were avoided for various reasons. In one instance, fighting was avoided simply because a U.S. naval cruiser never caught the Chilean ship that it was tracking and was supposed to return to the United States. The ship, the *Itata*, was sent by Chilean rebels to San Diego to obtain arms. When the United States felt that the vessel violated neutrality laws, it detained the ship prior to its obtaining the weapons. After the crew regained control of the vessel from the U.S. deputy marshal on board, the *Itata* returned to Chile. President Harrison sent a cruiser after it, with the charge to return it to the United States—by force if necessary. The *Itata* returned to Chile without ever meeting up with the cruiser.

In another instance, the nation was brought to the brink of war, as President Harrison submitted a war message against Chile to Congress before Chile backed down from the confrontation and acceded to the United States' demands. In 1891 Harrison sent three warships to protect U.S. interests during the Chilean civil war. While on shore leave, U.S. sailors were beaten by a mob, and two of them were killed. Diplomatic tensions rose as Harrison demanded restitution and threatened action, which led the Chilean leader to insult the United States and the president. After Harrison issued an ultimatum on January 21, 1892, which received no response, he sent his war message to Congress on January 25. The next day, the United States received Chile's note of surrender and apology and later a $75,000 payment to the injured sailors and the relatives of those killed. Other disputes, such as Germany's restriction of U.S. pork and compensation for the killing of Italian citizens and U.S. citizens of Italian origin in New Orleans, were settled in more traditional, diplomatic ways.

27. Strictly speaking, ten were conducted to protect U.S. lives and/or interests, mostly during times of unsettled political conditions in the other country. The eleventh instance was the continuing pursuit of Mexican bandits by military forces, which occurred from 1873 to 1882.

28. Unlike his policy successes in the Dominican Republic and Haiti, Wilson continually experienced setbacks in his policy toward Mexico (see Kendrick A. Clements, *The Presidency of Woodrow Wilson*, 96–103). In early 1913, Victoriano Huerta led a military coup and took control of the country. Wilson was determined to get Huerta to allow free elections in Mexico. When these efforts failed, Wilson sent a representative to interview leaders of Huerta's rebel opposition, the Constitutionalists. While the leaders sought social and political reforms that extended beyond the reinstitution of a democratic government, they did not wish any U.S. involvement in Mexican affairs.

In April 1914, U.S. sailors were arrested in Mexico after landing in error in a prohibited area. Although the sailors were immediately released, Wilson utilized the opportunity to send a thousand marines to Veracruz, Mexico. Designed to help eventually remove Huerta from power, the intervention had an unanticipated effect in which Mexican citizens took the action as a national affront. Mexican naval cadets fought the U.S. Marines, and mobs attacked U.S. consulates. Representatives from Argentina, Brazil, and Chile moderated a mediation conference to resolve the dispute, but it fell apart because of Wilson's insistence that Huerta relinquish power. Wilson received his wish, however, as Huerta left Mexico in July 1914, although due more in part to the military success that the Constitutionalists were experiencing. Wilson withdrew all of the troops from Veracruz by the fall.

Mexico remained in a state of political chaos into 1915, but a faction of the Constitutionalists headed by Venustiano Carranza eventually gained control. When Wilson recognized Carranza's government, the leader of another faction, Pancho Villa, accused Carranza of selling out to the United States and in March 1916 led a raid on a town in New Mexico, killing eighteen Americans.

Feeling a need to retaliate, Wilson ordered Gen. John J. Pershing to lead four thousand troops into Mexico to pursue Pancho Villa. Wilson did so without requesting permission from Carranza, as Wilson thought that he would not grant it. Pershing's troops eventually numbered ten thousand, but they never did find Villa. Instead, they engaged the Mexican military in June in a battle that cost nine American and thirty Mexican lives. Looking for a way to end the hostilities, Wilson and Secretary of State Robert Lansing eventually persuaded Mexico to create a joint commission. Although the commission did not achieve much by itself, the growing tensions in Europe in early 1917 gave the United States a reason to remove all of Pershing's troops out of Mexico.

29. From the universe of events, the first step was to select those cases that were of a sufficiently sustained nature. Specifically, the events considered were those in countries that had multiple interactions with the United States that were found in more than one of the three time periods. Next, the cases were reviewed to maximize their comparability, specifically in terms of the geographic location of the foreign country; the scope and size of the events; and, probably most importantly, the policy rationale for U.S. involvement. Finally, the events were examined to select a set of cases that were significant enough to have sufficient data to permit a detailed case study of the event. Based on this process, the aforementioned set of cases was selected.

In terms of comparability, possibly the hardest criterion to meet, the U.S. intervention in each of the cases resulted from the actual or threatened intervention by a European power that would have harmed U.S. interests, particularly its economic interests, in the nation. The other two criteria, while easier to achieve, are important nonetheless. Each of these three cases is sustained, in the sense that U.S. involvement with each nation stretched beyond the particular incident in question; there was both a history and the likelihood of future interactions with each nation. Finally, each of these matters has been deemed significant by their inclusion in the secondary sources utilized to develop the history that preceded this section.

Admittedly, there may be room for someone to question the selection of these particular cases. For example, one might ask whether the cases are sufficiently comparable since the incident in Samoa had prior congressional approval, whereas the others did not. The impetus for U.S. intervention in Samoa, however, stemmed from the 1878 treaty between the United States and the Samoan monarch, which stated that the United States would protect Samoan independence "against the designs of others" (Richard E. Welch Jr., *The Presidencies of Grover Cleveland*, 167). Since this treaty provides a policy justification similar to the other two incidents (i.e., to forestall the intervention of a European nation), this potential critique regarding prior congressional authorization does not undermine the appropriateness of this case.

Another potential critique is that the two Caribbean countries fall within the traditional purview of the Monroe Doctrine, whereas Samoa does not. Since the three interventions were carried out for the same policy reason (as stated earlier), the question of the Monroe Doctrine becomes moot. Further, as asserted previously, the goal of the selection process is to produce cases to make analytic generalizations. These cases maximize the three criteria for selection and thus are sufficient for study.

30. Sen. Joseph Dolph (R-OR), *Congressional Record,* 50th Cong., 2d sess., Jan. 30, 1889, 1325.

31. Malietoa was a name or title given to Samoan kings. It was the family name of a famous chief; as such, the title belonged to the Malietoa family.

32. *Congressional Record,* 50th Cong., 2d sess., Jan. 30, 1889, 1329.

33. Document no. 78, Senate Ex. Doc. 31, 50th Cong., 2d sess.

34. Document no. 79, Senate Ex. Doc. 31, 50th Cong., 2d sess.

35. Document no. 83, Senate Ex. Doc. 31, 50th Cong., 2d sess.

36. Document no. 94, Senate Ex. Doc. 31, 50th Cong., 2d sess.

37. Britain had one vessel at Samoa throughout this period.

38. Document no. 6, Senate Ex. Doc. 68, 50th Cong., 2d sess. The original message included the "(?)" shown in the quotation.

39. Allan Nevins, ed., *Letters of Grover Cleveland, 1850–1908,* 197.

40. Richardson, ed., *A Compilation,* 5389–90.

41. Senator Morgan's concern was generally limited to the narrow issue of the nature of the treaty relationship between Germany and Samoa.

42. These members include Senators Hale (R-ME), Reagan (D-TX), Sherman (R-OH), Spooner (R-WI), Hoar (R-MA), Morgan (D-AL), Gray (D-DE), Dawes (R-MA), Hawley (R-CT), Frye (R-ME), George (D-MS), Dolph (R-OR), Evarts (R-NY), Saulsbery (D-DE), Blair (R-NH), Eutis (D-LA), Platt (R-CT), Hampton (D-SC), Cockrell (D-MO), and Call (D-FL). Furthermore, many of these senators merely asked one to three questions but did not otherwise engage in the debate.

43. *Congressional Record,* 50th Cong., 2d sess., Dec. 10, 1888, 108–109.

44. Ibid., Jan. 30, 1889, 1337.

45. Ibid., Jan. 31, 1889, 1373.

46. At the time, the Senate was debating the following appropriations item (Reagan's amendment, which was rejected, is included and shown in italics):

> For the execution of the obligations and the protection of the interests of the United States existing under the treaty between the United States and the Government of the Samoan Islands, *for the protection of the rights of American citizens in said islands and to preserve the neutrality and independence of the people thereof,* $500,000, or so much thereof as may be necessary to be expended under the direction of the President, this appropriation to be immediately available.
>
> For the survey, improvement, and occupation of the bay and harbor of Pago Pago, in the island of Tutuila, Samoa, and for the construction of the necessary wharves and buildings for such occupation, and for a coaling station therein, under the direction of the President, $100,000, this appropriation to be immediately available.

47. *Congressional Record,* 50th Cong., 2d sess., Jan. 29, 1889, 1291.

48. Ibid., Jan. 30, 1889, 1332.

49. Ibid., Jan. 31, 1889, 1375.

50. See Senate Ex. Doc. 44, 59th Cong., 1st sess., 77. Hollander's assignment was "to examine the financial condition of that Government, with particular reference to the origin, the amount, and the validity of its public indebtedness" (ibid., 1). He characterized the thirty-five-year period prior to the U.S. intervention as follows: The period from 1869 to 1887 saw the genesis of the debt; that from 1888 to 1897 was termed the decade of bond issues; and the years from 1898 to 1905 constituted the period of floating debt accumulation. For an examination of the political turmoil in the Dominican Republic during this time, see Exhibit A of Senate Ex. Doc. 44.

51. Theodore Roosevelt, *The Works of Theodore Roosevelt,* vol. 16, 257. In Roosevelt's words, "[I]n the Western Hemisphere, the United States cannot ignore its duty" (quoted in DeConde, *A History of American Foreign Policy,* vol. 1, 352).

52. In his 1904 annual message, Roosevelt acknowledged that the obligation imposed upon the United States by the Monroe Doctrine might require it to undertake an action that it would not otherwise undertake (i.e., "reluctantly").

53. Senate Ex. Doc. 5, 58th Cong., 3d sess., 2.

54. In addition, the United States could provide assistance to restore the credit and increase the civil administration of the Dominican Republic. See ibid.

55. Letter to Robert Bridges, Mar. 21, 1905, in Elting E. Morison, ed., *The Letters of Theodore Roosevelt,* vol. 5, 1142.

56. Letter to Charles Joseph Bonaparte, Sept. 4, 1905, in Morison, ed., *Letters of Theodore Roosevelt,* vol. 5, 10.

57. On Mar. 13, 1905, Secretary of State John Hay wrote Senator Cullom that "The protocol was not drawn up by the Department of State and was never seen by any of its officials until it appeared in the newspapers on January 22nd last, as given out by the Dominican officials" (Shelby M. Cullom, *Fifty Years of Public Service: Personal Recollections of Shelby M. Cullom,* 388).

58. More specifically, in mid-March 1905, the Dominican president asked Roosevelt to implement the terms of the treaty until the U.S. Senate formally acted upon it.

59. See Lewis L. Gould, *Presidency of Theodore Roosevelt,* 178.

60. Senate Ex. Doc. 5, Feb. 15, 1905, 58th Cong., 3d sess., 9.

61. Letter to William George Tiffany, Mar. 14, 1905, in Morison, ed., *Letters of Theodore Roosevelt,* vol. 5, 1139.

62. March 6, 1905, in Richardson, ed., *A Compilation,* 6950.

63. Ibid.

64. Letter to John C. Spooner, July 7, 1905, in Morison, ed., *Letters of Theodore Roosevelt,* vol. 5, 1263.

65. Letter to William Howard Taft, July 29, 1905, in ibid., 1290–91.

66. Letter to Lyman Abbot, Dec. 14, 1905, in ibid., vol. 6, 111.

67. Letter to John Hay, Mar. 30, 1905, in Morison, ed., *Letters of Theodore Roosevelt,* vol. 5, 1150. Gen. Carlos F. Morales was president of the Dominican Republic at this time.

68. Morison, ed., *Letters of Theodore Roosevelt,* vol. 5, 1156–57.

69. On Jan. 24, 1905, the Senate heatedly discussed the fact that the press broke the story of the protocol. That debate comprised more than five pages of the *Congressional Record* and included comments from eleven senators. The debate in the special session comprised more than twelve pages of the *Congressional Record,* with almost all of the deliberations occurring on March 17 and 18, 1905. All told, twelve senators participated in the debate during the special session, with Lodge, Cullom, Teller, and Morgan among the most active.

70. *Congressional Record,* 58th Cong., 2d sess., Jan. 24, 1905, 1285.

71. Ibid., 59th Cong., special sess., Mar. 18, 1905, 29.

72. Ibid., 58th Cong., 2d sess., Jan. 24, 1905, 1288.

73. Sen. Shelby Cullom, ibid.

74. *Congressional Record,* 59th Cong., special sess., Mar. 18, 1905, 28.

75. Ibid., 30.

76. Ibid.

77. Ibid.

78. Ibid., 59th Cong., 1st sess., Jan. 23, 1906, 1418.

79. Ibid.

80. Ibid., Jan. 25, 1906, 1533.

81. Ibid., 1535.

82. Ibid., 1537.

83. See Gould, *Presidency of Theodore Roosevelt,* 179.

84. Arthur S. Link, ed., *The Papers of Woodrow Wilson,* vol. 32, 27.

85. Haiti traditionally had a strong French influence in its institutions and customs.

86. January 7, 1915, in Link, ed., *Papers of Woodrow Wilson,* vol. 32, 27.

87. Wilson, letter to Bryan, Jan. 13, 1915, in ibid., 62.

88. Wilson, letter from Bryan, Apr. 3, 1915, in ibid., 472. This quotation reflects Bryan's understanding of Wilson's position.

89. Wilson, letter to Bryan, Apr. 5, 1915, in ibid., 479.

90. William Jennings Bryan resigned as secretary of state on June 8, 1915, in protest of President Wilson's response to Germany after one of its submarines sank the British ocean liner RMS *Lusitania.*

91. Senate report 794, 67th Cong., 2d sess., 31.

92. Caperton, letter to Wilson, Aug. 11, 1915, in Link, *Papers of Woodrow Wilson,* vol. 34, 165.

93. Link, *Papers of Woodrow Wilson,* vol. 32, 27.

94. Wilson, letter to Bryan, Mar. 31, 1915, in ibid., 458.

95. Link, *Papers of Woodrow Wilson,* vol. 34, 70.

96. Wilson, letter to Lansing, Aug. 4, 1915, in ibid., 78.

97. This language is similar to that used by Theodore Roosevelt in the Dominican Republic case.

98. U.S. Department of State, *The Lansing Papers, 1914–1920,* vol. 2.

99. The treaty was introduced in the Senate on Jan. 11, 1916, and ratified on Feb. 23, 1916.

100. *Congressional Record,* 63rd Cong., 3d sess., Feb. 19, 1915, 4134.

101. Even searches of the personal papers of prominent congressional members who served during this interaction yielded no additional insight, only continued silence on this issue.

102. A total of fifteen members participated in this debate, with Representatives Padgett and Callaway speaking the most. The most substantive issue raised, for the purposes here, concerned whether the "president would . . . have the means of executing [the treaty] as he would like to" if the House did not approve the legislation (Rep. Lemuel P. Padgett, D-TN, chair of the House Naval Affairs Committee, *Congressional Record,* 64th Cong., 1st sess., May 4, 1916, 7426). Rep. Oscar Callaway (D-TX), also a member of the Naval Affairs Committee, vehemently argued that the "treaty will go on and operate just as well without this act and just as thoroughly as it will with it" (ibid.).

103. From "Woodrow Wilson and Preparedness" (1916), written by Hay (James Hay Papers).

104. For example, the escalating tensions in Europe and resolving the United States' dispute with Germany over the sinking of the RMS *Lusitania* were of great concern for all. Even in Latin America, the events in Haiti were not of most concern; Mexico held that distinction. Senator Spooner is said to have stated that "Mexico has become an international nuisance. It is our weak spot" (Robert Lansing Papers).

105. Before we draw conclusions from the case studies, we should consider two cases that could be seen as similar to those mentioned earlier. One possible situation is the U.S. intervention in Nicaragua in 1912, the most significant incident of U.S. involvement in Latin America pursuant to Taft's Dollar Diplomacy policy. After a revolution led to the resignation of dictator José Santos Zelaya, who was anti-American and had financed the country's debt through a European syndicate, Secretary of State Philander Knox negotiated a convention with the new Nicaraguan president that would have made Nicaragua a protectorate. The U.S. Senate, however, did not approve this convention. After another revolt broke out in 1912, the United States, at the request of the Nicaraguan president, intervened militarily to protect U.S. interests. However, another treaty that would have assisted Nicaragua financially also did not pass in the Senate.

Although this intervention may seem to be one in which the Senate asserted its institutional role in the policy-making process and did not defer to the president's lead, this case is not strictly comparable to the earlier ones. First, although Nicaragua's debt was financed through European investors, the threat of a European military intervention was not imminent. Second, Taft's attempt to establish a formal protectorate went beyond what even Roosevelt wanted. Roosevelt, in fact, expressly denied any interest in establishing a protectorate. Finally, whereas the cases discussed previously were isolated, the 1912 intervention in Nicaragua was part of Taft's larger Dollar Diplomacy policy, which had been widely discredited in Congress even before the United States became involved in Nicaragua. As a result, although this case possibly demonstrates the outside limits of presidential authority, it does not contradict any of the conclusions that can be drawn from the prior cases.

A second possible case is the U.S. involvement in the Dominican Republic in 1916. The problems that nation experienced a decade previously had not been fully resolved, and by 1916 it was facing decaying financial conditions and internal revolutions. Wilson undertook a policy similar to the one he pursued in Haiti. Although a U.S. military government was set up in both countries, Wilson did not negotiate a treaty for the Dominican Republic like the one used in Haiti.

CHAPTER 3

1. For example, federal supervision over other areas resulted in an increase in and a diversification of the government's regulatory and administrative agencies during the middle period from 1894 to 1907. The administrative agencies increased government involvement in science and information collection (Bureau of Plant Industry, Bureau of Forestry, National Bureau of Standards, and Bureau of the Census), commerce (National Bureau of Commerce and Bureau of Fisheries), land use (Bureau of Reclamation), and foreign affairs (Bureau of Insular Affairs). During the final period from 1908 to 1920, the national government maintained an interest in scientific research (the Naval Advisory Committee for Aeronautics) and provided additional economic-related agencies (the Shipping Board, the U.S. Tariff Commission, and the Federal Farm Loan Board).

2. For example, the Bureau of Animal Industry was created in response to widespread disease in livestock. Such a problem can be seen as a public health issue, which is generally considered within the purview of a state's police powers. The problem of diseased livestock, however, fell into the national government's purview as a foreign commerce issue when it affected the ability of U.S. meat producers to export their products to Europe. The function of the new bureau reflected this mixed purpose, as it was responsible for both preventing the exportation of diseased livestock (i.e., a foreign commerce function) and suppressing and eliminating pleuropneumonia and other diseases (i.e., a public health function).

The creation of the Bureau of Labor in the Interior Department in 1884 and a sub-Cabinet-level Department of Labor in 1888 also reflected the federal government's increased involvement in an area traditionally left to the states. The Bureau of Labor was charged with the responsibility of collecting data and other information on labor, its relation to capital, hours worked, earnings, and ways to promote laborers' material, social, intellectual, and moral prosperity. A state's governmental functions were generally considered to include promoting the safety and welfare of its citizens, as well as being responsible for their education and moral well-being. The information that the new bureau was supposed to collect falls squarely within areas of state responsibility.

In the latter part of the period, the national government created entities with police powers, namely the Bureau of Investigation, which delved into safety and health issues through the creation of the Bureau of Mines and the Interdepartmental Social Hygiene Board.

3. The notion of administrative apparatus is generally used in conjunction with examining the institution of the presidency. It is important to emphasize that such a connection is not made here. Instead, administrative apparatus is used herein solely to examine it as a tool of the federal government to execute its laws and regulations. The discussion contained in this work thus focuses on how this tool was used and affected by the institutions of the presidency and Congress.

4. The focus here is solely on the creation of new agencies or the elevation of existing ones to a higher position. For the most part, reorganizations of jurisdiction, personnel, and so on within and among agencies are not discussed. Although such reorganizations may be important for questions of institutional authority, they are beyond the scope of this discussion. In addition, the focus is solely on administrative agencies and therefore not on the military establishment. For a discussion of the military establishment during this era, see Skowronek, *Building a New American State*.

5. Both the Civil Service Commission and the Interstate Commerce Commission (ICC) were created within bills that dealt with a larger problem: civil service reform and regulation of the railroads, respectively. Their significance, however, is greater than simply the policy issues they were addressing. First, they were the first administrative agencies established outside the traditional, single-headed executive departmental structure. The commissions were under the control of a board (each member with essentially equal power) and had a degree of independence greater than other administrative agencies. The ICC, in fact, was even more important in that it was the first independent regulatory commission.

Second, these commissions can be seen as the first major administrative agencies created in response to the nationalization of U.S. politics. As stated earlier, the goal of civil service reform was to establish a more professional and efficient bureaucracy that would be better able to perform the growing administrative tasks of the federal government. The creation of the ICC stemmed from the fact that unfair railroad practices could not be resolved on a state-by-state basis. As a result, a national governmental solution was required to address what had become a national economic problem. In doing so, the national government expanded the role it could play in the nation to include the regulation of private business practices that unfairly affected people on a national (or at least an interstate) basis.

6. Some agencies created during the era, however, were of lesser importance. For example, the Bureau of Navigation, which supervised the Merchant Marine, and the Bureau of Immigration both fell under the heading of national government activities. In addition, the U.S. Weather Bureau and the Office of Road Inquiry were mostly data collection agencies for subjects that were more national than local in scope.

7. Developed in response to the need for additional development of power projects, the Federal Power Commission, composed of the secretaries of war, interior, and agriculture, was given the responsibility of regulating the development, utilization, licensing, and accounting of hydroelectric power projects. Although Congress was primarily responsible for the creation of this commission, it did so in name only, meaning that the final legislation was geared more toward establishing some form of commission rather than a necessarily effective one. See Bernard Schwartz, "Hepburn Act 1906: Commentary," 1822–23.

8. World War I increased the demands placed upon the federal government, which in turn responded by establishing several new agencies to fill its needs. The most prominent ones created included the Bureau of War Risk Insurance, the Coast Guard, the Council of National Defense, the War Industries Board, and the War Finance Corporation. The War Finance Corporation, originally designed to assist businesses that were necessary for or contributing to the war effort, continued after the war as well. Although intended as a temporary agency, the corporation was extended after the conflict to "embrace an entirely new activity, namely, the promotion of the export trade of the United States" (Lloyd M. Short, *The Development of National Administrative Organization in the United States*, 434).

9. Short states that "The development of national administration in the United States . . . has proceeded largely along lines laid down by successive enactments of Congress and with a view to meeting specific needs as they have arisen" (ibid., 459).

10. John A. Fairlie, *The National Administration of the United States of America*, 225. See also Justus D. Doenecke, *The Presidencies of James A. Garfield and Chester A. Arthur*, 67–69 and 136–37, for a discussion of the "pork war" and its role in the bureau's creation.

11. For a discussion of the particularized functions of the federal government between 1800 and 1933, see Theodore J. Lowi, *The Personal President*, 24–25.

12. Short, *Development of National Administrative Organization*, 383.

13. In some cases, the regulated interests favored the creation of an agency as a protection against "detrimental competitive practices." Peter Woll, *American Bureaucracy*, 42.

14. Gabriel Kolko, *Main Currents in Modern American History*, 35.

15. Martin J. Sklar, *The Corporate Reconstruction of American Capitalism, 1890–1916: The Market, the Law, and Politics*, 3. In other words, the period saw a movement from small or medium-sized, individually owned enterprises to associational ownership of private property "marked [by] a deep-going change in the capitalist mode of production and exchange" (Sklar, *The United States as a Developing Country*, 21).

16. The Hepburn Act of 1906 gave the Interstate Commerce Commission a set of teeth that it did not have before, "rescuing the Commission from futility" (Robert E. Cushman, *The Independent Regulatory Commissions*, 65). Despite the fact that the creation of the ICC represented a significant moment in administrative history, the Interstate Commerce Act left the commission with two damaging shortcomings: It could not set railroad rates, and it had no real enforcement power (Schwartz, "Hepburn Act 1906: Commentary," 593.) The Hepburn Act rectified these shortcomings by granting the ICC the authority to set maximum rates for the future; providing that the ICC's orders should be effective upon issuance and remain so unless overturned by a court; giving the ICC the power to issue reparation orders; extending the scope of the Interstate Commerce Act to include certain types of railway carriers; prohibiting railroads from transporting most of the commodities they owned; and enlarging the commission from five to seven members, with increased salaries and information collection powers. One of the driving forces behind the enactment of this bill was President Roosevelt, who endorsed the idea of greater regulation of the railroads as early as his December 1904 annual message. While Roosevelt may not have created the movement for additional railroad regulation (Southern and Midwestern shippers earned that distinction), he was instrumental in achieving it (Lewis L. Gould, *The Presidency of Theodore Roosevelt*, 150).

17. The Department of Agriculture was given additional and significant regulatory powers through the enactment of the Meat Inspection Act and the Pure Food and Drug Act in 1906. The passage of these bills benefited from President Roosevelt's involvement in the issue, as well as from *The Jungle*, a novel by Upton Sinclair that details the unsanitary practices followed in a Chicago meat-packing plant. The administrative powers of enforcing these acts fell to the Department of Agriculture's Bureau of Chemistry, whose chief had long been the leading proponent of pure food legislation.

18. Letter to Lyman Abbott, July 1, 1906, in Morison, ed., *Letters of Theodore Roosevelt*, vol. 5, 328.

19. By the 1890s a new consensus among manufacturers, bankers, farmers, workers, and reformers was established, replacing the old agreement that had favored largely competitive markets. This new, anticompetitive consensus framed the debate over the proper extent of government regulation. According to Sklar, "Conflicting proposals for government regulation of the market derived from small-producer fears of competition as well as of monopolistic oppression, from adversarial market interests such as those of shippers against

carriers, from positive and defensive corporate initiatives, from investors in negotiable securities seeking greater stability in the capital markets—that is, from all manner of bourgeois sources within the market, as well as from intellectuals, social reformers, independent professionals, trade unionists, and political leaders of various pro-corporate, populist, progressive, and socialist persuasions" (Sklar, *Corporate Reconstruction,* 17).

20. For example, some companies such as Standard Oil adapted by expanding the size of their legal departments to address this increased regulation.

21. Gabriel Kolko argues, for example, that even the railroad industry welcomed and advocated regulation (Kolko, *Railroads and Regulation 1877–1916*).

22. Clements, *Presidency of Woodrow Wilson,* 43. The need to revise the nation's banking and currency system was evident as early as the Panic of 1907. Despite previous efforts to address this need, the issue was not successfully dealt with until 1913. The Federal Reserve Act contained the following provisions: It created a system composed of twelve regional federal reserve banks under the direction of the Federal Reserve Board. These banks were to hold bank reserves and have directors that represented banking, commercial, industrial, and financial interests in the region, as well as the national board. In order to enhance economic and geographic diversity, the Federal Reserve Board was to consist of the secretary of the treasury, the comptroller of the currency, and five additional members. The act provided the board with managerial powers to fix the rediscount rate, control bank reserves, and issue bank notes, among other things. Finally, the act also granted the board supervisory powers over bank examinations and the removal of directors and officers of the reserve banks. See Cushman, *Independent Regulatory Commissions,* 150–51.

23. For a fuller discussion, see Robert H. Wiebe, *Businessmen and Reform: A Study of the Progressive Movement,* 10–14.

24. The importance of the nation's growing labor movement was reflected particularly in the establishment of new administrative agencies between 1908 and 1920. The separation of the Department of Labor from the Department of Commerce represented the most significant agency creation. Labor organizations finally achieved the unified Cabinet-level position they had been seeking since the 1880s. In addition, other labor-related agencies were created, including the Children's Bureau (1912), the Commission on Industrial Relations (1912), the Board of Mediation and Conciliation (1913), the Women's Bureau (1920), and the Railroad Labor Board (1920).

25. Wiebe, *Businessmen and Reform,* 6.

26. For example, James L. Sundquist states that the Progressive movement failed to result in a systemic change, such as a party realignment, because "(1) the major parties responded to the demands for reform, and (2) they responded at about the same time and to about the same degree" (Sundquist, *Dynamics of the Party System: Alignment and Realignment of Political Parties in the United States,* 170).

27. The Republicans, concerned about the potential loss of the White

House in 1884, wanted to limit the spoils system while their supporters still held patronage positions, thus allowing them to keep their jobs even if a Democrat were elected president in 1884. A committee of Democrats attempted to get Pendleton to withdraw the bill until after the presidential election so that the party could reap the benefits of the spoils system should it win, but Pendleton refused. See Skowronek, *Building a New American State,* 64–68.

28. See Leonard D. White, *The Republican Era: 1869–1901,* especially chapter 16.

29. For reform of the organization and methods of administrative agencies, see Woodrow Wilson, "The Study of Administration," 197–222. For separating politics and administration, see Frank J. Goodnow, *Politics and Administration: A Study in Government.* For scientific management, see Frederick Taylor's testimony before the U.S. House of Representatives on Jan. 25, 1912, in Jay M. Shafritz and Albert C. Hyde, eds. *Classics of Public Administration.*

30. For example, the Budget and Accounting Act passed in 1921 created the Bureau of the Budget in the Department of Treasury and the General Accounting Office as an agency of Congress. This act also gave the president the responsibility of crafting a national executive budget, something Taft's commission had suggested nine years earlier.

31. There are three approaches that could have been considered in selecting cases for this area. First was the transition of the administrative agency with jurisdiction over labor issues from the Bureau of Labor through to the Cabinet-level Department of Labor. This method would have provided a degree of comparability but would have fallen short with regard to other considerations. In particular, each of the institutional interactions within the transition was carried out for somewhat different policy reasons. Remember, however, the key component of the comparability criterion used previously was that each case was done for the same policy reason. As such, focusing solely on the interactions involving the Labor Bureau/Department would have sacrificed the key component for comparability in this study and thus was ruled out.

The second approach would have been to select cases in which a subdepartmental bureau was created. Doing so would enhance the comparability criteria in that three bureaus could have been selected that are similar in size, scope, and level within the government and were created for the same policy reasons. One possible set could have been the Bureau of Labor, the Bureau of Manufactures, and the Children's or Women's Bureau since all three are labor and industry related. The most significant limiting factor, however, with these is that they may not be significant enough to produce an adequate institutional interaction for study. On one hand, this point is telling; it may reflect the constitutional authority that Congress has over the creation of administrative agencies and also indicate that the formation of some agencies does not necessarily warrant the president's attention. On the other hand, presidents have been involved in the establishment of at least some administrative agencies. Thus, since the approach of selecting subdepartmental bureaus would not necessarily produce a set of significant institutional interactions, it was not pursued.

The one set of agency creations that did warrant the various presidents' attention throughout the period was that of top-level agencies, including independent regulatory commissions and executive departments. The formation of the Interstate Commerce Commission, the Department of Commerce and Labor (and the Bureau of Corporations within it), and the Federal Trade Commission each represented a major policy initiative to establish an administrative agency involved in the increasingly important and nationalized aspects of commerce, a set of issues that was found throughout the period. Therefore, these cases maximize the three selection criteria and were thus utilized for the case study analysis.

The most significant caveat in using these three cases has to do with the difference between Commerce and Labor as an executive department and the ICC and FTC as independent regulatory commissions. The board of an independent regulatory commission is not directly answerable to the president in the way that the secretary of an executive department would be. Therefore, this fact may limit the extent of the authority that the president may exercise over these commissions. Both the independent regulatory commissions and the department, however, would have presidential input on their personnel and would therefore still be subject to presidential influence. All of this might result in a difference in terms of the institutional interactions that create each of them. Given the importance and visibility of both types of agencies in the federal administrative system, one would expect that the issue of their creation would produce the most substantive institutional interactions. In addition, all three cases meet the following conditions: (1) They were top-level agencies; (2) they were high profile, meaning that both the president and Congress recognized the problem that led to their formation; (3) there was a debate over the level of presidential control of the agencies; and, most importantly, (4) the same policy reason was given for their establishment (i.e., commerce/trade issues). Therefore, these additional conditions seem to compensate for the possible drawbacks mentioned earlier.

32. Woll, *American Bureaucracy*, 32.

33. Richard D. Stone, *The Interstate Commerce Commission and the Railroad Industry: A History of Regulatory Policy*, 2–3.

34. William E. Nelson, *The Roots of American Bureaucracy, 1830–1900*, 126–27.

35. I. L. Sharfman, *The Interstate Commerce Commission: A Study in Administrative Law and Procedure*.

36. Bernard Schwartz, ed., "Interstate Commerce Act, 1887: Commentary," 18.

37. See ibid. See also Cushman, *Independent Regulatory Commissions*, 42.

38. "Argument of the Hon. John D. Reagan, of Texas, before the Committee on Commerce of the House of Representatives on the Railroad Problem."

39. Ibid.

40. Cullom, *Fifty Years of Public Service*, 305.

41. Definition used by Sen. Orville Platt (R-CT) in floor debate, *Congressional Record*, 49th Cong., 2d sess., Jan. 5, 1887, 361.

42. House Report 902, U.S. House of Representatives, 49th Cong., 1st sess., 3.

43. Of particular note, on July 27, 1886, Rep. Frank Hiscock (R-NY) proposed an amendment that would have substituted the Cullom bill for the alternate (i.e., Reagan) bill that the House was considering. For a discussion of this maneuver, see Scott C. James, "A Party System Perspective on the Interstate Commerce Act of 1887: The Democracy, Electoral College Competition, and the Politics of Coalition Maintenance," especially footnote 7. See also Elizabeth Sanders, "Response to James."

44. The Senate was represented by Cullom and Sen. Isham G. Harris (D-TN); House members included Reagan, Rep. Charles Crisp (D-GA), and Rep. Archibald J. Weaver (R-NE).

45. *Wabash, St. Louis, and Pacific Railway Company v. Illinois.* In this case, the Supreme Court ruled that states could not validly regulate railroad rates within their boundaries for carriers involved in interstate commerce and that commerce that crossed over state lines was under the regulatory jurisdiction of the federal government.

46. Gerald Berk argues that, although the ICA represented a "middle course, regional republicans had won a limited victory." The success of the act, however, depended on the cooperation of the railroads (Berk, *Alternative Tracks: The Constitution of American Industrial Order, 1865–1917,* 100).

47. Regarding the conference committee, Cullom wrote: "The contention finally centered on the pooling provisions. Reagan had yielded on nearly everything else; but Platt of Connecticut was bound there should be no prohibition against pooling. Reagan affirmed that the whole matter would have to drop, that he would never yield on that. I came back and consulted the leaders in the Senate, Allison among others, and they advised me to yield; that the country demanded a bill, and I had better accept Reagan's anti-pooling prohibition section than offer no measure at all—which I did" (*Fifty Years of Public Service,* 322).

48. Cleveland's public speeches and private papers reflect a virtual absence of presidential activity in substantively trying to promote, secure, or otherwise affect legislation in this regard. Further, to quote from Elizabeth Sanders, "Cleveland played hardly any role in the ICA's passage (except to sign it)" ("Response to James," 205).

49. Richardson, ed., *A Compilation,* 5111.

50. See Welch Jr., *The Presidencies of Grover Cleveland,* 79. Here he states that Cleveland "had doubts about the constitutional soundness of 'government by commission.' "

51. James claims that "the ICA was written with an eye to the interests of groups in states that were central to the maintenance of the Democratic Party's electoral college majority and the goal of party victory in the 1888 presidential

elections" ("A Party System Perspective," 191). Specifically, James argues that Democratic party leaders, secure in the support they would receive from Southern agrarian interests, supported the commission approach to the ICA to win support in key swing states in the electoral college, most notably New York.

52. The ICA provided that "any Commissioner may be removed by the President for inefficiency, neglect of duty, or malfeasance in office." One possible interpretation of this language is that it limits the presidency's removal power to only those instances set forth in the act. However, a subsequent Supreme Court decision, *Shurtleff v. United States* (1903), found that this same language in another statute creating a board of general appraisers did not limit the presidency's removal power. Further, the Supreme Court in *Myers v. United States* (1926) noted that *Shurtleff*'s approach allowed the seeming limitation placed upon the president's removal power in the Interstate Commerce Act and other similar legislation to be reconciled with the unrestricted power of the president to remove.

53. In addition, no more than three commissioners could come from the same political party, which was meant to "defus[e] the fear of partisanship that had figured prominently in the debates" surrounding the commission's creation (Skowronek, *Building a New American State*, 149).

54. Although both Reagan and Cullom had kept their respective bills on the congressional docket for a number of years, this analysis is limited to the 49th Congress, in which the legislation became law. In doing so, I examine the behavior and rhetoric of the members of Congress and their implications for the institutional authority of the presidency.

55. *Congressional Record*, 49th Cong., 1st sess., May 12, 1886, 4422.

56. Ibid.

57. Ibid.

58. Ibid.

59. *Congressional Record*, 49th Cong., 2d sess., Jan. 20, 1887, 848.

60. Ibid., 839.

61. Ibid., 840.

62. In *Building a New American State*, Skowronek stated, "Throughout the debate, [Reagan] and his more adamant supporters would denounce commissions as an unnecessary bureaucratic burden on the people, as an illegitimate delegation of judicial and legislative power, as a hindrance to speedy and effective redress, and most especially, as a concentration of authority in an agency too easily controlled by the railroads" (144).

63. See ibid. (149) regarding these regional differences.

64. *Congressional Record*, 49th Cong., 2d sess., July 21, 1886, 7281.

65. Ibid., 49th Cong., 1st sess., Apr. 16, 1886, 3556.

66. Ibid., 49th Cong., 2d sess., Jan. 20, 1887, 846.

67. Ibid., 49th Cong., 1st sess., July 21, 1886, 7296. In the course of this same speech, immediately before making this statement, Reagan said, "If the most fertile minds in either House of Congress could have been employed to

devise means to retard, embarrass, mystify, hinder, and delay the redress of wrongs and the punishment of violations of law they could not in my opinion have succeeded better than the distinguished framer of the Senate bill."

68. With the administrative approach, Congress granted its power to the new independent regulatory agency. With the legislative approach, Congress would have depended on the judiciary for enforcement of the legislation. In both cases, Congress provides authority to another entity to regulate interstate commerce. See Morris P. Fiorina, "Legislative Choice of Regulatory Forms: Legal Process or Administrative Process?"; Morris P. Fiorina, "Group Concentration and the Delegation of Legislative Authority"; and Morris P. Fiorina, "Legislator Uncertainty, Legislative Control, and the Delegation of Legislative Power."

69. See, for example, Rep. Byron Cutcheon (R-MI), *Congressional Record,* 49th Cong., 2d sess., Jan. 20, 1887, 843.

70. *Congressional Record,* 49th Cong., 1st sess., July 21, 1886, 7285.

71. Ibid., May 12, 1886, 4399.

72. Ibid., Apr. 14, 1886, 3471.

73. Ibid., 49th Cong., 2d sess., Jan. 18, 1887, 784.

74. Ibid., Jan. 20, 1887, 843.

75. Ibid., 850.

76. See, for example, Short, *Development of National Administrative Organization in the United States.*

77. Richardson, ed., *A Compilation,* 6649.

78. The bill Nelson introduced (S. 569) was one of nine similar measures in the 57th Congress alone. For the most part, the other bills died in committee.

79. *Congressional Record,* 57th Cong., 1st sess., Jan. 13, 1902, 598.

80. Ibid., 599.

81. Samuel Gompers, president of the American Federation of Labor, sent a letter dated Jan. 20, 1902, to Sen. William Frye (R-ME), which Frye read into the *Congressional Record.* In the letter, Gompers wrote, "The creation of a department of commerce with the provision for the subordination of the Department of Labor, will minimize the importance of labor's interests and minimize the present Department of Labor. Against such a procedure, in the name of American labor, I enter my most solemn protest" (ibid., Jan. 22, 1902, 863). On the other hand, the Knights of Labor sent a letter to the Senate via Senator Nelson, stating that "The great mass of organized labor will be glad to see it included in the new department so that there may be a competent and responsible head to direct its work" and that the organization "looked upon the proposed department of commerce as a decided step forward in the interests of the workingman" (ibid., Jan. 27, 1902, 1000).

82. Sen. Marcus A. Hanna (R-OH), Senator Nelson, Sen. Alexander C. Clay (D-GA), Rep. William P. Hepburn (R-IA), Rep. James A. Mann (R-IL), and Rep. William Richardson (D-AL).

83. *Congressional Record,* 57th Cong., 2d sess., Jan. 19, 1902, 946. Com-

mon carriers subject to the Interstate Commerce Act were exempt from such investigation.

84. In fact, Richardson referred to the Nelson Amendment as "an ultra dilution of a homeopathic dose of so-called antitrust legislation . . . a travesty upon what its friends represent and claim to be its only virtue—publicity" (ibid., Feb. 10, 1903, 2003).

85. On one hand, the creation of the Department of Commerce and Labor in 1903 may not seem as significant as the formation of a new executive department would imply. Most of the subdepartmental agencies that were placed in the new department were already-existing agencies that were transferred from another department; only two new bureaus—the Bureau of Corporations and the Bureau of Manufactures—were created. Under this view, the new department merely unified most of the existing agencies involved in administering commerce laws into one department (see Fairlie, *National Administration,* 231, for a general discussion of this view). The establishment of this department, though, was more significant than just an attempt at administrative reorganization.

86. Elizabeth Sanders, "Industrial Concentration, Sectional Competition, and Antitrust Politics in America, 1880–1980," 161 (emphasis in the original). On another note, as mentioned in the previous chapter, the bill also created a Bureau of Manufactures—the only other new entity. The remaining bureaus, offices, and so on that fell under the new department's jurisdiction were existing entities transferred into it.

87. Annual message, December 2, 1902 (Richardson, ed., *A Compilation,* 6716). Roosevelt also reiterated that he "earnestly hoped that a secretary of commerce may be created, with a seat in the Cabinet."

88. Letter to Lawrence Fraser Abbott, Feb. 3, 1903. In Morison, ed., *Letters of Theodore Roosevelt,* vol. 3, 417.

89. Annual message, Dec. 3, 1901 (Richardson, ed., *A Compilation,* 6649). The Senate briefly discussed the possibility of transferring the ICC into the new department but did not pursue doing so in part because of the unique powers, including its *"quasijudicial"* ones, which are not shared by other government bureaus. See John C. Spooner (R-WI), *Congressional Record,* 57th Cong., 1st sess., Jan. 23, 1902, 921. See also George Hoar's (R-MA) comments on the same page of the *Congressional Record.* As an aside, Hoar voted against the Interstate Commerce Act, whereas Spooner voted for it. Even Senator Hanna (R-OH), who was not in Congress when the ICC was formed, referred to it as "purely a judicial body" (ibid., 912).

90. See L. White Busbey, *Uncle Joe Cannon: The Story of a Pioneer American,* 219–23. This book is Cannon's autobiography as told to his private secretary for twenty years. For another example of the role Roosevelt played behind the scenes regarding Section 6 of the bill, see a personal letter from George Courtelyou to Sen. Nelson Aldrich, dated Feb. 5, 1903 (Nelson W. Aldrich Papers). In this letter Courtelyou wrote, "The President requests me to ask if you will

be good enough to inform him what the situation is with regard to Section 6 of the Department of Commerce and Labor bill. He would like to know if there is any need for him to see you in regard to the matter."

91. Letter to Lyman Abbott, Sept. 5, 1903, in Morison, *Letters of Theodore Roosevelt,* vol. 3, 591 (emphasis added).

92. Some of the nation's economic problems from 1881 to 1920 and the ways in which the federal government addressed them are discussed further in the next chapter (relating to the tariff).

93. A full examination of this argument is outside the scope of the discussion here.

94. *Congressional Record,* 57th Cong., 1st sess., Jan. 23, 1902, 915.

95. Ibid., 916.

96. Ibid.

97. Ibid., 918.

98. Ibid., 919.

99. Ibid.

100. Ibid., 920.

101. Ibid., 57th Cong., 2d sess., Jan. 17, 1903, 911.

102. For a review of both Sections 6, see Representative Richardson, *Congressional Record,* 57th Cong., 2d sess., Feb. 10, 1903, 2003–2004.

103. Richardson, however, voted for the final passage of the bill. In concluding his remarks on the conference bill and the Nelson Amendment, he stated, "I do not believe that anything good for the people against the trusts can come out of the [Nelson Amendment]. I was anxious to have and requested a separate vote on this substitute. This was declined or refused. I think that there is nothing whatever in it to alarm the trusts, and I do not think they are alarmed. The Republican party is responsible. No one should be allowed hereafter to say to us that we obstructed or hindered any legislation that promised or claimed to check the trusts. In that spirit I shall vote for the conference report" (ibid., 2006).

104. Ibid., 2007.

105. Annual message, Dec. 3, 1901 (Richardson, ed., *A Compilation,* 6649).

106. *Congressional Record,* 57th Cong., 1st sess., Jan. 13, 1902, 599.

107. The movement that led to the Federal Trade Commission can be traced back to the Sherman Antitrust Act of 1890. Some people viewed this legislation as ineffective in addressing the problems caused by trusts and left them "groping for [a] more effective administrative apparatus" (Cushman, *Independent Regulatory Commissions,* 178). Although the creation of the Department of Commerce and Labor was seen as a step in the right direction in terms of regulating trusts, the opponents of trusts sought a body with greater regulatory authority. The Supreme Court further ruled, in *Standard Oil Co. v. United States* and *United States v. American Tobacco Co.,* that only trusts that unreasonably restrained trade were prohibited under the Sherman Act. Congress was stimulated into action.

108. In Arthur M. Schlesinger Jr., ed., *History of American Presidential Elections, 1789–1968,* 2180.

109. Ibid., 2190.

110. Special message, Jan. 20, 1914, Richardson, ed., *A Compilation,* 7917.

111. Rep. Frederick Stevens (R-MN) said that he could not complain about the Democrats because "not so very long ago some of our Republican administrations had been accustomed to abstract some of the treasures of your Democratic platforms without an especial credit for it, and we turned them to our advantage without any thanks to you. So turn about is fair play" (*Congressional Record,* 63rd Cong., 2d sess., May 19, 1914, 8849).

112. Scott C. James, "Building a Democratic Majority: The Progressive Party Vote and the Federal Trade Commission," 334.

113. Special message, Jan. 20, 1914, in Richardson, ed., *A Compilation,* 7916.

114. Cushman, *Independent Regulatory Commissions,* 186–87.

115. Among other things, the Clayton Act prohibited discriminating pricing; tie-in selling; exclusive dealing; and interlocking directorates among banks, railroads, and large corporations. See Clements, *Presidency of Woodrow Wilson,* 48–49. The Rayburn Act directed the ICC to supervise the issuance of securities by railroad companies. See *Congressional Record,* 63rd Cong., 2d sess., July 21, 1914, 12410, for further discussion of this bill.

116. Congressional concern regarding presidential control over the functioning of the FTC was also manifested in another way. As E. M. House wrote to Wilson, "The papers state that the sensibilities of the Senate are hurt because you are not consulting them in regard to the appointments of this Commission. This, taken in connection with what Culberson told me, indicates that they will hesitate to confirm any member of this board to whom there may be any possible objection" (Dec. 25, 1914, in Link, ed., *Papers of Woodrow Wilson,* vol. 31, 524).

117. *Congressional Record,* 63rd Cong., 2d sess., Aug. 1, 1914, 13105.

118. Representative Covington (D-MD) argued that the act that originally created the Bureau of Corporations "omitted to confer powers, perhaps not then though useful, but now believed to be most necessary to assist in effectuating the definite policy and functions for the proposed commission" (*Congressional Record,* 63rd Cong., 2d sess., May 19, 1914, 8842).

119. Senator Newlands (D-NV), for example, spoke of the benefits that could be obtained because of the "authority or prestige which attaches to an independent commission" (*Congressional Record,* 63rd Cong., 2d sess., June 25, 1914, 11089).

120. Ibid., May 21, 1914, 8986.

121. Ibid., May 19, 1914, 8857.

122. Ibid., 8842.

123. Following the division of the Department of Commerce and Labor into two Cabinet-level agencies, the Bureau of Corporations remained in the Department of Commerce in 1913.

124. Rep. J. Harry Covington, *Congressional Record*, 63rd Cong., 2d sess., May 19, 1914, 8842.

125. *Congressional Record*, 63rd Cong., 2d sess., July 2, 1914, 11529–30.

126. Ibid., 11529.

127. Ibid., Sept. 10, 1914, 14935.

128. Ibid., July 31, 1914, 13057.

129. Ibid., July 27, 1914, 12806.

130. Ibid., July 13, 1914, 12030.

131. The Supreme Court had already addressed such matters. See, for example, *Texas and Pacific Railroad Co. v. Abilene Cotton Oil Co.* regarding the doctrine of primary jurisdiction.

132. *Congressional Record*, 63rd Cong., 2d sess., May 19, 1914, 8840.

133. Wilson, letter to Covington, Aug. 27, 1914, in Link, ed., *Papers of Woodrow Wilson*, vol. 30, 454.

134. Newlands, letter to Wilson, Aug. 22, 1914, in ibid., 434.

135. See Sanders, "Industrial Concentration, Sectional Competition, and Antitrust Politics."

136. Skowronek, *Building a New American State*, 175.

137. James, "Building a Democratic Majority," 374.

138. Although the creation of new agencies and the reorganization of existing ones escalated throughout this period (and certainly beyond), only two cases—both during the Wilson administration—are similar enough to warrant a brief reference at this point. Possibly the most significant new entities created between 1881 and 1920 (other than those discussed in this chapter) were the Federal Reserve Board and related regional banks. Stemming from the banking and currency problems that plagued the nation as far back as the Cleveland administration, the Federal Reserve System was needed to impart stability to the nation's financial system. Although the act that created this structure established new government organizations (i.e., the Federal Reserve Board and banks), they were only one component of the new legislation. In that regard, the creation of the Federal Reserve Board and banks is somewhat akin to that of the ICC; however, the Federal Reserve Act set up an entire system rather than a single agency. Further, although some of the authority issues addressed were similar (such as whether the government should regulate in this area), the Federal Reserve Board case was dissimilar because it was expanding the authority of the national government to address long-standing currency and banking problems, not unfair business practices.

The second case that merits a brief discussion is that of the separation of the Department of Commerce and Labor into two Cabinet-level departments. The experience of the ten years between the creation of the department and its disaggregation demonstrated one point that had been made in congressional debates in 1903: Commercial interests and labor interests are vastly different and often in conflict. Although this legislation provided the labor interests with one thing that it wanted—a Cabinet official representing their concerns alone—from the perspective of establishing new agencies, it did not reflect a significant new endeavor. This case also did not shed much light on presidential and congressional authority issues because the status quo was essentially maintained (i.e., the agencies remained at cabinet level).

139. For further discussion of congressional "counteroffensives" in other areas, see, for example, Skowronek and Sklar.

CHAPTER 4

1. For example, tariffs were passed in 1842 and 1864 due to the government's need for revenues. See F. W. Taussig, *The Tariff History of the United States,* 230–31.

2. Ibid., 231.

3. See George Crompton, *The Tariff: An Interpretation of a Bewildering Problem,* 117, and Taussig, *Tariff History,* 1–2. See also S. Walter Poulshock, *The Two Parties and the Tariff in the 1880s.*

4. Crompton also reviews other reasons for a protectionist tariff, including providing a home market for surplus domestic farm produce, continuing business interests that were developed subsequent to government policies, and protecting against foreign dumping (*The Tariff,* 105–109). See also Percy Ashley, *Modern Tariff History: Germany-United States-France.*

5. Raymond L. Bridgman, *The Passing of the Tariff,* 164. Also see Crompton, *The Tariff,* chapter 4.

6. Poulshock, *Two Parties and the Tariff,* 22.

7. See U.S. Tariff Commission, *The Tariff and Its History,* 88–96, for further discussion and definitions of free trade and protectionism.

8. Although agricultural interests, for the most part, opposed protective tariffs, they occasionally wavered on this position. Specifically, some agricultural interests were persuaded to a more protectionist stance under the guise of the home market theory.

9. Poulshock, *Two Parties and the Tariff,* 18.

10. Southern politics during this era was virtually exclusively Democratic. As a result, Southerners tended to oppose protective tariffs favored by Republicans. Furthermore, Southern congressmen were encouraged by Midwestern leaders to take such a position (ibid., 102–103).

11. See Lowi, *The Personal President.* Lowi argues that tariff policy during this era, like other policies under the purview of the national government, was an "area of patronage"—that is, one in which the government, acting as a patron, shared its resources with others at its discretion (25). Lowi's argument, however, that tariff policy was particularistic throughout this period seems not to have fully appreciated the breadth of this matter. As we will see, the tariff issue became one that divided the parties and influenced the outcomes of elections on a national basis. It had greater meaning than just granting government resources to specific interests.

12. See Poulshock, *Two Parties and the Tariff,* 54.

13. For example, the Democratic Party had a tariff-for-revenue plank in its 1880 national platform (ibid., 60). Furthermore, Poulshock has stated that agricultural interests outside the South were persuaded to vote Republican in the 1880 election because of their belief that a protectionist tariff at this time would provide a home market for surplus domestic farm produce.

14. At the time, Congress, as well as those whom the president appointed to the commission, was controlled by a majority of those subscribing to the protectionist position. The commission's original report was given to Congress at the beginning of the 1882–1883 session. In it, the commission surprisingly "proposed average reductions of from 20 to 25 percent, applying to commodities of necessary general consumption, such as sugar and molasses, rather than to luxuries, and to raw rather than to manufactured materials" (U.S. Tariff Commission, *The Tariff and Its History,* 77). In addition, Poulshock raises the possibility that the outcome of the 1882 congressional elections, in which the Democrats gained control of the House of Representatives, may have affected the commission's position on the issue (*Two Parties and the Tariff,* 80).

15. See Taussig, *Tariff History* (232) for more information about this maneuver.

16. Ibid., 233. The original passage vote was 42 to 29.

17. Ibid.

18. In 1884 Rep. William Morrison (D-IL) proposed an overall reduction of twenty percent and the "entire remission of duties on iron ore, coal, lumber, and other articles" (ibid., 251). When this bill did not pass the House, he proposed more detailed reductions in 1886, but they too were not considered in Congress.

19. By the summer of 1887, the government had accumulated sizable surplus revenues, which served as the basis of Cleveland's December 1887 State of the Union message. This address dealt with surplus revenues and protectionist tariffs exclusively and delivered "a bitter tirade against protectionism, the machinations of business, and Republicans in general." (Tom E. Terrill, *The Tariff, Politics, and American Foreign Policy, 1874–1901,* 140.) The reaction to Cleveland's speech was split along partisan lines. While the Republicans used the tariff as an issue around which the party rallied, the Democrats achieved a level of internal unity on the matter only by overcoming a strong protectionist minority within its ranks (Poulshock, *Two Parties and the Tariff,* 183). See Ida M. Tarbell, *The Tariff in Our Times,* for a discussion of Cleveland's involvement with the tariff. For a more general discussion, see Welch Jr., *Presidencies of Grover Cleveland.*

20. The McKinley Tariff, although reducing the duties on steel and copper and allowing for sugar to be imported tariff free, was still considered to continue prohibitive rates. The McKinley Tariff also extended the free list and increased duties on wool and other assorted goods. The tariff legislation for the most part made the duties on these goods prohibitive. The act also extended

the minimum-value principle (for further discussion of this principle, see Taussig, *Tariff History*, 269) and increased the duty on tin and wheat, while placing a bounty on domestic sugar. Finally, the act established a system of commercial reciprocity and enacted several reforms of the customs administration. The McKinley Tariff heralded a dramatic shift toward expanding the protective system.

21. The Senate, however, amended the bill more than six hundred times; consequently, it was significantly different from the one produced by the House (Welch, *Presidencies of Grover Cleveland*, 135; see 131–39 for a general discussion of this tariff). Those favoring tariff reductions did not perceive the final legislation as fully satisfactory. For the fiscal years of 1894–1897, the average rates on dutiable goods dropped to 41 percent—eight percentage points below the McKinley Tariff's very high rate of 49 percent. The tariff rates for free and dutiable goods decreased from 22 percent to 21 percent. The rates on items such as wool and woolens, cotton, silk goods, pig iron, steel rails, coal, iron ore, chinaware, and tin plate were lowered. This act also reinstated the duty placed on imported raw sugar. The lack of extensive changes, however, emanated from the fact that this attempt at reducing tariff rates occurred during an economic downturn (Welch refers to Cleveland's "poor timing" among other factors contributing to the bill's limited scope. See *Presidencies of Grover Cleveland*, 137).

22. See U.S. Tariff Commission, *The Tariff and Its History*, 78–79.

23. The bill was easily approved in the House due to the large Republican majority and the control exercised by Speaker Thomas Reed. In the Senate, a special subcommittee of the Finance Committee was created to help pass a tariff revision bill in the Senate. Eventually, the House and the Senate agreed to a conference report. Under the Dingley Tariff, many of the reductions made under the Wilson-Gorman Tariff were reversed, in some cases fully reinstating the tariff rates of the McKinley Tariff of 1890. The tax on sugar was restructured, in part to protect the developing domestic beet-sugar industry (U.S. Tariff Commission, *The Tariff and Its History*, 79). Overall, the act allowed for increases of protective rates that reached an average rate as high as fifty-two percent.

24. Taussig, *Tariff History*, 361.

25. See Gould, *Presidency of Theodore Roosevelt*, 27. Gould also states that Roosevelt was both uncertain about the tariff and "unwilling to risk his political future as president" on the issue. Since the tariff was not an important issue for Roosevelt—but was for Republican leaders in Congress—the president occasionally made concessions to them that favored protectionist tariffs. See John Morton Blum, *The Progressive Presidents*.

26. Following the elections, the House Ways and Means Committee held hearings on tariff revisions.

27. For a discussion of Taft's role in the Payne-Aldrich Tariff, see Peri E. Arnold, "Effecting a Progressive Presidency: Roosevelt, Taft and the Pursuit of Strategic Resources."

28. Robert M. La Follette of Wisconsin was the primary progressive critic of the Payne-Aldrich Tariff. He explicitly told Taft that the president should veto the measure. The progressives also "renounced the leadership of Aldrich and pointedly noted the difference between themselves and the 'regular' Republicans, tools of eastern corporations and trusts" (Paolo E. Coletta, *The Presidency of William Howard Taft*, 65).

29. Taussig, *Tariff History*, 497. In looking at what the tariff did provide, we can see that its one significant aspect was that it was "less aggressively protectionist than the previous Republican measure" (ibid., 408), as it reduced rates in 584 instances (twenty percent of imports) (U.S. Tariff Commission, *The Tariff and Its History*, 79). In many ways, these reductions reflected a shift in the sentiment that had prevailed throughout this time, ushering in a period during which extreme protectionism was no longer in favor. In addition to its effects on tariff rates, the Payne-Aldrich Tariff provided authorization for the establishment of a tariff board.

30. Theodore Roosevelt formed the Bull Moose Progressive Party, which served to divide the Republican Party between its old-guard conservatives, who backed Taft as the Republican candidate, and the progressive insurgents, who backed Roosevelt. For a further discussion of this see Coletta, *Presidency of William Howard Taft*, and Clements, *Presidency of Woodrow Wilson*.

31. The next major tariff revisions were the passage of the Emergency Tariff of 1921 and the Tariff Act of 1922 (Fordney-McCumber Tariff), outside the period under study here.

32. The most vigorous opposition came from the Louisiana delegation, which opposed efforts to phase out sugar tariffs.

33. See, for example, the discussion in Cynthia A. Hody, *The Politics of Trade: American Political Development and Foreign Economic Policy*, 20–26.

34. This number becomes fifteen if one includes a joint resolution that corrected a punctuation error in the text of the Tariff Act of 1890 (the McKinley Tariff).

35. Congress sustained each of the vetoes. Taft's vetoes all occurred during the Sixty-second Congress, in which the Democrats controlled the House, and the Republicans the Senate. Wilson's vetoes occurred during the Sixty-sixth Congress, in which the Republicans had a majority in both houses.

36. From the preceding historical review, one can see that the acts that shaped the nation's tariff policy at any given time were generally comprehensive bills that remained in place for several years. Therefore, only a handful of the institutional interactions between Congress and the presidency over tariff policy decisions meet the "significant" criterion established for selecting cases. Furthermore, as tariff questions represent one of the most important economic issues of the era, each case would meet the requirement of being ongoing. As a result of the nature of the institutional interactions regarding tariff policy, the comparability criterion becomes the most important in selecting the cases for empirical study. Based on the comparability reasons discussed elsewhere,

the three cases selected were the 1890 McKinley Tariff, the 1897 Dingley Tariff, and the 1913 Underwood Tariff. Each of these bills was passed for the same general policy reason: to provide an omnibus revision to the nation's established general tariff policy, as well as to change specific tariff rates on a large number of individual products. In addition, these three bills each represent a distinct movement toward one end of the protectionism–free trade philosophical debate.

The most important potential critique that one should consider regarding these cases relates to the partisan and ideological forces that shaped the bills. More specifically, the McKinley and Dingley tariffs were protectionist in nature and passed under Republican leadership. The Underwood Tariff—a Democratic initiative—sought to reduce tariff rates. Although these differences might be said to limit the comparability of these acts, they do not appreciably do so at the level of analysis; these acts were institutional interactions attempting to make a significant and definitive revision in the tariff. Despite the differences in terms of the directions of the tariff revision between the McKinley and Dingley tariffs and the Underwood Tariff, they are comparable in that each embraced and implemented a specific philosophy. Furthermore, each revision took place at a time of undivided government, with the majority in both houses of Congress and the presidency being of the same party, thereby enhancing the comparability among the cases as well.

One should also consider the three other major tariff revisions between 1881 and 1920 to determine whether their inclusion would enhance the three selection criteria, particularly comparability. The Tariff Act of 1883 was passed during a time of partially divided government, as the presidency and the Senate were held by the Republicans and the House by the Democrats. Furthermore, the "mongrel tariff" ended as a set of compromises and did not tend toward either side of the debate. The Wilson-Gorman Tariff is unique in that it became law without the president's signature. Although this fact may provide us with special insight into institutional interactions between Congress and the president, it also limits its comparability with the other potential cases. Finally, the Payne-Aldrich Tariff, similar to the 1883 tariff, did not send any clear signals regarding the direction of tariff policy. Although it maintained protectionist-level tariffs, it also reflected an initial movement away from extremely protectionist tariffs. Thus, each of these cases, while comparable to the three selected on a base level, is sufficiently limited in comparability to warrant exclusion from the case studies.

37. George F. Parker, *The Writings and Speeches of Grover Cleveland*, 72.
38. Welch Jr., *Presidencies of Grover Cleveland*, 89. See also 83–89 generally.
39. Schlesinger Jr., ed., *History of American Presidential Elections*, 1654–55.
40. Ibid., 1657.
41. Cleveland captured the popular vote 48.6 percent to 47.8 percent by winning large margins in Southern states while narrowly losing in the North. Harrison carried the electoral college 233 to 168.

42. John Sherman, *Recollections of Forty Years in the House, Senate, and Cabinet,* 1032.

43. Taussig, *Tariff History,* 256.

44. Ibid., 258.

45. This amendment lists a variety of products designed to be exported from the United States into such countries without any duties.

46. Homer E. Socolofsky and Allan B. Spetter, *The Presidency of Benjamin Harrison,* 50.

47. The House conferees included Rep. William McKinley (R-OH), Rep. Julius C. Burrows (R-MI), Rep. Thomas Bayne (R-PA), and Rep. Nelson Dingley (R-ME). The Senate was represented by Sen. Nelson Aldrich (R-RI), Sen. John Sherman (R-OH), Sen. William B. Allison (R-IA), and Sen. Frank Hiscock (R-NY).

48. For example, 95 of the 325 (27.7 percent) of the House members were absent on the vote for final passage; 24 of the 84 senators (28.6 percent) were absent for final passage. As Sen. Orville Platt (R-CT) wrote to President Harrison on September 19, 1890, "we have a bare quorum in the city. I don't think we have fifty members, and our ranks are constantly being thinned" (Benjamin Harrison Papers).

49. Parker, *Writings and Speeches,* 87.

50. As Welch argues, "Cleveland appeared to believe that he had done his duty once his message was published and he had successfully urged Democrats in the House to pass the Mills bill" (*Presidencies of Grover Cleveland,* 89).

51. Parker, *Writings and Speeches,* 73 and 84 respectively.

52. Ibid., 77.

53. Sherman, *Recollections,* 1032.

54. Dec. 3, 1889. See Richardson, ed., *A Compilation,* 5473–74 (emphasis added).

55. The only specific items that Harrison mentioned in his message were tobacco and "spirits used in the arts and in manufactures" (ibid., 5474).

56. Ibid., 5509.

57. For example, in early September, Harrison and McKinley engaged in a "wire conversation" regarding the status of the bill. Harrison also received several letters from party leaders urging that, if a special session were needed to complete any unfinished business, it should not be called until after the November elections. See *Harrison Papers.*

58. The Dictionary of Tariff Information sets out three ways in which the imposition of tariffs influences foreign countries: Domestic tariff policy affects foreign industries; tariff policies may shape another state's friendliness toward the United States; and they generally influence "world peace and harmony." See excerpt from Dictionary of Tariff Information, in U.S. Tariff Commission, *The Tariff and Its History,* 721–22.

59. Socolofsky and Spetter, *Presidency of Benjamin Harrison,* 51.

60. *Congressional Record,* 51st Cong., 1st sess., Sept. 27, 1890, 10587.

61. Ibid., 10588.

62. Ibid., 10638.

63. Ibid., Sept. 29, 1890, 10659.

64. Ibid.

65. Ibid., 10658–59.

66. Ibid., Sept. 27, 1890, 10595.

67. Ibid., 10597.

68. Ibid., 10640.

69. Schlesinger Jr., ed., *History of American Presidential Elections,* 1828.

70. Ibid., 1832.

71. Dingley Tariff, section 4.

72. Richardson, ed., *A Compilation,* 6238–39.

73. Ibid., 6239.

74. Ibid., 6242 (emphasis added).

75. Ibid., 6246.

76. *Congressional Record,* 55th Cong., 1st sess., July 19, 1897, 2730.

77. Ibid., July 21, 1897, 2789.

78. Ibid., Mar. 22, 1897, 136. Representative Hopkins referred specifically to Germany, France, Belgium, and "all of northern Europe" (ibid.).

79. See, for example, William Chandler, June 27, 1897, letter to Sen. Edward O. Wolcott (R-CO), *William E. Chandler Papers.*

80. *Field v. Clark,* 143 U.S. Reports.

81. See comments made by Sen. George Graham Vest (D-MO), *Congressional Record,* 55th Cong., 1st sess., July 2, 1897, 2227–28. Senator Vest did not originally hear the inclusion of this phrase when the amendment was read—it was not included in the printed version—and he protested the amendment, thinking that it was similar in nature to the McKinley Tariff provision. Senator Vest recanted from this particular criticism after he was informed of the inclusion of the "advice and consent" clause.

82. Sen. William Lindsay (D-KY; ibid., 2231).

83. *Congressional Record,* 55th Cong., 1st sess., July 2, 1897, 2231.

84. Sen. William B. Allison (R-IA; ibid., 2227).

85. Ibid., 2228.

86. *Congressional Record,* 55th Cong., 1st sess., July 2, 1897, 2232.

87. Ibid., 2234. Besides referencing it in this passage, Gray emphasized elsewhere that the House of Representatives had the power to pass legislation needed to implement the terms of many treaties. In other words, the House had its own source of institutional authority separate from the treaty-making powers the Constitution granted to the presidency and the Senate.

88. William Chandler, June 27, 1897, letter to Sen. Edward O. Wolcott, *Chandler Papers.*

89. *Congressional Record,* 55th Cong., 1st sess., July 19, 1897, 2705–2706. The "applause" comments were included in the text of the *Congressional Record.*

90. Ibid., July 22, 1897, 2837. Silver Republicans were a faction in the

Republican Party who differed from the majority in the party over the issue of bimetallism in the 1890s. Primarily from western mining states, Silver Republicans favored a monetary policy employing both gold and silver, whereas most Republicans supported a gold-only standard.

91. Ibid., July 24, 1897, 2883.

92. Taussig, *Tariff History,* 407.

93. Schlesinger Jr., ed., *History of American Presidential Elections,* 2167.

94. Ibid., 2180.

95. Ibid., 2194.

96. U.S. Tariff Commission, *The Tariff and Its History,* 80.

97. Richardson, ed., *A Compilation,* 7871.

98. Colonel House wrote in his diary that Underwood sought to "let some interim lapse between the death of the old Congress and the birth of the new, so that the members might go home and leave the committee free to work to the best advantage. He thought that, if the members were there, his time would be largely taken up in committee assignments and other matters" (Link, ed., *Papers of Woodrow Wilson,* vol. 27, 20). Wilson, however, initially wanted the session to start on March 18, 1913.

99. See, for example, Wilson, letter from Underwood (Feb. 20, 1913); Wilson, letter to Underwood (Mar. 14, 1913); Wilson, letter from Underwood (Mar. 17, 1913); and Colonel House's diary (Apr. 1, 1913), all in ibid.

100. Wilson was originally quoted in the *New York World* (Apr. 10, 1913). This article appears in Link, ed., *Papers of Woodrow Wilson,* vol. 27, 278. This article also reported that President Wilson's meeting with senators at the Capitol was a practice that had been abandoned since the Grant administration.

101. Link, ed., *Papers of Woodrow Wilson,* vol. 27, 328.

102. Ibid., 335.

103. Ibid., 347.

104. Ibid., vol. 28, 35. Link adds as a point of reference that "The Senate Democratic caucus debated the Underwood bill from June 20 through July 7, 1913. The members voted on the latter date to make the bill a party measure."

105. Quoted in ibid., vol. 27, 322 (emphasis added).

106. *Congressional Record,* 63rd Congress, 1st sess., Sept. 30, 1913, 5255.

107. Ibid., 5256.

108. Ibid., 5266.

109. Ibid., 5252.

110. Ibid., 5273.

111. Unlike the other issue areas examined previously, the intervening cases relating to tariff policy must be taken into consideration when examining the McKinley, Dingley, and Underwood tariffs. The major revisions of tariff policy, which include these three tariffs, as well as the Wilson-Gorman and Payne-Aldrich tariffs, represent a string of connected policies. For any given tariff, the one that preceded it served as a foil on which the policy changes were based; similarly, any given tariff would serve as a foil for the policy that followed it.

For example, one can consider Congress's treatment of reciprocity over the McKinley, Wilson-Gorman, Dingley, and Payne-Aldrich tariffs.

In addition, both the presidency and Congress faced similar policy and institutional authority issues within the context of each tariff debate. For example, should the tariff be protectionist or for revenue purposes only? Moreover, what role, if any, should the president play? The substance, process, and outcomes of any one interaction could affect any subsequent on the connected string of tariff revisions.

The preceding analysis reviewed the political, institutional, and policy connections that tied the McKinley, Wilson-Gorman, Dingley, Payne-Aldrich, and Underwood tariffs together. The McKinley, Dingley, and Underwood tariffs were selected because they maximized the three case-selection criteria. By quickly reviewing the linkages that connected the various tariffs, however, the foils upon which these three tariffs were based are better understood.

CHAPTER 5

1. In Rossiter, ed., *The Federalist Papers*, "The Federalist No. 51," 290, Madison wrote of how human nature would lead government officials to pursue their own self-interest in fulfillment of their public responsibilities. This assumption leads to his famous rationale for the dual systems of separation of powers and checks and balances ("Ambition must be made to counteract ambition. The interest of the man must be connected with the constitutional rights of the place. It may be a reflection on human nature, that such devices should be necessary to control the abuses of government. But what is government itself, but the greatest of all reflections on human nature? If men were angels, no government would be necessary. If angels were to govern men, neither external nor internal controls on government would be necessary. In framing a government which is to be administered by men over men, the great difficulty lies in this: you must first enable the government to control the governed; and in the next place oblige it to control itself.")

2. See note 58 in chapter 1.

3. For a historical, economic approach that explores the origins of policy, see, for example, Sanders, "Industrial Concentration." For a historical, party-based approach to the adoption of a specific policy alternative, see, for example, James, "Building a Democratic Majority," and James, "A Party System Perspective." For a work that employs the same question but utilizes a rational choice framework, see Jack Knight, "Models, Interpretations and Theories: Constructing Explanations of Institutional Emergence and Change."

4. As I have noted previously, President Cleveland also attempted to expand the boundaries of presidential initiatives in the context of the tariff. Congress, however, rebuffed his attempts at leadership in this area and failed to pass legislation prior to the election of 1888. This exemplifies the point made here

that it is only through the development of shared understandings of expected behavior that authority can shift.

5. See Kernell, *Going Public*.

6. The discussion of the 1970s-era reforms and the examples cited are for illustrative purposes only. They are not intended to be directly comparable or necessarily connected in any way to the case studies discussed here.

7. The catalytic event that prompted Congress to believe that an independent counsel position was necessary was the "Saturday Night Massacre," when Richard Nixon had special prosecutor Archibald Cox fired. With regard to Congress's implied constitutional power of oversight, Frederick M. Kaiser states that, "Although the Constitution grants no formal, express authority to oversee or investigate the executive or program administration, oversight is implied in Congress's impressive array of enumerated powers" (Kaiser, "Congressional Oversight," 3).

8. For a more detailed discussion of the transfer of authority resulting from the War Powers Resolution, see Victoria A. Farrar-Myers, "Transference of Authority: The Institutional Struggle over the Control of the War Power."

9. This quotation comes from the foreword written by John F. Kennedy to Theodore Sorensen's book *Decision-making in the White House: The Olive Branch or the Arrows*. The president's foreword, reprinted by special permission, was written from the White House and is dated June 1963.

Bibliography

Aldrich, Nelson W., Papers. Manuscript Division, Library of Congress.

Almond, Gabriel A. 1973. "Approaches to a Developmental Causation." In *Crisis, Choice, and Change: Historical Studies of Political Development,* edited by Gabriel A. Almond, Scott C. Flanagan, and Robert J. Mundt. Boston: Little, Brown.

——, Scott C. Flanagan, and Robert J. Mundt, eds. 1973. *Crisis, Choice, and Change: Historical Studies of Political Development.* Boston: Little, Brown.

"Argument of the Hon. John H. Reagan, of Texas, before the Committee on Commerce of the House of Representatives, on the Railroad Problem." March 28, 1882. Washington, D.C.: Government Printing Office.

Arnold, Peri E. 1993. "The Institutionalized Presidency and the American Regime." In *The Presidency Reconsidered,* edited by Richard W. Waterman. Itasca, Ill.: F. E. Peacock.

——. 2002. "Effecting a Progressive Presidency: Roosevelt, Taft and the Pursuit of Strategic Resources." Paper presented at the 2002 annual meeting of the American Political Science Association, August 29–September 1, 2002, Boston.

Asher, Herbert B. 1973. "The Learning of Legislative Norms." *American Political Science Review* 67: 499–513.

Ashley, Percy. 1970. *Modern Tariff History: Germany-United States-France.* New York: Howard Fertig.

Axelrod, Robert. 1986. "An Evolutionary Approach to Norms." *American Political Science Review* 80: 1095–1111.

Barber, James David. 1977. *The Presidential Character: Predicting Performance in the White House.* Englewood Cliffs, N.J.: Prentice-Hall.

Bas v. Tingy. 4 U.S. 37 (Dall.) (1800).

Baumgartner, Frank R. 1989. "Presidential Leadership of Congress: The Role of Legislative Skills." In *Leadership and Politics: New Perspectives in Political Science,* edited by Bryan D. Jones. Lawrence: University Press of Kansas.

Bayard, Thomas, Papers. Manuscript Division, Library of Congress.

Bell, Wendell, Richard J. Hill, and Charles R. Wright. 1961. *Public Leadership.* San Francisco: Chandler.

Bemis, Samuel Flagg. 1950. *A Diplomatic History of the United States,* 3d ed. New York: Henry Holt.

Berk, Gerald. 1994. *Alternative Tracks: The Constitution of American Industrial Order, 1865–1917.* Baltimore: Johns Hopkins University Press.

Bessette, Joseph M., ed. 1995. *Toward a More Perfect Union: Writings of Herbert J. Storing.* Washington, D.C.: AEI Press.

Bidwell, Percy W. 1933. *Tariff Policy of the United States: A Study of Recent Experience*. New York: National Institute of Economic and Social Research.

Bilmes, Jack. 1986. *Discourse and Behavior*. New York: Plenum.

Blum, John Morton. 1980. *The Progressive Presidents*. New York: Norton.

Bond, Jon R., and Richard Fleisher. 1990. *The President in the Legislative Arena*. Chicago: University of Chicago Press.

———, and Glen S. Krutz. 1996. "An Overview of the Empirical Findings on Presidential-Congressional Relations." In *Rivals for Power: Presidential-Congressional Relations,* edited by James A. Thurber. Washington, D.C.: CQ Press.

Brady, David W., and Phillip Althoff. 1974. "Party Voting in the U.S. House of Representatives 1890–1910: Elements of a Responsible Party System." *Journal of Politics* 36: 753–74.

Brady, David W., Joseph Cooper, and Patricia A. Hurley. 1979. "The Decline of Party in the U.S. House of Representatives." *Legislative Studies Quarterly* 4: 381–408.

Bridgman, Raymond L. 1909. *The Passing of the Tariff.* Boston: Sherman, French.

Bryan, William Jennings, Papers. Manuscript Division, Library of Congress.

Bryant, Clifton D., ed. 1990. *Deviant Behavior: Readings in the Sociology of Norm Violations*. New York: Hemisphere.

Burke, John P. 1995. "The Institutional Presidency." In *The Presidency and the Political System,* 4th ed., edited by Michael Nelson. Washington, D.C.: CQ Press.

Burns, James MacGregor. 1978. *Leadership*. New York: Harper and Row.

Busbey, L. White. 1927. *Uncle Joe Cannon: The Story of a Pioneer American*. New York: Henry Holt.

Chandler, William E., Papers. Manuscript Division, Library of Congress.

Chubb, John E., and Paul E. Peterson, eds. 1985. *New Direction in American Politics*. Washington, D.C.: Brookings Institution.

Clemens, Elisabeth, and James M. Cook. 1999. "Politics and Institutionalism: Explaining Durability and Change." *Annual Review of Sociology* 25: 441–66.

Clements, Kendrick A. 1992. *The Presidency of Woodrow Wilson*. Lawrence: University Press of Kansas.

Cleveland, Grover, Papers. Manuscript Division, Library of Congress.

Cohen, Jeffrey E. 1995. "Presidential Rhetoric and the Public Agenda." *American Journal of Political Science* 39: 87–107.

Coletta, Paolo E. 1973. *The Presidency of William Howard Taft*. Lawrence: University Press of Kansas.

Collier, Ruth Berins, and David Collier. 1991. *Shaping the Political Arena: Critical Junctures, the Labor Movement, and Regime Dynamics in Latin America*. Princeton, N.J.: Princeton University Press.

Combs, Jerald A. 1983. *American Diplomatic History: Two Centuries of Changing Interpretations*. Berkeley: University of California Press.

Committee on Foreign Affairs, House of Representatives. 1973. *War Powers: Hearings before the Subcommittee on National Security Policy and Scientific Developments of the Committee on Foreign Affairs*. House of Representatives, 93rd Cong., 1st sess. Washington, D.C.: Government Printing Office.

Congressional Quarterly's Guide to Congress, 3d ed. 1982. Washington, D.C.: Congressional Quarterly, Inc.

Cooper, Joseph, and David Brady. 1981. "Institutional Context and Leadership Style: The House from Cannon to Rayburn." *American Political Science Review* 75: 411–25.

Corwin, Edward S. 1957. *The President: Office and Powers, 1787–1957: History and Analysis of Practice and Opinion*, 4th ed. New York: New York University Press.

Crawford, Sue E. S., and Elinor Ostrom. 1995. "A Grammar of Institutions." *American Political Science Review* 89: 582–600.

Crompton, George. 1927. *The Tariff: An Interpretation of a Bewildering Problem*. New York: Macmillan.

Cullom, Shelby M. 1911. *Fifty Years of Public Service: Personal Recollections of Shelby M. Cullom*. Chicago: A. C. McClurg.

Cushman, Robert E. 1972. *The Independent Regulatory Commissions*. New York: Octagon Books.

Davidson, Roger H. 1996. "The Presidency and Congressional Time." In *Rivals for Power: Presidential-Congressional Relations*, edited by James A. Thurber. Washington, D.C.: CQ Press.

DeConde, Alexander. 1978a. *A History of American Foreign Policy*. Vol. 1: *Growth to World Power (1700–1914)*, 3d ed. New York: Scribner.

———. 1978b. *A History of American Foreign Policy*. Vol. 2: *Global Power (1900 to the Present)*, 3d ed. New York: Scribner.

DeRidder, Richard, and Rama C. Tripathi, eds. 1992. *Norm Violation and Intergroup Relations*. New York : Oxford University Press.

DiMaggio, Paul J., and Walter W. Powell. 1991. "Introduction." In *The New Institutionalism in Organizational Analysis*, edited by Walter W. Powell and Paul J. DiMaggio. Chicago: University of Chicago Press.

Dodd, Lawrence C., and Calvin Jillson, eds. 1994. *The Dynamics of American Politics: Approaches and Interpretations*. Boulder, Colo.: Westview.

Doenecke, Justus D. 1981. *The Presidencies of James A. Garfield and Chester A. Arthur*. Lawrence: University Press of Kansas.

Dulles, Foster Rhea. 1956. *The Imperial Years*. New York: Thomas Y. Crowell.

Eastland, Terry. 1992. *Energy in the Executive: The Case for the Strong Presidency*. New York: Free Press.

Eckler, A. Ross. 1972. *The Bureau of the Census*. New York: Praeger.

Edwards, George C., III. 1980. *Presidential Influence in Congress*. San Francisco: W. H. Freeman.

———. 1989a. *At the Margins: Presidential Leadership of Congress*. New Haven: Yale University Press.

———. 1989b. "Presidential Leadership of Congress: The Role of Legislative Skills." In *Leadership and Politics: New Perspectives in Political Science,* edited by Bryan D. Jones. Lawrence: University Press of Kansas.

———, John H. Kessel, and Bert A. Rockman, eds. 1993. *Researching the Presidency: Vital Questions, New Approaches.* Pittsburgh: University of Pittsburgh Press.

Edwards, George C., III, and Stephen J. Wayne, eds. 1983. *Studying the Presidency.* Knoxville: University of Tennessee Press.

Elster, Jon. 1989a. *The Cement of Society: A Study of Social Order.* New York: Cambridge University Press.

———. 1989b. *Solomonic Judgments: Studies in the Limitations of Rationality.* New York: Cambridge University Press.

Emerson, J. Terry. 1972. "War Powers Legislation." *West Virginia Law Review* 74: 53–119.

Evens, Peter B., Dietrich Rueschemeyer, and Theda Skocpol, eds. 1985. *Bringing the State Back In.* New York: Cambridge University Press.

Fairlie, John A. 1909. *The National Administration of the United States of America.* New York: Macmillan.

Farrar-Myers, Victoria A. 1998. "Transference of Authority: The Institutional Struggle over the Control of the War Power." *Congress and the Presidency* 25: 183–97.

Ferejohn, John A., and Charles R. Shipan. 1989. "Congressional Influence on Administrative Agencies: A Case Study of Telecommunications Policy." In *Congress Reconsidered,* 4th ed., edited by Lawrence C. Dodd and Bruce I. Oppenheimer. Washington, D.C.: CQ Press.

Field v. Clark. 143 U.S. 649 (1892).

Finkle, Jason L., and Richard W. Gable, eds. 1971. *Political Development and Social Change,* 2d ed. New York: Wiley.

Fiorina, Morris P. 1982. "Legislative Choice of Regulatory Forms: Legal Process or Administrative Process?" *Public Choice* 39: 33–66.

———. 1985. "Group Concentration and the Delegation of Legislative Authority." In *Regulatory Policy and the Social Sciences,* edited by Roger G. Noll. Berkeley: University of California Press.

———. 1986. "Legislator Uncertainty, Legislative Control, and the Delegation of Legislative Power." *Journal of Law, Economics, and Organization* 2: 33–51.

———, and Kenneth A. Shepsle. 1989. "Formal Theories of Leadership: Agents, Agenda Setters, and Entrepreneurs." In *Leadership and Politics: New Perspectives in Political Science.* edited by Bryan D. Jones. Lawrence: University Press of Kansas.

Fleisher, Richard, and Jon R. Bond. 1988. "Are There Two Presidencies? Yes, but Only for Republicans." *Journal of Politics* 50: 747–67.

Genovese, Michael A. 1995. *The Presidential Dilemma: Leadership in the American System.* New York: Harper Collins.

Goldstein, Judith, and Robert O. Keohane, eds. 1993. *Ideas and Foreign Policy.* Ithaca: Cornell University Press.

Goodnow, Frank J. 1900. *Politics and Administration: A Study in Government.* New York: Russell and Russell.

Gould, Lewis L. 1980. *The Presidency of William McKinley.* Lawrence: University Press of Kansas.

———. 1991. *The Presidency of Theodore Roosevelt.* Lawrence: University Press of Kansas.

Greenstein, Fred I. 1975. *Personality and Politics: Problems of Evidence, Inference, and Conceptualization.* New York: Norton.

———. 1978. "Change and Continuity in the Modern Presidency." In *The New American Political System,* edited by Anthony King. Washington, D.C.: American Enterprise Institute for Public Policy Research.

———. 1982. *The Hidden-hand Presidency: Eisenhower as Leader.* New York: Basic Books.

———, Larry Berman, and Alvin S. Felzenberg, eds. 1977. *Evolution of the Modern Presidency: A Bibliographical Survey.* Washington, D.C.: American Enterprise Institute for Public Policy Research.

Grover, William F. 1989. *The President as Prisoner: A Structural Critique of the Carter and Reagan Years.* Albany: State University of New York Press.

Hacker, Jacob S. 2002. *The Divided Welfare State: The Battle over Public and Private Social Benefits in the United States.* New York: Cambridge University Press.

Harrington, Fred Harvey. 1957. "The New World Power." In *Problems in American History,* 2d ed., edited by Richard W. Leopold and Arthur S. Link. Englewood, N.J.: Prentice-Hall.

Harrison, Benjamin, Papers. Manuscript Division, Library of Congress.

Harsanyi, John C. 1960. "Explanation and Comparative Dynamics in Social Science." *Behavior Science* 5: 136–45.

Hay, James, Papers. Manuscript Division, Library of Congress.

Heclo, Hugh. 1983. "One Executive Branch or Many?" In *Both Ends of the Avenue: The Presidency, the Executive Branch, and Congress in the 1980s,* edited by Anthony King. Washington, D.C.: American Enterprise Institute for Public Policy Research.

Helmke, Gretchen, and Steven Levitsky. 2004. "Informal Institutions and Comparative Politics." *Perspectives on Politics* 2: 725–40.

Henderson, Gerald C. 1924. *The Federal Trade Commission: A Study in Administrative Law and Procedure.* New Haven, Conn.: Yale University Press.

Hess, Stephen. 1988. *Organizing the Presidency,* 2d ed. Washington, D.C.: Brookings Institution.

Hody, Cynthia A. 1996. *The Politics of Trade: American Political Development and Foreign Economic Policy.* Hanover, N.H.: University Press of New England.

Holt, W. Stull. 1964. *Treaties Defeated by the Senate: A Study of the Struggle between President and Senate over the Conduct of Foreign Relations.* Gloucester, Mass.: Peter Smith.

Hopkins, Raymond F. 1975. "Political Roles: Micro Analysis and Macro Process." In *Political Development and Change: A Policy Approach,* edited by Gary D. Brewer and Ronald D. Brunner. New York: Free Press.

Humphrey's Executor v. United States. 295 U.S. 602 (1935).

Huntington, Samuel. 1968. *Political Order in Changing Societies.* New Haven, Conn.: Yale University Press.

In re Neagle, 135 U.S. 1, 67 (1890).

Jackson, John E., ed. 1990. *Institutions in American Society: Essays in Market, Political, and Social Organizations.* Ann Arbor: University of Michigan Press.

James, Scott C. 1992. "A Party System Perspective on the Interstate Commerce Act of 1887: The Democracy, Electoral College Competition, and the Politics of Coalition Maintenance." *Studies in American Political Development* 6: 163–200.

———. 1995. "Building a Democratic Majority: The Progressive Party Vote and the Federal Trade Commission." *Studies in American Political Development* 9: 331–85.

Jepperson, Ronald L. 1991. "Institutions, Institutional Effects, and Institutionalism." In *The New Institutionalism in Organizational Analysis,* edited by Walter W. Powell and Paul J. DiMaggio. Chicago: University of Chicago Press.

Jervis, Robert. 1997. *System Effects: Complexity in Political and Social Life.* Princeton, N.J.: Princeton University Press.

———. 2000. "Timing and Interaction in Politics: A Comment on Pierson." *Studies in American Political Development* 14: 93–100.

Jessup, Philip C. 1938. *Elihu Root,* vol. 1. New York: Dodd, Mead.

Jillson, Calvin. 1994. "Patterns and Periodicity in American National Politics." In *The Dynamics of American Politics: Approaches and Interpretations,* edited by Lawrence C. Dodd and Calvin Jillson. Boulder, Colo.: Westview.

Jones, Bryan D., ed. 1989. *Leadership and Politics: New Perspectives in Political Science.* Lawrence: University Press of Kansas.

Jones, Charles O. 1994. *The Presidency in a Separated System.* Washington, D.C.: Brookings Institution.

———. 1995. *Separate but Equal Branches: Congress and the Presidency.* Chatham, N.J.: Chatham House.

Kaiser, Frederick M. 2001. "Congressional Oversight." CRS report no. 97-936 GOV. Washington, D.C.: Congressional Research Service.

Katzenstein, Peter J. 1993. "Coping with Terrorism: Norms and Internal Security in Germany and Japan." In *Ideas and Foreign Policy,* edited by Judith Goldstein and Robert O. Keohane. Ithaca, N.Y.: Cornell University Press.

Katznelson, Ira. 1997. "Structure and Configuration in Comparative Politics." In *Comparative Politics: Rationality, Culture, and Structure,* edited by Mark Irving Lichbach and Alan S. Zuckerman. New York: Cambridge University Press.

Keller, Morton. 1977. *Affairs of State: Public Life in Late Nineteenth-century America.* Cambridge, Mass.: Belknap Press of Harvard University Press.

———. 1996. *Regulating a New Economy: Public Policy and Economic Change in America, 1900–1933.* Cambridge, Mass.: Harvard University Press.

Kendall v. United States. 37 U.S. 524 (1838).

Kernell, Samuel. 1986. *Going Public: New Strategies of Presidential Leadership.* Washington, D.C.: CQ Press.

Keyssar, Alexander. 2000. *The Right to Vote: The Contested History of Democracy in the United States.* New York: Basic Books.

Khan, R. F. 1968. "A Note of the Concept of Authority." In *Leadership and Authority: A Symposium,* edited by Gehan Wijeyewardene. Singapore: University of Malaya Press.

King, Anthony, ed. 1978. *The New American Political System.* Washington, D.C.: American Enterprise Institute for Public Policy Research.

———, ed. 1983. *Both Ends of the Avenue: The Presidency, the Executive Branch, and Congress in the 1980s.* Washington, D.C.: American Enterprise Institute for Public Policy Research.

King, Gary, and Lyn Ragsdale. 1988. *The Elusive Executive: Discovering Statistical Patterns in the Presidency.* Washington, D.C.: CQ Press.

Kingdon, John W. 1989. *Congressmen's Voting Decisions,* 3d ed. Ann Arbor: University of Michigan Press.

Knight, Jack. 1995. "Models, Interpretations, and Theories: Constructing Explanations of Institutional Emergence and Change." In *Explaining Social Institutions,* edited by Jack Knight and Itai Sened. Ann Arbor: University of Michigan Press.

———, and Itai Sened, eds. 1995. *Explaining Social Institutions.* Ann Arbor: University of Michigan Press.

Kolko, Gabriel. 1965. *Railroads and Regulation 1877–1916.* Princeton, N.J.: Princeton University Press.

———. 1976. *Main Currents in Modern American History.* New York: Harper and Row.

Krasner, Stephen D. 1983a. "Structural Causes and Regime Consequences: Regimes as Intervening Variables." In *International Regimes,* edited by Stephen D. Krasner. Ithaca, N.Y.: Cornell University Press.

———, ed. 1983b. *International Regimes.* Ithaca, N.Y.: Cornell University Press.

Kratochwil, Friedrich V. 1989. *Rules, Norms, and Decisions: On the Conditions of Practical and Legal Reasoning in International Relations and Domestic Affairs.* New York: Cambridge University Press.

Lansing, Robert, Papers. Manuscript Division, Library of Congress.

Larkin, John Day. 1936. *The President's Control of the Tariff.* Cambridge, Mass.: Harvard University Press.

LeLoup, Lance T., and Steven A. Shull. 1979. "Congress versus the Executive: The 'Two Presidencies' Reconsidered." *Social Science Quarterly* 59: 704–19.

Leopold, Richard W., and Arthur S. Link, eds. 1957. *Problems in American History,* 2d ed. Englewood, N.J.: Prentice-Hall.

Lichbach, Mark Irving, and Alan S. Zuckerman, eds. 1997. *Comparative Politics: Rationality, Culture, and Structure.* New York: Cambridge University Press.

Lieb, Hermann. 1888. *The Protective Tariff: What It Does for Us!* Chicago: Hermann Lieb.

Lieberman, Robert C. 2002. "Ideas, Institutions, and Political Order: Explaining Political Change." *American Political Science Review* 96: 697–712.

Lieberson, Stanley. 1985. *Making It Count: The Improvement of Social Research and Theory.* Berkeley: University of California Press.

Light, Paul C. 1991. *The President's Agenda: Domestic Policy Choice from Kennedy to Reagan.* Baltimore: Johns Hopkins University Press.

Link, Arthur S., ed. 1966. *The Papers of Woodrow Wilson.* 69 vols. Princeton, N.J.: Princeton University Press.

Lord, Clifford, ed. 1979. *List and Index of Presidential Executive Orders, Unnumbered Series, 1789–1941.* Wilmington, Del.: Michael Glazier.

Lowi, Theodore J. 1985. *The Personal President.* Ithaca, N.Y.: Cornell University Press.

———. 1994. "Foreword: Political History and Political Science." In *The Dynamics of American Politics: Approaches and Interpretations,* edited by Lawrence C. Dodd and Calvin Jillson. Boulder, Colo.: Westview.

Mahoney, James. 2000. "Path Dependence in Historical Sociology." *Theory and Society* 29: 507–48.

———. 2001. *The Legacies of Liberalism: Path Dependence and Political Regimes in Central America.* Baltimore: Johns Hopkins University Press.

———, and Dietrich Rueschemeyer. 2003. *Comparative Historical Analysis in the Social Sciences.* Princeton, N.J.: Princeton University Press.

March, James, ed. 1965. *Handbook of Organizations.* Chicago: Rand McNally.

———, and Johan P. Olsen. 1989. *Rediscovering Institutions: The Organizational Basis of Politics.* New York: Free Press.

Martin v. Mott. 25 U.S. (12 Wheat.) 19 (1827).

May, Ernest R. 1961. *Imperial Democracy: The Emergence of America as a Great Power.* New York: Harcourt, Brace, and World.

McCubbins, Mathew D., and Talbot Page. 1987. "A Theory of Congressional Delegation." In *Congress: Structure and Policy,* edited by Mathew D. McCubbins and Terry Sullivan. New York: Cambridge University Press.

McCubbins, Mathew D., and Terry Sullivan, eds. 1987. *Congress: Structure and Policy.* New York: Cambridge University Press.

McDonald, Forrest. 1994. *The American Presidency: An Intellectual History.* Lawrence: University Press of Kansas.

McGerr, Michael E. 1986. *The Decline of Popular Politics: The American North, 1865–1928.* New York: Oxford University Press.

Meier, Robert F. 1990. "Norms and the Study of Deviance: A Proposed Research Strategy." In *Deviant Behavior: Readings in the Sociology of Norm Violations,* edited by Clifton D. Bryant. New York: Hemisphere.

Milkis, Sidney M. 1993. *The President and the Parties.* New York: Oxford University Press.

Milkis, Sidney M., and Michael Nelson. 1990. *The American Presidency: Origins and Development, 1776–1990.* Washington, D.C.: CQ Press.

Milner, Helen, and Ira Katznelson, eds. 2002. *The State of the Discipline.* New York: Norton.

Miroff, Bruce. 1980. "Beyond Washington." *Society* 17: 66–72.

———. 1993. *Icons of Democracy: American Leaders as Heroes, Aristocrats, Dissenters, and Democrats.* New York: Basic Books.

Moe, Terry M. 1984. "The New Economics of Organization." *American Journal of Political Science* 28: 739–76.

———. 1985. "The Politicized Presidency." In *The New Direction in American Politics,* edited by John E. Chubb and Paul E. Peterson. Washington, D.C.: Brookings Institution.

———. 1987. "Interests, Institutions, and Positive Theory: The Politics of NLRB." *Studies in American Political Development* 2: 236–99.

———. 1993. "Presidents, Institutions, and Theory." In *Researching the Presidency: Vital Questions, New Approaches,* edited by George C. Edwards III, John H. Kessel, and Bert A. Rockman. Pittsburgh: University of Pittsburgh Press.

Morgan, John Tyler, Papers. Manuscript Division, Library of Congress.

Morison, Elting E., ed. 1951–1954. *The Letters of Theodore Roosevelt.* 8 vols. Cambridge, Mass.: Harvard University Press.

Myers v. U.S. 27 U.S. 52 (1926).

Nathan, Richard P. 1983. *The Administrative Presidency.* New York: Macmillan.

Nelson, Garrison. 1994. "The Modernizing Congress, 1870–1930." In *Encyclopedia of the American Legislative System: Studies of the Principal Structures, Processes, and Policies of Congress and State Legislatures since the Colonial Era,* edited by Joel Silbey. New York: Charles Scribner's Sons.

Nelson, Michael. 1987. "Introduction: Rossiter Revisited." In *The American Presidency,* by Clinton Rossiter. Baltimore: Johns Hopkins University Press.

———, ed. 1995. *The Presidency and the Political System.* Washington, D.C.: CQ Press.

Nelson, William E. 1982. *The Roots of American Bureaucracy, 1830–1900.* Cambridge, Mass.: Harvard University Press.

Neustadt, Richard E. 1990. *Presidential Power and the Modern Presidents: The Politics of Leadership from Roosevelt to Reagan.* New York: Free Press.

Nevins, Allan, ed. 1933. *Letters of Grover Cleveland, 1850–1908.* Boston: Houghton Mifflin.

Nichols, David K. 1994. *The Myth of the Modern Presidency.* University Park: Pennsylvania State University Press.

Noll, Roger G., ed. 1985. *Regulatory Policy and the Social Sciences.* Berkeley: University of California Press.

North, Douglass C. 1990. *Institutions, Institutional Change, and Economic Performance.* New York: Cambridge University Press.

Olcott, Charles S. 1972. *William McKinley*. New York: AMS Press.

Oldfield, Duane, and Aaron Wildavsky. 1989. "Reconsidering the Two Presidencies." *Society* 26: 54–59.

Orren, Karen, and Stephen Skowronek. 1994. "Beyond the Iconography of Order: Notes for a 'New Institutionalism.'" In *The Dynamics of American Politics: Approaches and Interpretations,* edited by Lawrence C. Dodd and Calvin Jillson. Boulder, Colo.: Westview.

———. 2004. *The Search for American Political Development*. New York: Cambridge University Press.

Ostram, Charles W., Jr., and Dennis M. Simon. 1985. "Promise and Performance: A Dynamic Model of Presidential Popularity." *American Political Science Review* 79: 334–58.

Parker, George F. 1892. *The Writings and Speeches of Grover Cleveland*. New York: Cassell.

Parker, Glenn R., ed. 1985. *Studies of Congress*. Washington, D.C.: CQ Press.

Parsons, Karen Toombs. 1994. "Exploring the 'Two Presidencies' Phenomenon: New Evidence from the Truman Administration." *Presidential Studies Quarterly* 24: 495–514.

Pellow, David N. 1999. "Framing Emerging Environmental Movement Tactics: Mobilizing Consensus, Demobilizing Conflict." *Sociological Forum* 14: 659–83.

Peppers, Donald A. 1975. "'The Two Presidencies': Eight Years Later." In *Perspectives on the Presidency,* edited by Aaron Wildavsky. Boston: Little, Brown.

Peters, Ronald M., Jr. 1990. *The American Speakership: The Office in Historical Perspective*. Baltimore: Johns Hopkins University Press.

Peterson, Mark A. 1990. *Legislating Together: The White House and Capitol Hill from Eisenhower to Reagan*. Cambridge, Mass.: Harvard University Press.

———. 1995. "The President and Congress." In *The Presidency and the Political System,* edited by Michael Nelson. Washington, D.C.: CQ Press.

Peterson, Merrill D., ed. 1984. *Thomas Jefferson: Writings*. New York: Library of America.

Pfiffner, James. 1991. *The Managerial Presidency*. Pacific Grove, Calif.: Brooks/ Cole.

Pierson, Paul. 1993. "When Effect Becomes Cause: Policy Feedback and Policy Change." *World Politics* 45: 595–628.

———. 2004. *Politics in Time: History, Institutions, and Social Analysis*. Princeton, N.J.: Princeton University Press.

———, and Theda Skocpol. 2002. "Historical Institutionalism and Contemporary Political Science." In *The State of the Discipline,* edited by Helen Milner and Ira Katznelson. New York: Norton.

Pious, Richard. 1979. *The American Presidency*. New York: Basic Books.

Polsby, Nelson C. 1968. "The Institutionalization of the House of Representatives." *American Political Science Review* 62: 144–68.

Poulshock, S. Walter. 1965. *The Two Parties and the Tariff in the 1880s*. Syracuse, N.Y.: Syracuse University Press.

Powell, Walter W., and Paul J. DiMaggio, eds. 1991. *The New Institutionalism in Organizational Analysis*. Chicago: University of Chicago Press.

Pratt, Julius W. 1967. *Challenge and Rejection: The United States and World Leadership, 1900–1921*. New York: Macmillan.

Prize Cases. 67 U.S. (2 Black) 635 (1863).

Protector. 79 U.S. (12 Wall.) 700 (1871).

Pyle, Christopher H., and Richard M. Pious. 1984. *The President, Congress, and the Constitution: Power and Legitimacy in American Politics*. New York: Free Press.

Ragsdale, Lyn. 1995. "Studying the Presidency: Why Presidents Need Political Scientists." In *The Presidency and the Political System*, 4th ed., edited by Michael Nelson. Washington, D.C.: CQ Press.

———, and John J. Theis. 1997. "The Institutionalization of the American Presidency, 1924–1992." *American Journal of Political Science* 41: 1280–1318.

Renka, Russell D., and Bradford S. Jones. 1991. "The 'Two Presidencies' and the Reagan Administration." *Congress and the Presidency* 18: 17–35.

Rhode, David, and Dennis Simon. 1985. "Presidential Vetoes and Congressional Response: A Study in Institutional Conflict." *American Journal of Political Science* 29: 397–427.

Richardson, James D. 1911. *A Compilation of the Messages and Papers of the Presidents*. Washington, D.C.: Bureau of National Literature.

Rieselbach, Leroy. 1996. "One Vote at a Time: Building Presidential Coalitions in Congress. In *Rivals for Power: Presidential-congressional Relations*, edited by James A. Thurber. Washington, D.C.: CQ Press.

Rivers, Douglas, and Nancy L. Rose. 1985. "Passing the President's Program: Public Opinion and Presidential Influence in Congress." *American Journal of Political Science* 29: 183–96.

Rockman, Bert A. 1984. *The Leadership Question: The Presidency and the American System*. New York: Praeger Special Studies.

———. 1985. "Legislative-executive Relations and Legislative Oversight." In *Handbook of Legislative Research*, edited by Gerhard Loewenberg, Samuel C. Patterson, and Malcom E. Jewell. Cambridge, Mass.: Harvard University Press.

Rohde, David W., Norman J. Ornstein, and Robert L. Peabody. 1985. "Political Change and Legislative Norms in the U.S. Senate, 1957–1974." In *Studies of Congress*, edited by Glenn R. Parker. Washington, D.C.: CQ Press.

Roosevelt, Theodore. 1926. *The Works of Theodore Roosevelt*. 20 vols. New York: Scribner.

Roosevelt, Theodore, Papers. Manuscript Division, Library of Congress.

Root, Elihu, Papers. Manuscript Division, Library of Congress.

Rose, Richard. 1993. "Evaluating Presidents." In *Researching the Presidency: Vital Questions, New Approaches*, edited by George C. Edwards III, John H. Kessel, and Bert A Rockman. Pittsburgh: University of Pittsburgh.

Rossiter, Clinton. 1963. *The American Presidency*. [Editor's preface]. New York: Time, Inc., Book Division.

———, ed. 1999. *The Federalist Papers.* New York: Mentor.

Rueschemeyer, Dietrich, Evelyne Huber Stephens, and John D. Stephens. 1992. *Capitalist Development and Democracy.* Chicago: University of Chicago Press.

Sanders, Elizabeth. 1986. "Industrial Concentration, Sectional Competition, and Antitrust Politics in America, 1880–1980." *Studies in American Political Development* 1: 142–214.

———. 1992. "Response to James." *Studies in American Political Development* 6: 201–205.

Scharpf, Fritz W. 1997. *Games Real Actors Play: Actor-centered Institutionalism in Policy Research.* Boulder, Colo.: Westview.

Schickler, Eric. 2001. *Disjointed Pluralism: Institutional Innovation and the Development of the U.S. Congress.* Princeton, N.J.: Princeton University Press.

Schlesinger, Arthur M., Jr., ed. 1971. *History of American Presidential Elections 1789–1968.* New York: Chelsea House.

Schulzinger, Robert D. 1994. *American Diplomacy in the Twentieth Century,* 3d ed. New York: Oxford University Press.

Schwartz, Bernard. 1973a. "Hepburn Act 1906: Commentary." In *The Economic Regulation of Business and Industry: A Legislative History of U.S. Regulatory Agencies,* edited by Bernard Schwartz. New York: Chelsea House.

———. 1973b. "Interstate Commerce Act, 1887: Commentary." In *The Economic Regulation of Business and Industry: A Legislative History of U.S. Regulatory Agencies,* edited by Bernard Schwartz. New York: Chelsea House.

———, ed. 1973c. *The Economic Regulation of Business and Industry: A Legislative History of U.S. Regulatory Agencies.* New York: Chelsea House.

Selections from the Correspondence of Theodore Roosevelt and Henry Cabot Lodge, 1884–1918. 1925. New York: Charles Scribner's Sons.

Seligman, Lester G., and Cary R. Covington. 1996. "Presidential Leadership with Congress: Change, Coalitions, and Crisis." In *Rivals for Power: Presidential-congressional Relations,* edited by James A. Thurber. Washington, D.C.: CQ Press.

Selznick, Philip. 1957. *Leadership in Administration.* Evanston, Ill.: Row, Peterson.

Shafritz, Jay M., and Albert C. Hyde, eds. 1992. *Classics of Public Administration,* 3d ed. Pacific Grove, Calif.: Brooks/Cole.

Sharfman, I. L. 1931. *The Interstate Commerce Commission: A Study in Administrative Law and Procedure.* New York: Commonwealth Fund.

Sherman, John. 1895. *Recollections of Forty Years in the House, Senate, and Cabinet.* Chicago: Werner.

Short, Lloyd M. 1923. *The Development of National Administrative Organization in the United States.* Baltimore: Johns Hopkins Press.

Shull, Steven A., and Lance T. LeLoup. 1981. "Reassessing the Reassessment: Comment on Sigelman's Note on the 'Two Presidencies' Thesis." *Journal of Politics* 43: 563–64.

Shurtleff v. United States. 189 U.S. 311 (1903).

Sigelman, Lee. 1979. "A Reassessment of the Two Presidencies Thesis." *Journal of Politics* 41: 1195–1205.

———. 1981. "Response to Critics." *Journal of Politics* 43: 565.

Silbey, Joel H. 1991. *The American Political Nation, 1838–1893*. Stanford, Calif.: Stanford University Press.

———, ed. 1994. *Encyclopedia of the American Legislative System*: *Studies of the Principal Structures, Processes, and Policies of Congress and State Legislatures since the Colonial Era*. New York: Scribner.

Sklar, Martin J. 1988. *The Corporate Reconstruction of American Capitalism, 1890–1916: The Market, the Law, and Politics*. New York: Cambridge University Press.

———. 1992. *The United States as a Developing Country: Studies in U.S. History in the Progressive Era and the 1920s*. New York: Cambridge University Press.

Skocpol, Theda. 1992. *Protecting Soldiers and Mothers: The Political Origins of Social Policy in the United States*. Cambridge, Mass.: Belknap Press of Harvard University Press.

Skowronek, Stephen. 1982. *Building a New American State: The Expansion of National Administrative Capacities, 1877–1920*. New York: Cambridge University Press.

———. 1993. *The Politics Presidents Make: Leadership from John Adams to George Bush*. Cambridge, Mass.: Belknap Press of Harvard University Press.

Snow, David, and Robert Benford. 1992. "Master Frames and Cycles of Protest." In *Frontiers in Social Movement Theory*, edited by Aldon Morris and Carol Mueller. New Haven, Conn.: Yale University Press.

Socolofsky, Homer E., and Allan B. Spetter. 1987. *The Presidency of Benjamin Harrison*. Lawrence: University Press of Kansas.

Sorensen, Theodore. 1963. *Decision-making in the White House: The Olive Branch or the Arrows*. New York: Columbia University Press.

Spooner, John Coit, Papers. Manuscript Division, Library of Congress.

Standard Oil Co. v. United States. 221 U.S. 1 (1911).

Stanley, Harold W., and Richard G. Niemi. 1994. *Vital Statistics on American Politics*, 4th ed. Washington, D.C.: CQ Press.

Stern, Clarence A. 1971. *Protectionist Republicanism: Republican Tariff Policy in the McKinley Period*. Ann Arbor, Mich.: Edwards Brothers.

Stinchcombe, Arthur L. 1965. "Social Structure and Organizations." In *Handbook of Organizations*, edited by James March. Chicago: Rand McNally.

———. 1968. *Constructing Social Theories*. New York: Harcourt, Brace.

———. 1978. *Theoretical Methods in Social History*. Orlando: Academic Press.

———. 1991. "The Conditions for Fruitful Theorizing about Mechanisms in Social Science." *Philosophy of the Social Sciences* 21: 367–87.

Stone, Richard D. 1991. *The Interstate Commerce Commission and the Railroad Industry: A History of Regulatory Policy*. New York: Praeger.

Sundquist, James L. 1983. *Dynamics of the Party System: Alignment and*

Realignment of Political Parties in the United States. Washington, D.C.: Brookings Institution.

Talbot v. Seeman. 5 U.S. (1 Cranch) 1 (1801),

Tarbell, Ida M. 1912. *The Tariff in Our Times.* New York: Macmillan.

Tariff: A Bibliography, The. 1934. Washington, D.C.: Government Printing Office.

Tariff Hearings before Committee on Ways and Means. 1896–1897. Vols. 1–2. Washington, D.C.: Government Printing Office.

Taussig, F. W. 1967. *The Tariff History of the United States.* New York: Augustus M. Kelley.

Terrill, Tom E. 1973. *The Tariff, Politics, and American Foreign Policy, 1874–1901.* Westport, Conn.: Greenwood.

Texas and Pacific Railroad Co. v. Abilene Cotton Oil Co. 204 U.S. 426 (1907).

Thelen, Kathleen. 1999. "Historical Institutionalism and Comparative Politics." *Annual Review of Political Science* 2: 369–404.

———. 2003. "How Institutions Evolve: Insights from Comparative-historical Analysis." In *Comparative Historical Analysis in the Social Sciences,* edited by James Mahoney and Dietrich Rueschemeyer. New York: Cambridge University Press.

Thurber, James A. 1996. " An Introduction to Presidential-congressional Rivalry." In *Rivals for Power: Presidential-congressional Relations,* edited by James A. Thurber. Washington, D.C.: CQ Press.

———, ed. 1996. *Rivals for Power: Presidential-congressional Relations.* Washington, D.C.: CQ Press.

Tolbert, Pamela S., and Lynne G. Zucker. 1983. "Institutional Sources of Change in the Formal Structure of Organizations: The Diffusion of Civil Service Reform, 1880–1935." *Administrative Science Quarterly* 28: 22–39.

Tulis, Jeffrey K. 1987. *The Rhetorical Presidency.* Princeton, N.J.: Princeton University Press.

———. 1995. "The Two Constitutional Presidencies." In *The Presidency and the Political System,* edited by Michael Nelson. Washington, D.C.: CQ Press.

U.S. Congress. *Congressional Record.* 49th Cong., 1st sess.

———. 49th Cong., 2d sess.

———. 50th Cong., 2d sess.

———. 51st Cong., 1st sess.

———. 55th Cong., 1st sess.

———. 56th Cong., 1st sess.

———. 57th Cong., 1st sess.

———. 57th Cong., 2d sess.

———. 58th Cong., 2d sess.

———. 59th Cong., 1st sess.

———. 59th Cong., Special sess.

———. 63d Cong., 1st sess.

———. 63d Cong., 2d sess.

———. 64th Cong., 1st sess.

U.S. Department of State. 1940. *The Lansing Papers, 1914–1920*, vol. 2. Washington, D.C.: Government Printing Office.

U.S. House of Representatives. *House Report No. 902*. 49th Cong., 1st sess.

U.S. Senate. 1923. *Treaties, Conventions, International Acts, Protocols, and Agreements between the United States of America and Other Powers*. Washington, D.C.: Government Printing Office.

———. *Senate Ex. Doc. No. 31*. 50th Cong., 2d sess.

———. *Senate Ex. Doc. No. 44*. 59th Cong., 1st sess.

———. *Senate Ex. Doc. No. 68*. 50th Cong., 2d sess.

———. *Senate Ex. Doc. V*. 58th Cong., 3d sess.

———. *Senate Report No. 794*. 67th Cong., 2d sess.

U.S. Tariff Commission. 1934. *The Tariff and Its History*. Washington, D.C.: Government Printing Office.

United States v. American Tobacco Co. 221 U.S. 106 (1911).

United States v. Kendall. 26 Fed. Cas. 702, 752 (1837).

Wabash, St. Louis, and Pacific Railway Company v. Illinois. 118 U.S. 557 (1886).

Waterman, Richard W., ed. 1993. *The Presidency Reconsidered*. Itasca, Ill.: F. E. Peacock.

Wayne, Stephen J. 1983. "Approaches." In *Studying the Presidency*, edited by George C. Edwards III and Stephen J. Wayne. Knoxville: University of Tennessee Press.

Weber, Gustavus A. 1925. *The Bureau of Standards: Its History, Activities, and Organization*. Baltimore: Johns Hopkins Press.

Weingast, Barry R. 1979. "A Rational Choice Perspective on Congressional Norms." *American Journal of Political Science* 23: 245–62.

Weir, Margaret, and Theda Skocpol. 1985. "State Structures and the Possibilities for 'Keynesian Responses to the Great Depression in Sweden, Britain, and the United States." In *Bringing the State Back In,* edited by Peter B. Evens, Dietrich Rueschemeyer, and Theda Skocpol. New York: Cambridge University Press.

Welch, Richard E., Jr. 1988. *The Presidencies of Grover Cleveland*. Lawrence: University Press of Kansas.

White, Leonard D. 1958. *The Republican Era: 1869–1901: A Study in Administrative History*. New York: Macmillan.

Whitney, Donald R., ed. 1983. *Government Agencies*. Westport, Conn.: Greenwood.

Widenor, William C. 1980. *Henry Cabot Lodge and the Search for an American Foreign Policy*. Berkeley: University of California Press.

Wiebe, Robert H. 1962. *Businessmen and Reform: A Study of the Progressive Movement*. Cambridge, Mass.: Harvard University Press.

Wijeyewardene, Gehan, ed. 1968. *Leadership and Authority: A Symposium*. Singapore: University of Malaya Press.

Wildavsky, Aaron. 1966. "The Two Presidencies." *Transaction* 4: 7–14.

———. 1989. "A Cultural Theory of Leadership." In *Leadership and Politics: New Perspectives in Political Science,* edited by Bryan D. Jones. Lawrence: University Press of Kansas, 98.

———, ed. 1975. *Perspectives on the Presidency.* Boston: Little, Brown.

Williams, William Appleman. 1959. *The Tragedy of American Diplomacy.* Cleveland: World Publishing.

Willoughby, W. F. 1919. *An Introduction to the Study of the Government of Modern States.* New York: Appleton-Century.

Willoughby, W. W. 1910. *Constitutional Law of the United States.* New York: Baker, Voorhis.

Wilson, Woodrow. 1885. *Congressional Government: A Study in American Politics.* New York: Houghton Mifflin.

———. 1887. "The Study of Administration." *Political Science Quarterly* 2: 197–222.

Woll, Peter. 1963. *American Bureaucracy.* New York: Norton.

Woolley, John T. "Institutions, the Election Cycle, and the Presidential Veto." *American Journal of Political Science* 35: 279–304.

Wright, Russell O. 1995. *Presidential Elections in the United States: A Statistical History, 1860–1992.* Jefferson, N.C.: McFarland.

Yin, Robert K. 1989. *Case Study Research: Design and Methods.* Newbury Park, Calif.: Sage.

Youngstown Sheet and Tubing Co. v. Sawyer. 343 U.S. 579 (1952).

Zevin, Robert. 1972. "An Interpretation of American Imperialism." *Journal of Economic History* 32: 316–60.

Index

Congress, tariff legislation: actions listed, 190–97; in case comparisons, 115–17, 146–47; creation context, 234nn13–14, n18, 236n32, nn34–36; Dingley bill, 129, 131–37, 235n23, 239n81; McKinley bill, 117, 121, 124–28, 234n20, 238n48; Payne-Aldrich bill, 236nn28–29, n36; as treaty-making power, 134, 239n87; Underwood Act, 138–40, 141–46, 240n98, n104; Wilson-Gorman bill, 235n21

Congress, troop commitments: generally, 34; cases comparisons, 66–68, 154–56; Dominican Republic debate, 36, 49–59, 217n69; Haiti conflict, 61, 63, 64–66, 218n99, n102; Samoa conflict, 36, 37–38, 39, 40–47

Congressional Budget and Impoundment Control Act (1974), 169–70

Connecticut, USS, 61

Constitution, U.S., 1–2, 3–4, 10–11, 123, 199n5, 200n11

"cooling off" treaties, 31, 210n14

coordinated scripting, overview, 1–2, 6–7, 10–12, 14–17, 149–54, 199n4. *See also specific topics, e.g.,* administrative agencies *entries;* tariff legislation *entries;* troop commitment *entries*

corporate capitalism era, 71–72, 222n15, n19

Corporations, Bureau of: in case comparisons, 75, 76, 108–109, 157; Roosevelt's policy approach, 75, 90, 91; in trade commission legislation, 76, 97, 99, 100, 101–102, 107, 231n118

Courtelyou, George, 229–30n90

Covington, J. Harry, 101–102, 105, 231n118

Cox, Archibald, 242n7

Crawford, Sue E. S., 199n4

Crisp, Charles, 86–87, 226n44

Crumpacker, Edgar, 95

Cuba, 32, 210–11n19

Cullom, Shelby, 54, 78, 86, 216n57, 226n47

Cummins, Albert, 102–103

database development, 20–26, 175–97

Democratic Party, 30, 208–209n11, 223–24n27, 226–27n51. *See also* Congress *entries;* tariff *entries*

Dibble, Samuel, 83

Dingley, Nelson, 135–36

Dingley Tariff: in case comparisons, 115–16, 146–47, 159; congressional debate/actions, 129, 131–37, 235n23, 239n81; creation context, 114, 128–29; McKinley's policy approach, 129–31, 132, 137; methodology issues, 236–37n36, 240–41n111

Dollar Diplomacy, 207–208n10, 218–19n105

Dolph, Joseph, 37–38, 42, 45, 46

Dominican Republic: in case comparisons, 8–9, 36–37, 66–68, 109, 155; congressional debate/actions, 49–59, 217n69; intervention context, 47–50, 216n50; Roosevelt policy approach, 48–49, 50–54, 58–59, 216n54, nn57–58; Wilson's policy approach, 218–19n105

Dulles, Foster Rhea, 205–206n1

economic factors, foreign policy: Dominican Republic, 47–48, 49, 216n50; in expansionist objectives, 29–30, 206–207n7, n9, 210n15; Haiti, 59–60, 61, 62, 207–208n10

Edmunds, George F., 82, 132

Edwards, George C. III, 201–202n24

Elkins, Stephen, 92–93, 94

Emergency Tariff, 236n31

Emerson, J. Terry, 210n18

England, 37, 206n9, 209nn12–13, 212n24

Ethics in Government Act (1978), 169–70

executive branch: creation goals, 3–4, 199–200n8, n10; growth potential, 4, 10–11, 35–36, 200n11. *See also* presidential authority, institutionalization processes

expansionist policy: as presidential authority opportunity, 35–36; U.S. beginnings, 28–31, 206–209n7, nn9–13

facilitative leadership, 201–202n24

Federal Power Commission, 70, 221n6

Federal Reserve Act, 72, 223n22, 232n138

Federal Reserve Board, 70, 223n22, 232n138

Federal Trade Commission (FTC): in case comparisons, 76, 108–109, 157–58; congressional debates/actions, 98–99, 100–107, 231nn118–19; creation context, 70, 97–99, 230n107; Wilson's policy approach, 98–99, 105–107

Finance Committee, Senate, 141

Foraker, Joseph B., 53, 54

foreign policy: expansionist beginnings, 28–31, 206–209n7, nn9–13; as presidential authority opportunity, 35–36; shared understanding of, 151. *See also* troop commitment *entries*

Foreign Relations Committee: Dominican Republic debate, 49,

54; Samoan conflict, 37–38, 42, 44–45

Foster, John W., 208–209n11

framing, defined, 199n4

France, 209n13

free trade. *See* tariff legislation *entries*

Frelinghuysen, Frederick, 206–207n9, 210n15

frontier thesis, 206n7

Frye, William, 228n81

FTC. *See* Federal Trade Commission (FTC)

Fuller, Paul, Jr., 61

Fuller, William, 87

Gallinger, Jacob H., 56

Germany, 37–39, 41, 48, 60, 217n90, 218n104

Goldwater, Barry, 210n18

Gompers, Samuel, 228n81

Gould, Lewis L., 235n25

grammar of institutions, 199n5

Gray, George, 43, 134, 239n87

Great Britain, 37, 206n9, 209nn12–13, 212n24

Greenstein, Fred I., 201n18

Grover, William, 201n18

Guam, 32, 211n20

Hague Conference, 209n13

Haiti: in case comparisons, 8–9, 37, 66–68, 155–56; congressional debates/actions, 64–66, 216n50; intervention context, 59–61; Wilson's policy approaches, 61–64, 65–66, 207–208n10

Hale, Eugene, 42, 45, 46, 119

Hamilton, Alexander, 3, 200n10

Handy, Levin I., 131

Hanna, Marcus A., 228n82, 229n89

Harris, Isham G., 226n44

Harrison, Benjamin: Chile disputes, 212–13n26; election of, 113, 118, 121, 237n41

Harrison, Benjamin (tariff policy): congressional relations, 122–24, 127–28, 159, 238*n*55, *n*57; context of legislation, 116, 118, 119, 120
Hawaiian Islands, 208–209*n*11
Hay, James, 64
Hay, John, 29, 53, 209*n*13, 216*n*57
Hepburn, William P., 228*n*82
Hepburn Act, 71, 222*n*16
Herbert, Hillary A., 125
Hiscock, Frank, 226*n*43
historical causes explanation, 203*n*34
historical context, importance, 4–6
Hoar, George, 229*n*89
Hollander, Jacob H., 47–48, 49, 216*n*50
Holt, W. Stull, 209*n*12
Honduras, 207*n*10
Hopkins, Albert J., 132
House, E. M., 231*n*116, 240*n*98
House of Representatives: Haiti treaty, 64, 218*n*102; Samoan debate, 42–43. *See also* Congress *entries*
House of Representatives, administrative agency legislation: commerce and labor department bill, 89–90, 95, 228*n*82, 230*n*103; interstate commerce legislation, 76, 78–80, 81–82, 83–87, 88, 226*nn*43–44, 227*n*62, *n*67; trade commission creation, 98, 99, 100, 101–107
House of Representatives, tariff legislation: Dingley bill, 129, 132, 134, 135–36, 235*n*23; McKinley bill, 116, 117, 120, 124–27, 238*n*48; Underwood bill, 139, 143–44; summarized, 112–15
Huerta, Victoriano, 213*n*28

ICA (Interstate Commerce Act), 69, 222*n*16

ICC. *See* Interstate Commerce Commission (ICC)
Illinois, Wabash, St. Louis, and Pacific Railway Company v., 77, 78, 226*n*45
imperialism debate, 28–30, 206*n*7
Independent Counsel Act (1978), 169–70, 242*n*7
Ingalls, John, 86
institutionalization process. *See* presidential authority, institutionalization processes
international stature objective, 28–29
Interstate Commerce Act (ICA), 69, 222*n*16
Interstate Commerce Commission (ICC): in case comparisons, 74–75, 108–109; Cleveland's policy approach, 80–81, 156, 226*n*48; Commerce and Labor department creation compared, 90–91, 229*n*89; congressional debates/actions, 13, 77–88, 156, 226–27*n*43, *nn*46–47, *nn*51–53, *n*62, *n*67; creation context, 69, 71, 77–80, 220–21*n*5, 226*nn*43–44, *nn*46–47, *n*51; enforcement legislation, 222*n*16, 231*n*115; trade commission creation compared, 99–100
isolationism policy, 205–206*n*1. *See also* expansionist policy
Italy, 48, 49
Itata, 212*n*26

James, Scott C., 226–27*n*51
Japan, 208–209*n*11, 211–12*n*21
Jefferson, Thomas, 1, 199*n*1

Kaiser, Frederick M., 242*n*7
Katzenstein, Peter J., 202*n*32
Kennedy, John F., 173, 242*n*9
Kernell, Samuel, 201*n*18
Kimberly, Lewis A., 38–39, 41, 42

Knights of Labor, 228n81
Knox, Philander C., 207n10, 209n13, 218–19n105
Kolko, Gabriel, 223n21
Korea, 211n21

Labor, Bureau of, 88, 219–20n2
Labor, Department of, 88, 89, 92–94, 93, 223n24, 228n81. *See also* Commerce and Labor, Department of
labor movement, 223n24
La Follette, Robert M., 236n28
Lansing, Robert, 61, 62, 63–64, 213–14n28
leadership: components of, xv–xvi, 9–10; types of, 201–202n24. *See also* presidential authority, institutionalization processes; *specific presidents, e.g.,* Cleveland, Grover; Roosevelt, Theodore; Wilson, Woodrow
League for the Preservation of American Independence, 32
League of Nations, 32–33, 212n22
Leary, Commander, 38
legislative branch, creation, 3–4, 10–11, 200n11. *See also* Congress *entries*
Light, Paul, 201n18
Liliuokalani, Queen, 208–209n11
Lodge, Henry Cabot, 29, 53, 54, 56, 212n22
Lowi, Theodore, 4, 233n11
Lusitania, RMS, 217n90, 218n104

Madison, James, 3, 148, 241n1
Malietoa Laupepa, 37
Malietoa Mataafa, 37
manifest destiny philosophy, 28
Mann, James A., 95, 228n82
Manufactures, Bureau of, 229n86
Martin, John, 84–85
Martin, Thomas, 94

Maxey, Samuel, 82
McKinley, William: Boxer Rebellion, 211n21; in case comparisons, 9–10, 146–47, 159; Cuba policy, 210–11n19; Guam policy, 211n20; Hawaiian Islands annexation, 208–209n11; as institutional leader, 165; tariff policy approach, 116, 117, 127, 129–31, 132, 137
McKinley Tariff: in case comparisons, 115–16, 146–47; Cleveland's policy approach, 120–22, 128; congressional debate/actions, 117, 121, 124–28, 238n48; creation context, 113, 117–20; Harrison's policy approach, 122–24, 128; methodology issues, 236–37n36, 240–41n111; provisions in, 234n20
McMillin, Benton, 125–26
Meat Inspection Act, 71, 222n17
methodology approach: case selection issues, 23–26, 205nn54–57, 214n59, 220nn3–4, 224n31, 236n36, 240n111; database development, 20–26, 175–97; policy area focus, 19–20, 204n46; time period selection, 17–19
Mexico, 209n12, 213–14nn27–28, 218n104
Milkis, Sidney M., 204n44
Mills bill, 113, 117
Miroff, Bruce, 201–202n24
missionary diplomacy, 207–208n10
Mole Saint Nicholas, 60
Money, Hernando D., 54, 55, 57, 93–94
Monroe Doctrine: and canal projects, 206–207n9; and Dominican Republic conflict, 29, 48, 52, 54, 58; and Haiti conflict, 61
Montague, Andrew J., 101, 144

Moore, Hampton J., 143
Morgan, Dick, 101
Morgan, John T., 42, 54, 82–83, 126, 134
Morrison, William, 234n18
Mullan, Commander, 38
Myers v. United States, 227n52

National Bank of Haiti, 59
Navigation, Bureau of, 221n6
Navy, U.S.: Dominican Republic conflict, 49; Haiti conflict, 61; Samoan conflict, 38–39, 41
Nelson, Knute, 89, 91, 96–97, 228n78
Nelson, Michael, 204n44
Nelson Amendment, 90, 91, 95, 229–30n84, n90, n103
Neustadt, Richard E., 200n12
Newlands, Francis, 56–57, 105, 231n119
Nicaragua, 206–208nn9–10, 209n12, 218–19n105
NIpsic, USS, 38, 41
Nixon, Richard, 242n7
norms and patterned behavior: overview, 6–7, 13–15, 149–54, 202–203nn32–33; case studies summarized, 154–61; Congress' role, 10, 161–63; methodology approach, 21–22, 23, 205n54
North, Douglass C., 203n36

Oates, William C., 83
Olney-Pauncefote Convention, 209n13
Ostrom, Elinor, 199n4

Padgett, Lemuel P., 218n102
Pago Pago, 37, 39
Panama, 206–207n9
Pan American Trade Conference, 31, 210n15
partisanship theory, 150

passive-reactive position, Congress. *See* Haiti
patronage jobs, and civil service reform, 72–73, 223–24n27
patterned behavior. *See* norms and patterned behavior
Patterson, Thomas M., 56
Payne-Aldrich Tariff, 114, 137–38, 236nn28–29, n36
Pendleton, George, 73, 223–24n27
Pendleton Act, 69, 73
Pepper, I. S., 144
periodization, 5, 200n15
Pershing, John J., 213–14n28
personal power argument, limitations, 4, 164–65
Pettigrew, Richard F., 136
Pettus, Edward W., 133
Philippines, 29, 30, 32, 211–12n21
Pierson, Paul, 203n37
Platt, Orville, 82, 132, 226n47, 238n18
Platt Amendment, 210–11n19
pooling provision, interstate commerce legislation, 79, 226n47
power: authority compared, 7–8; components of, xiv–xv
presidential authority, institutionalization processes: overview, xii–xv, 6–7, 10–17, 148–54; case studies summarized, 154–61; Congress' role, 10–11, 161–63; contemporary implications, 166–73; continuous nature, 163–64; foreign policy opportunities, 35–36; personal power theory compared, 164–65. *See also specific presidents, e.g.,* Cleveland, Grover; Roosevelt, Theodore; Wilson, Woodrow
Progressive Era, characterized, 71–73, 222n19, 223n21, n24, n26
Progressive Party, 97, 98, 138, 236n30
protectionism. *See* tariff legislation *entries*

Treaty of Versailles, 209n12
Trenton, USS, 39, 41
troop commitments: overview of
era, 31–36, 66–68, 185; China,
211n21; Cuba, 210–11n19;
Hawaiian Islands, 208–209n11;
Panama's revolution, 206–207n9;
Philippines, 211n21; seal dispute,
212n24; in Taft's Dollar Diplomacy, 207–208n10, 218–19n105;
in Wilson's missionary diplomacy,
207–208n10
troop commitments, case studies: comparisons, 8–9, 36–37,
66–68, 154–56, 160; Dominican
Republic, 8–9, 47–59, 109, 155,
216n50, n54, nn57–58, 217n69;
Haiti, 8–9, 37, 59–68, 155–56,
207–208n10, 216n50; methodology issues, 20, 23–26; Samoan
conflict, 37–47, 154–55, 214n29
trust legislation. *See* Federal Trade
Commission (FTC)
Turner, Frederick Jackson, 206n7
Turner, Henry G., 124
Tutuila, 37

Underwood, Oscar, 141, 143, 147,
240n98
Underwood Tariff: in case comparisons, 115–16, 117, 146–47,
159–60; congressional debate/
actions, 141–46, 240n98, n104;
creation context, 114, 137–40;
methodology issues, 236–37n36;
Wilson's policy approach, 140–43,
145–46
Upolu, 37

Vandalia, USS, 39
Vest, George Graham, 239n81
Villa, Pancho, 213–14n28

Wabash, St. Louis, and Pacific Rail-

way Company v. Illinois, 77, 78,
226n45
War Finance Corporation, 221n7
War Powers Resolution (1978),
169–71
War Powers Subcommittee, Senate,
210n18
Ways and Means Committee, House,
129, 132, 141, 145
Weaver, Archibald J., 226n44
Welch, Richard E., 238n50
Whitney, W. C., 38
Wilkinson, Theodore S., 126–27
Williams, William Appleman, 29–30,
206n7
Wilson, William L., 113, 128
Wilson, Woodrow: "cooling off"
treaties, 31, 210n14; Dollar Diplomacy, 207–208n10;
Dominican Republic intervention,
218–19n105; League of Nations,
32–33; Mexico conflicts, 213–
14n28; and Progressive Party, 72;
on the 1880s, 204n40; World War
I diplomacy, 32
Wilson, Woodrow (in case studies):
Haiti conflict, 8–9, 37, 59–68,
155–56; trade commission legislation, 76, 98–99, 105–107, 108,
157–58
Wilson, Woodrow (in tariff case
study): congressional relations,
138–39, 140–43, 145, 146, 147;
context of legislation, 114, 115;
leadership comparisons, 117,
138–39, 159–60
Wilson-Gorman Tariff Act, 113, 116,
235n21, 236–37n36
Wolcott, Edward, 135
Women's Bureau, 71
wool tariffs, 119, 129, 139, 142–43
World War I, 32, 218n104, 221n7

Zelaya, José Santos, 207n10

ISBN-13: 978-1-58544-585-1
ISBN-10: 1-58544-585-1

54995

9 781585 445851